THE BOOK
OF
MERLIN

THE BOOK
OF
MERLIN

MAGIC, LEGEND AND HISTORY

JOHN MATTHEWS

AMBERLEY

First published 2020

Amberley Publishing
The Hill, Stroud
Gloucestershire, GL5 4EP

www.amberley-books.com

Copyright © John Matthews, 2020

The right of John Matthews to be identified as
the Author of this work has been asserted in
accordance with the Copyrights, Designs and
Patents Act 1988.

ISBN 978 1 4456 9920 2 (hardback)
ISBN 978 1 4456 9921 9 (ebook)

British Library Cataloguing in Publication Data.
A catalogue record for this book is available
from the British Library.

Typesetting by Aura Technology and Software
Services, India. Printed in the UK.

CONTENTS

DEDICATION

To R.J. Stewart, Gareth Knight and Robin Williamson
for their work on the figure of Merlin
and for their continuing friendship.
J.M.

ACKNOWLEDGEMENTS

Many thanks to my wife Caitlín Matthews for allowing me to quote her translation of the poem 'Commanding Youth', and for her advice throughout the process of writing this book, which as ever has been of great help. To David Elkington for reading the MSS and commenting on it; to Dr Kresimir Vukovic for his support; to Joe Machine, Nicole Ryan and Will Worthington for giving their permission to reproduce their art works in the book, and to Steven O'Brien for permission to quote his poem 'Nimue of the Pallid Countenance' at the head of Chapter 4. I am also grateful to the editors and staff at Amberley Books for making the process of bringing this book to fruition as painless as possible.

INTRODUCTION

THE COMING OF MERLIN

For most of us he is Merlin the Magician, Merlin the Enchanter, Merlin the Wizard. He lives backwards, in a crystal cave, growing younger every day. He wears a pointed hat and starry cloak and carries a staff. But there is much more to him than this composite of medieval and modern imagery, drawn from varying sources. The titles listed here were never used until the seventeenth century. Merlin's roots go far deeper, and he is far older than any of these ideas of his history, none of which are present in the oldest accounts of his life. He has had many incarnations since he first arrived on the scene, sometime in the fifth century AD, as a warrior, a prophet and a shaman. From this shadowy beginning he has reappeared over the succeeding centuries as a medieval magician, an alchemist, a sage and even as a desolate lover. In our own time these elements have been combined into the figure we recognise from countless novels, films, plays and even a couple of operas.

Yet, despite the fact that he is one of the most well-known characters in myth, legend and literature, Merlin remains one of the most enigmatic and subtle players in the vast tapestry that makes up the Arthurian legends. The oldest stories in which he features derive from the treasure trove of myth and legend belonging to the Celts. These sources, often forgotten or neglected, are important for an understanding of who Merlin was; for while the Arthurian legends in which he plays such a leading part betray the influence of French and German storytellers, the myth of Merlin, in its purest form, draws entirely upon native British traditions dating from long before any of those were written.

In the later tales, Merlin's greatest vision is of the Round Table, where all men would meet as equals – his idea rather than Arthur's. In time this image of a perfect society that would be broken apart by quarrels among the knights, by the illicit love of the great knight Lancelot for Arthur's queen, Guinevere, and by the bitterness of Arthur's own incestuous son, Mordred, took over. Small wonder if in the end Merlin is said to have fled the world of men – retreating to a celestial observatory where he would live out his days in the study of the starry heavens – a far more productive subject than human deeds and frailty.

But Merlin has since re-emerged from his tower in a variety of new guises. He can be recognised in the characters of Obi Wan Kenobi and Yoda from George Lucas's *Star Wars* franchise, and again in the powerful character of Gandalf from J. R. R. Tolkien's *Lord of the Rings*, and Dumbledore in J. K. Rowling's *Harry Potter* books. New myths have been made and are being created each year, including a successful TV series, a recent movie in which he appears as a shaman and freedom fighter and a more recent film *The Kid Who Would be King*, in which he is an eccentric wizard advising a modern boy how to 'become' Arthur.

Within years of his first appearance in literature and tradition, his personality changed from a demonic spawn of hell to a wise and beneficent being whose actions and purpose, while seldom wholly revealed, suggest an ongoing influence in the affairs of the human race. It is in this guise he is, still, largely perceived.

* * *

In this book I have set out to explore the complex figure of Merlin through as many as the different guises he has worn throughout his long career as possible: as an historical figure, as a character from literature, and above all as a carrier of ideas and dreams that still move us today. With new books, movies and plays appearing every year, there seems no foreseeable end to the fascination with this character. Trends come and go, but Merlin's story outlasts all such ephemeral events, making him as fascinating to us in the twenty-first century as he was in the fifth.

I would like to acknowledge my debt to three friends, each of whom have taught me to see Merlin through different eyes: Bob Stewart, Robin Williamson and Gareth Knight all contributed to my understanding of his character (though of course they are not responsible for the conclusions I have reached or any mistakes I may have made). In addition, I would like to pay tribute to the intrepid band who took part in a deeper exploration of Merlin's magic in Wales at the dawn of the twenty-first century. And last, but by no means least, to my wife Caitlín, who, as ever, read every word I wrote and gave me the benefit of her own wide knowledge in this area, and who advised me throughout my work on Merlin's enigmatic poems, which run like a golden thread throughout this book. She also kindly allowed me to include her translation of 'Peiryan Vaban' ('Commanding Youth') among the other poems attributed to Myrddin.

John Matthews
Oxford, 2020

MERLIN THE SHAMAN

I set myself to sing
of the madness of the bard of prophecy,
an entertaining tale of Merlin

Geoffrey of Monmouth:
Vita Merlini

Despite his legendary fame, Merlin remains one of the most obscure characters in the entire Arthurian cycle. It is as though he is always in the act of turning away from us, allowing only a glimpse of his face, the gleam of an eye, the echo of a smile – a voice dying into silence. Perhaps because of this he has been perceived in many different ways by the writers, artists and storytellers who have portrayed him over the centuries. The medieval authors who made him famous saw him first of all as a demon, then a magician, and then as a prophet. In our own time, researchers and historians seeking his roots have turned to the figure of the shaman for the oldest aspect of his character.

The first shamans certainly fulfilled many of the roles later attributed to Merlin: they were lore-keepers, healers, prophets, diviners and ceremonialists, as well as ambassadors to and interpreters of the gods. A shaman was born, not made; he was literally a walker between the worlds, one whose attunement to both tribal consciousness and the world of spirits was so fine that he or she could slip between the hidden walls of life and death, move between the worlds, and report on what they saw. It is upon the shaman's revelations and visions that much of our oldest known religious practice and beliefs are founded. While tribal members had only a vague notion of the threshold dividing the worlds, the shamans could not only divine future events through interaction with the spirits of nature and of elemental forces but were also supremely sensitive to the will of the ancestors, the first gods. The oldest stories of deity arose from a weaving of relationships between such animistic powers and the people who understood and interpreted them.[1]

In each of these aspects of the shaman we can find something of the character and actions of Merlin. He too is a mover and shaker, a seer who offers profound insights into the inner worlds of the spirit. Even in the later, medieval figure of the magician, weaving his spells and shaping the destiny of Arthur and his people, we can catch a glimpse of the shaman, while in the earliest records in which the name Merlin appears it is central to his character.

These early records are themselves enigmatic and offer a number of problems for anyone seeking the origins of Merlin. Many were not written down for several hundred years after they were first composed, in the form of poems meant to be spoken or sung by court bards in the halls of early Welsh chieftains. Since oral tradition is notoriously difficult to establish, this makes the evidence for the actual existence of Merlin hard to prove. Favourable to this is the rigorous discipline of memorising vast amounts of poetry practised by the early bards. Distrusting writing, they committed everything they composed to memory, ensuring that the versions that were written down by later transcribers are more likely to be accurate, at least to a reasonable degree – though we should not forget the tendency of copyists to 'improve' on the original or, since most were Christian monks, to deliberately omit pagan references or substitute pious prayers to Christ. With these provisos in mind we may look at the earliest records in which the name or character of Merlin makes an appearance, always bearing in mind that within this shifting tapestry of words and images, we can do no more than catch a glimpse of our prey.

The Oldest Records

The first recorded mention of the name Merlin (in its Old Welsh form Myrddin or Mirdyn) appears in one of the oldest surviving pieces of epic Celtic literature – a ninth-century poem called '*Y Gododdin*' ('The Gododdin'), which describes a fateful expedition of a band of warriors from an area close to modern day Edinburgh, to a place known as Catraeth (identified as lying close to the North Yorkshire town of Catterick), where they fought a battle against the Saxons in which almost all were slain.[2] Among those mentioned by name is a warrior called 'Mirdyn'. But nothing more is said of his character or role, and we have no means of knowing whether this character is in any way related to the more famous Merlin. However, as we shall see, the idea of Merlin as a warrior is clearly part of the earliest texts, so this may be the earliest glimpse we have of our elusive character.

Another Welsh poem, the '*Armes Prydein*' ('Prophecy of Britain') which dates from roughly the same period as 'The Gododdin', uses the phrase '*Dysgogan Myrdin*', 'Merlin foretells' as the opening words to several of its stanzas. The poem as a whole, which we shall examine more closely later, foretells various events that are to come and establishes this version of Merlin as a prophet.[3]

These brief references suggest that the name Merlin, or a version of it, was known as long ago as the eighth or ninth centuries, possibly earlier since these references had almost certainly been preserved in oral tradition for several hundred years before this. Again, whether this Merlin has anything to do with the later character or not, the references are intriguing enough to give us pause for thought.

Elsewhere, in a collection of poetic triplets used by the native British bards as a kind of aide-mémoire for storytellers and poets, we also find mention of Merlin, who is even given a pedigree of sorts. These enigmatic writings, known as *Trioedd Ynys Prydein* (*The Triads of Britain*),[4] date in manuscript from the thirteenth century, but their origins are again much earlier – being traceable to sixth century sources at least, or even earlier if we refer them to oral tradition. Triad 87 lists

> Three Skillful Bards of Arthur's Court:
> Myrddin son of Morfren,
> Myrddin Emrys,
> and Taliesin.[5]

This reference is particularly important as it is the first time that Merlin is associated with Arthur, as well as suggesting that there may have been more than one Merlin – the Son of Morfren, and Myrddin Emrys, a name that was to re-occur extensively in some of the best-known works in which he features. This is an idea to which we shall return as we delve further into the complex history of his origins. For the moment we should note that here Merlin is presented as a bard, a role which at this point in time was assumed to include not only the ability to write poetry and to sing, but also to be possessed of prophetic insight.

The identity of Morfren remains something of a mystery. There is only one other character who bears a name close to this in Celtic tradition, and while there is nothing to link him directly with Merlin, the presence of his name in this context is interesting.

Morfran ab Tegid, who is also known as Avagddu (Utter Darkness, or possibly Great Crow) is the hideously ugly son of the wise-woman Ceridwen (sometimes described as a goddess), for whom she brews a magical drink that will make him all-wise.[6] The distillation of this wisdom, known as 'the three drops of inspiration', is accidentally imbibed by a youth set to watch over Ceridwen's cauldron for a year and a day. He at once has access to all knowledge, and after a chase in which he and Ceridwen shapeshift through several forms, the youth is reborn – as Taliesin, the most famous bard and shaman of sixth-century Britain, who is listed alongside Merlin in this triad.

As we shall see, Taliesin was to reappear later on in the story of Merlin as a friend and possible successor, who would come to be described as possessing many of Merlin's own skills as a prophet and guardian of wisdom.

Whether the presence of his name, along with that of Morfren/ Morfran, in Triad 87 is an accident, or whether there has been a transferal from the story of Taliesin to the story of Merlin, is impossible to say, but this small and seemingly insignificant detail points to an early association between the two poets which was to grow considerably in later accounts. It may also point to the way in which Merlin acquired his wisdom – if he was the son of Morfran, who was originally intended to be the recipient of Ceridwen's brew, this links Merlin to a source of knowledge very much like that of the shaman.

The Warrior-Poet

In his next appearance in the early literature of Wales, Merlin is not only a poet but also a warrior. A few enigmatic references, scattered through a collection of medieval poems, some of which are actually attributed to Merlin himself, tell us a little more, and hint at a story which was only to be fully told in the eleventh century. *The Black Book of Carmarthen* is one of four collections of early Welsh poetry now held in the National Library of Wales and known collectively as *The Four Ancient Books of Wales*.[7] The manuscript dates from the thirteenth century, but like many of these texts, contains material which originated much earlier. Linguistic evidence shows that there are fragments of older verse embedded in the later, medieval texts, suggesting that the pious monks who copied these poems sought to 'update' and 'improve' them, rather as if someone chose to rewrite Shakespeare today. Within the collection are several poems said to have been written by someone named Myrddin (a full translation of these will be found at the end of this book).

They may well date from a period after the time of any real historical character who bore the name, and there is no direct evidence to suggest that this Myrddin is the same as the more familiar character – however, there are aspects of the story glimpsed between the lines of the poems which were destined to become a central part in the developing story of Merlin, and for this reason we cannot ignore these early works as an important part of his developing character. Essentially there are three poems we need to look at – they are more personal than the rest, which are either prophetic or political and show clear signs of having been doctored by later scribes. The first of the three is called 'Oianau' ('Greetings'). It describes a man living alone in a wild forest, apparently the Wood of Celyddon – the great Caledonian forest which once stretched over more than half of the lands between the Grampian mountains and the old Roman wall built at the command of the Emperor Hadrian. The poem is addressed to his only companion, a pig.

Listen, small pig,
O happy, small pig!
Don't go rooting
On the mountain;
Stay here,
Secluded in this wood,
Hidden from the dogs
Of Rhydderch the Generous.

Listen, small pig,
We should both hide
From Mordei's huntsmen
Lest we be discovered.
If we escape –
I won't complain of fatigue –
Instead I'll predict,
From the back of the ninth wave…

Listen, small pig!
I lack sleep –
Such a tumult of grief is in me.
I have endured fifty years of pain.
Once I saw Gwenddolau,
With the gift of Princes,
Gathering prey in battle;
Now he lies beneath the sod –
Restless still.
He was the chief of the North,
And the gentlest…

Listen, small pig,
Go to Gwynedd,

Seek a mate.
Rhydderch Hael feasts in his hall
But does not know
What sleeplessness I suffer
Every night:
Snow to my knees,
Ice in my hair –
Sad my fate!

Listen, small pig –
blessed pig!
If you had seen
All I have seen
You would not sleep
Or root on the hill.

Listen, small pig,
Is the mountain not green?
In my thin cloak
I get no repose!
I grow pale because
Gwenddydd no longer comes...

Listen small pig,
O little trembling one!
Under this thin blanket,
There's no rest.
Since the battle of Arderydd
I no longer care,
If the sky falls
Or the seas overflow...

From these enigmatic verses we learn a number of things. Firstly, the poet (let us call him Merlin, since this story will become very much a part of his own) is living alone in the forest, an outcast in fear of his life, hiding from 'the dogs of Rhydderch' and the 'huntsmen of Mordei'. He is cold, hungry and has endured 'fifty years of pain' because of the death of a man named Gwenddolau, in battle at a place named Arderydd, and above all because of the absence of someone named Gwenddydd.

The Wild Man

On the face of it, the information contained in the poems is not much to go on. But if we look more closely at some of the details and put them together with those in the other poems attributed to Myrddin, a picture begins to emerge.

First of all, there are the names: Rhydderch is almost certainly to be identified with Ryderch Hael (the Generous) an historical figure who lived towards the end of the sixth century AD. A prominent chieftain, he ruled over the kingdom of Alt Clut (Clyde Rock) in the area known as 'The Old North' or *Hen Ogledd*. According to an episode in the thirteenth-century book of law codes known as *The Black Book of Chirk*,[8] Rhydderch was involved in a conflict between the Lords of the North and Rhun, the son of Maelgwyn of Gwynedd, who is named in the accounts of both Merlin and his shadowy associate Taliesin. The actual engagement is possibly invented – however, the references in the *Triads* suggest it may be based on historical events.

Perhaps because of the story of these military engagements, which presented Rhydderch as a famous warrior, he is also said to have been part of an alliance of British kings who fought against the Saxons in the sixth century. This would make him a probable contemporary of Arthur, into whose story Merlin would become drawn from the eleventh century onwards. He is also mentioned in Adamnan's *Life of St Columba*,[9] which refers to him ruling over Strathclyde during the lifetime of the saint. Since Columba died in 597, this places Rhydderch clearly in the sixth century, when Merlin is believed to have lived, in an area not far from the setting of the poems.

The second name which helps us anchor the poem in an historical context is Gwenddolau, whose death Myrddyn mourns. The name Gwenddolau appears in *The Annales Cambriae* (*The Welsh Annals*), a list of events complied in the ninth century but incorporating older materials. There, against the date 573, we find the following entry:

> The battle of Arderydd between the sons of Eliffer
> and Gwenddolau son of Ceidio, in which battle Gwenddolau fell;
> Merlin went mad.[10]

Gwenddolau ap Ceidio is said to have ruled over the kingdom of Arderydd (modern Arthuret) in the sixth century, in what is now the south-west of Scotland and the north-west of Britain and covers the area around Hadrian's Wall and Carlisle. Remains of a fortified structure at Carwinley near Longtown is thought to be a corruption of *Caer Wenddolau* or Gwenddolau's Fort.

Some historians have argued that these are retrospective references, added later, when Merlin was already a familiar figure, but in fact there is no reason to doubt the veracity of the *Annales*, despite their late date in manuscript, and this entry establishes an historical date for the battle in which Gwenddolau fell, as well as providing us with the interesting fact that in this same year (though not necessarily at the same place) Merlin went mad.

Apart from the references in the Myrddin poems, Gwenddolau's name appears three times in the *Triads*: in Number 6, where he is listed as one of the 'Three Bull-nobles of the Island of Britain';

and in Number 29 where we find listed, among the 'Three Faithful War-Bands of the Island of Britain ....[including] the War-Band of Gwenddolau son of Ceidiaw at Arderydd, who continued the battle for two weeks and a month after their lord was slain'.

Finally, in Triad 32, we hear of the otherwise unknown character of Gall son of Dysgyfdawt who 'slew the two birds of Gwenddolau.' What these birds were, or why their deaths were significant, is no longer known with any certainty, though it may be possible to hazard a guess – *see* below.[11]

The Battle of Arderydd

The important reference here is to the Battle of Arderydd, mentioned in both the Myrddin poems and the *Annales Cambriae*. Little is known of this battle beyond these few oblique references, which suggest that it was once the subject of a larger body of material, perhaps an epic poem, subsequently lost. The inference is that the battle was fought between rival chieftains from the areas around Strathclyde.

A rather curious passage in a note attached to an early, unpublished edition of the *Triads*, assembled in the eighteenth century by the antiquary Robert Vaughn, suggests a cause for the battle. Vaughn says:

> It chanced that the shepherds of Rhydderch and Aeddan aforesaid, by the instigation of the Devil, fell out for no other cause than a lark's nest; who, having beaten one another to the effusion of their blood, at last acquainted their lords of the whole strife, and they presently engaged themselves in the quarrel, entering into open hostility with such eagerness and hatred that having mustered their forces and committed some outrages, they appointed a day and place to try the matter by dint of sword. And Aeddan fearing to be too weak to encounter Rhydderch, drew to his side Gwenddolau

[*sic*] the son of Ceidiaw of the tribe of Coel Godeboc, a very powerful prince, and they joining their forces met Rhydderch at a place called Arderydd, where upon the first encounter Gwenddolau was slain, and with him Llywellyn, Gwgawn, Einiawn, and Rhiwallan, the sons of Morfryn, Merlin Caledonius's brethren; and in the end after a great slaughter on both sides, Rhydderch obtained the victory, and Aeddan fled the country.[12]

When placed side by side with the enigmatic reference to the killing of two birds mentioned in the *Annales Cambriae*, this note, though obviously of much later origin, offers us some pointers towards the cause of the strife between the two lords.

As with all such references, we must not forget that they were written down long after the events described, but nor should we forget that such periods are the merest blink of an eye in the history and folklore of place. Many manuscripts, held in the possession of high-ranking families until as recently as the nineteenth century, were lost or destroyed over time. But if some remained in obscure collections to which Robert Vaughn had access, they almost certainly retained materials from a much earlier time, and in this instance the account of the Battle of Arderydd rings true to what little we know of the time.

Here, again, we find reference to Merlin's brethren falling in the battle. Aeddan, who replaces the sons of Ellifer mentioned in the *Annales Cambriae* as the opponent, is almost certainly Aedan mac Gabhran, a formidable Irish leader who seems to have regularly raided across the sea into Britain at this time. The reference to the cause of the battle being over a lark's nest is obscure, but there are a number of similar battles listed in Celtic literature which begin over a seeming trifle and end in bloodshed. Nor should we forget the mention in the *Triads* of the death of Gwenddolau's birds. Celtic tradition mentions the Birds of Rhiannon, which put those who heard them into a trance in which they failed to notice the passage of time. Perhaps there was once a story in which Gwenddolau possessed two miraculous birds, the death of which caused a war to begin – or perhaps the writer simply wanted to point to the way fights can break out over the smallest thing. The wanton killing of these birds could very well have been the cause of conflict between Gall and Gwenddolau.

In any case, the death of Gwenddolau at Arderydd is well attested in all of these references, and in the passage by Vaughn we also have another reference to Merlin – this time as 'Caledonius', a title which seems to place him firmly in the area of Strathclyde and the Caledonian Forest and which will come to be applied to the figure of Merlin – whose kin fell in the battle. This last point is not without significance, as we shall see.

So far, then, we have a story about a man (the poet) who is alone in the woods because of something that happened at the Battle of Arderydd. This battle took place in the sixth century and involved the followers of two chieftains: Rhydderch Hael of Strathclyde and Gwenddolau ap Ceidaw, who are both mentioned elsewhere as historical characters. There are sufficient references to Merlin to place him at this battle, and to suggest that he may have gone mad as a result.

A Lovely, Wanton Girl

The other name mentioned in the poem is Gwenddydd, who is described as no longer coming to see the sorrowful poet. Her identity, with further details of the story, are found in the second of the poems from *The Black Book of Carmarthen*. This is 'Afallenau', or ('Apple Trees') in which each stanza begins with the poet praising the wondrous apple trees that grow close by. But there are other references which raise an intriguing question.

Sweet appletree of luxuriant growth!
Once I found food left at its foot,
When, because of a girl,
I slept alone in the woods of Celyddon,
Shield on shoulder, sword on thigh.
Hear, O small pig! listen to my words....

Sweet appletree in the glade,
The earth beaten round its base.
The men of Rhydderch see me not.
Gwenddydd neither loves nor greets me,
And I am hated by Rhydderch's son.
I have destroyed both his son and daughter:
Death visits them all – why not me?
Since Gwenddolau, no one will honour me,
No diversions attend me,
No fair women visit me.
Though I wore a golden torque at Arderydd
The swan-white woman despises me now.

Sweet appletree, growing by the river,
Who will thrive on your wondrous fruit?
When my reason was intact
I used to lie at its foot
With a lovely, eager girl of delicate form.
Now, for fifty years the plaything of lawless men
I wandered in gloom among the spirits.
After great wealth, and vociferous minstrels,
I have been here so long
Not even sprites can lead me astray.
I never sleep, but tremble at the thought
Of my Lord Gwenddolau, and our native folk.

The Book of Merlin

Long have I suffered unease and longing –
May I get freedom in the end.

Sweet appletree, with delicate blossom
Growing, hidden, in the wood!
At daybreak I heard how
My words offended the most powerful man –
Not once, not twice, but three times in a single day.
Ah! that my end had come
Before the death of Gwenddydd's son
Was upon my hands!

Here we learn much more about the state of the nameless poet. Again, the small pig is mentioned, and once more he speaks of being outcast in the wilderness for fifty years. At one time he was visited by a woman, 'a lovely, eager girl' who disported with him beneath the trees and brought him food. Now, she comes no more, this swan-white woman whose name seems to by Gwenddydd. Again, there are references to the death of Gwenddolau and additionally to Gwenddydd's son, possibly the offspring of these two characters. Throughout, the poet continues to blame himself for these deaths and to bemoan his outcast state.

Who, then, is Gwenddydd, and are we to assume that she and Merlin were once lovers? Or is the 'lovely, eager girl' another woman altogether? These details, small enough in themselves, will have a long-lasting effect on the development of Merlin's story.

The Secret of the Sister
The secret of Gwenddydd's identity is actually no secret at all. It is given away in the title and content of another of the poems from one of the *Four Ancient Books of Wales*. In *The Black Book of Carmarthen,* we find 'A Dialogue Between Myrddyn & His Sister

Gwenddydd'. Only in one other source, an important one in the history of Merlin which we shall discuss shortly, is Gwenddydd described as Merlin's sister.

Here she is described as his twin – the word used being *llallogan* which, as we shall see, may well be significant. Later, all mention of such a person vanished, or is so transformed that it gives a completely different take on the story. Most of the long poem (a full version will be found in the appendix at the back of this book) is taken up with Gwenddydd asking Merlin for the names of kings who will rule over the Cymry (Welsh) in future times and is full of the kind of riddling replies so beloved of Celtic bards. We are, however, able to glean a few more personal details. The poem opens as follows, with Gwenddydd naming herself a powerful woman who has 'rule' in the North.

GWENDDYDD
I have come to tell
Of the rule I have in the North –
The region's beauty known to me.

MYRDDIN
Since the action at Arderydd and Erydon
Gwenddydd, and all that has happened to me,
I am dull of wits.
Where shall I look for delight?

GWENDDYDD
I will ask of you, my twin brother,
Myrddin, wise man and diviner,
Who so often speaks the truth
When a girl goes to him.

MYRDDIN

I will sing like a simpleton,
Ominous with fears for the Cymry.
The wind tells me
Rhydderch Hael's standard cannot fall.

GWENDDYDD

Rhydderch is pre-eminent
And all the Cymry beneath him.
Who can possibly follow him?

MYRDDIN

Rhydderch Hael, feller of foes,
Dealt many wounds
On a blissful day at the ford of Tawy.

GWENDDYDD

Rhydderch Hael, while he is the enemy
Of the bardic city in Clyd
When will he reach the ford of death?

MYRDDIN

I will tell lovely Gwenddydd –
Since she has asked so skilfully –
After tomorrow Rhydderch will cease to be.

GWENDDYDD

I ask my far-famed twin,
Most intrepid fighter –
Who comes after Rhydderch?

MYRDDIN

As Gwenddolau was slain at bloody Arderydd,

And I have come to into the wild –
It shall be Morgant Mawr, son of Sadyrnin.

GWENDDYDD
I ask my far-famed brother,
Who sings amid the streams –
Who will rule after Morgant?

MYRDDIN
As Gwenddolau was slain at bloody Arderydd,
And as I wonder why anyone should visit me –
The country will call out to Urien.

GWENDDYDD
As your hair is white as hoar frost
And God has answered your need –
Who will rule after Urien?

MYRDDIN
Great affliction has fallen upon me.
I am sick of life –
Maelgwyn Hir will rule over Gwynedd.

GWENDDYDD
I pine every time I leave my brother,
Tears furrow my tired cheeks –
After Maelgwyn, who will rule?

MYRDDIN
Rhun is his name, impetuous in battle,
Foremost in the rank of the army –
Woe to Prydain when his day dawns.

GWENDDYDD
As both friend and companion of slaughter
That men will name as a leader –
Who will rule Gwynedd after Rhun?

MYRDDIN
Rhun, renowned in battle!
What I say will come to pass!
Gwynedd will fall next to Beli...

In each verse the pattern is the same – first, two lines that refer to events in Myrddin's own life, then one line in which Gwenddydd asks him to name the next king to rule after the death of Rhydderch, which he then lists. She continues to question her 'far-famed, twin brother', whom she refers to also as 'wise', 'prophetic', 'a diviner' and as 'blessed' and 'profound'. Finally, she ends on a mournful note:

Alas, dear one, for our separation.
After the tumult to come
You may well be placed in the earth
By a brave and fearless king.

I am left cheerless by the thought
Of your death –
Yet time offers a respite
For one that speaks truth.

Arise from your rest,
Open the Book of Awen without fear. [inspiration]
Hear the discourse of a girl,
Give repose to your dreams...

This remarkable poem, full of rich allusion and flashes of personal detail, finally gives us a more complete portrait of the events that drove Merlin to hide in the forest. I have included this lengthy extract both to give the feel of the bardic poetry in which it is expressed and because of its importance to the decipherment of Merlin's life. Again, we find references to Arderydd, to Rhydderch, and to Gwenddolau and to the death of Gwenddydd's son, for which Merlin blames himself. Could it be that this youth fought at his side in the battle and fell there? Is this what caused him to go mad, to escape into the forest and hide there with only animals for companions? Everything points to this, but the conclusions would only be speculative if it were not for another text, which draws upon these and other sources and wove them into a new pattern.

The Child of Wonder

The text known as the *Vita Merlini* (Life of Merlin)[13] dates from the twelfth century and was written by a Welsh cleric named Geoffrey of Monmouth, who played a central role in the creation of the Arthurian mythos. He is best known for his *Historia Regum Brittaniae* (History of the Kings of Britain)[14] which, despite its title actually deals more with King Arthur than any of the other (semi-legendary) kings of Britain. Geoffrey's book, completed in 1138, caused a sensation and was copied over and over again for the noble patrons of Norman England, who sought among the remains of the Arthurian legends their own roots and by inference their right to rule over Britain.

Included in the book was an account of Merlin which established him as a seer of astonishing power. Described as the offspring of a forbidden union between a human woman and a demon, the child named Merlin is brought before a usurping tyrant named Vortigern, who is trying to build a tower in which to hide from his enemies. When the tower falls down each night, Vortigern's magical advisors tell him to seek a fatherless child and to let out his blood on the foundations. The child, discovered conveniently at the town of Carmarthen (once held to derive its name from *Caer Merddyn*), confounds Vortigern's magicians by revealing the real reason why the tower will not stand and then by uttering a long series of profound prophecies, listing events to come in the far future. We shall be looking at this story more closely when we examine Merlin's prophetic abilities; for the moment, it is sufficient to note that in his first major literary appearance Merlin is shown as having recognisably shamanic powers and as coming from otherworldly stock – both factors that were to become a permanent aspect of his character from then onwards.

This part of the story was borrowed by Geoffrey of Monmouth from an earlier book, the *Historia Brittonum* (History of the Britons), attributed to a monk named Nennius and written during the seventh century.[15] This is still the only nearly contemporary account dating from close to the Arthurian period, and it remains a pivotal source in the argument for and against the historical existence of Arthur in the sixth century. The version of the story retold by Geoffrey originally featured a boy named Emrys (an Anglicisation of the Latin *Ambrose*) and seems to have originated as a folk story then circulating throughout Wales.

Geoffrey's choice of the town of Carmarthen for the home of his young hero is no accident, any more than is the fact that the title of the collection containing the Myrddyn poems is *The Black Book of Carmarthen*. Since at least the Middle Ages, there has been an implicit identification of the Welsh town with the figure of Merlin. This actually derives from a false etymology which sought to interpret *Caer Myrddyn* as Merlin's Town, but in fact the oldest name for the city was *Moridunum*, 'the Fortress of the Sea'. This is itself of interest as from it, it is possible to trnaslate Merlin's Welsh name as 'Man of the Sea'.

The association with Merlin only came later, however, though it gave rise to some interesting local traditions, including the story of an ancient oak tree, said to have been planted by Merlin himself. According to this belief, its roots may still be viewed in the town hall. The presence of the poems attributed to Merlin, in a book which also bears the name of the town believed to be associated with him, is interesting. It suggests that either the original collector or scribe of the poems was local and felt it appropriate to collect Merlin's work there, or that the presence of these poems themselves helped establish the connection between Merlin and Carmarthen.

The success of Geoffrey's book is attributable, in part at least, to the presence of Merlin's *Prophecies*, which he had previously issued as a separate book – the first of many to be appear throughout the ages, each one bearing Merlin's name and 'updated' to include prophecies of more recent events. The success of his earlier efforts seems to have prompted Geoffrey to embark on a third book, this time focusing entirely on Merlin. He based it on the poems from *The Black Book of Carmarthen* and, following up on the hints and clues he found in these, he told a wholly new and different tale of the great prophet. This book, the *Vita Merlini* (Life of Merlin), was less popular than the *Historia*, but it enshrined the older myths of a Merlin whose shamanic origins can still be clearly seen within its pages.

The Life of Merlin

At the beginning of the *Vita*, Merlin is described as a king, a bard, and a prophet to the South Welsh, famed far and wide for his wisdom and power. Then war breaks out between Gwenddolau, here named as the king of Scotland, and Peredur, a prince of North Wales. Merlin fights alongside Peredur, together with Rodarchus (Geoffrey Latinises the names throughout, so this is his version of Rhydderch). Peredur, of course, is the Welsh form of Perceval, the name of the hero of the earliest surviving version of the medieval Grail quest. There are also three 'brothers of the Prince' who are mighty warriors and slay many of the enemy until they are themselves slain. The effect of this on Merlin is profound. He movingly laments their death and commands a tomb to be raised over them. Finally, the weight of sorrow overthrows his mind and he runs mad, fleeing from the battlefield into the forest. The wording of the text makes it unclear whether the three young men are Merlin's brothers, or perhaps those of Peredur. Looking back to the references to the death of Gwenddydd's son in the 'Dialogue of Myrddyn and Gwenddydd' one cannot help wondering if these three brothers were not actually her sons. This would certainly explain Merlin's sense of guilt, even his madness – though the reference from the *Annales Cambriae* seems to suggest it was the death of Gwenddolau that drove Merlin into the wild. In either event the effect is the same, Merlin now becomes a 'Man of the Woods', living on roots and grasses, observing the wild animals and even conversing with them, and generally displaying aspects of the traditional figure of the shaman.

When winter comes, he finds it increasingly hard to survive. He complains of this aloud in verse that clearly show Geoffrey's indebtedness to the Myrddin Poems:

Where on earth can I live!
The is nothing here to eat –
No grass, no acorns on the tree.
Once nineteen apple trees stood here
With their abundant fruit.
Now they are gone [...]
The forest stands leafless, fruitless [...]
There is no cover for me
Since the wind took away all the leaves.

If I dig for turnips
Hungry swine and greedy boars
Rush to steal them from me.
Wolf, my old companion,
So weak are you become
You can barely crop the field;
All that is left to you
Is to fill the air with howling![16]

This is so close to the tone of 'Greetings' and 'Appletrees' that it is clear that they were current at the time Geoffrey was writing, and that he knew them.

One day a man hears Merlin's lament. He is from the court of King Rodarchus (Rhydderch) who is now married to Merlin's sister Ganeida (Gwenddydd). He reports what he has seen and heard, and a party is at once dispatched to the forest to capture the wild man and bring him back to court. They send a bard with the soldiers and it is this man's playing that brings Merlin back to the edge of sanity. Through music he remembers both his sister and his wife – a shadowy figure named Guendolena, who has almost no part to play in the story, though her existence will contribute to Merlin's story later on.

The Triple Death

Once back at court, the sights and sounds and the large gathering of people drive Merlin back into his shell of madness. He begs to be allowed to return to the woods he has grown to love, but Rodarchus has him incarcerated until he can be restored to health.

A famous episode now follows, which was to be repeated several times in the later stories of Merlin. When he sees Ganeida with her husband he laughs aloud. Puzzled, the king demands to know what causes this mirth. For answer Merlin says that when he saw

Rodarchus remove a leaf from his wife's hair he laughed because he knew that she had got it while meeting with her lover in the woods. Furious, the king rounds on Ganeida, but she conceals her guilt by dismissing her brother's words as those of a madman. She then offers to put the king's mind a rest by proving just how mad Merlin is. She sends for a boy and asks Merlin how he will die. He replies that the boy will drown. Ganeida then sends the boy away, has his hair cut and different clothes put on him and presents him again to Merlin, asking the same question. This time he says the boy will die by falling from a cliff. Finally, Ganeida has the boy dressed as a girl and asks the same question for a third time. Merlin laughs and says that 'he' will hang.

By this time everyone is convinced that Merlin is truly mad, and they prepare to release him back into the wild. Ganeida and Guendolena make impassioned pleas to persuade him to stay, but he refuses. Ganeida at this point asks him if his wife should be allowed to remarry, and Merlin says that she may do as she pleases, but that any man who marries her should watch out and never come near him for fear of their lives. He then returns to the forest.

Shortly after, the boy for whom Merlin predicted three separate deaths is out riding and falls from the back of his horse over a cliff. His foot is caught in a tree branch and as he hangs there upside down his head goes beneath the water of a river and he drowns. Thus, Merlin's prediction is proved true as the boy falls, is hung and drowns in the same moment.

This whole episode focusses on a very ancient theme indeed. Among the early Celts such a triple death would have marked out the one who suffered it as chosen by the gods. Evidence has come to light in recent years which suggests that those chosen for sacrifice may have been killed in this way. The body of a man found in a peat bog in Cheshire and dating from the first century

AD, was found to have been strangled and had his throat cut before he was thrown into the water. The contents of his stomach indicated that he had eaten a ritual meal just before his death, suggesting that he was indeed a chosen victim, offered to the gods, whose otherworldly kingdom was believed to be accessed through water. The presence of this episode in the *Vita Merlini* points to a genuinely ancient source for this part of the story, perhaps a distant memory of a time when a figure not unlike Merlin would have served as a priest and may himself have delivered the triple death to a chosen sacrificial victim. It is very much in line with the shamanic aspects of his character, and as we shall see shortly it is preserved in more than one tale associated with Merlin.

Merlin and the House of Stars

In the *Vita* time passes and Guendolena finally plans to remarry, having given up any hope of seeing Merlin again. He, watching the stars, reads of this coming event and feels abandoned. He summons a herd of deer, and riding on the back of a stag, drives them before him to the court. There, seeing Guendolena's would-be bridegroom standing in a window laughing at him, Merlin wrenches off the stag's antlers and flings them at him, killing the man instantly. Officers from the court pursue him and catch him when he falls into a river. He is brought back to the court in chains, and on the way laughs aloud twice more, apparently without reason.

When he hears this Rodarchus is consumed with curiosity and demands to know why. At first Merlin refuses to explain anything, but finally agrees to talk if he is allowed to return to the forest. Rodarchus agrees, and Merlin explains that the first time he laughed was when he saw a man begging in the street, little knowing that he was sitting on top of a hoard of gold. The second time was when he saw a man buying a new pair of shoes, though in fact he would drown in the river a few hours later. Once again, both predictions prove to be accurate and Merlin is set free.

Before he departs Gwenddydd again begs him not to leave, but Merlin is adamant. 'Why, my dear sister, do you strive so hard to hold me back? Neither winter with its storms, nor the chill north wind when it rages with savage blast and lashes the flocks of bleating sheep with sudden hail shower ... will be able to deter me from seeking the forest wilderness and the green glades...'[17] Then he relents. After all, food might grow short, so he lets his sister build him a house, with seventy doors and windows, through which he may study the stars and read the future of the nation. Further, 'let there be many secretaries trained to record what I say and let them concentrate on committing my prophetic songs to paper. Come here often yourself dear sister, and you will be able to stay my hunger with food and drink.'

So Ganeida builds Merlin a house with seventy doors and windows as requested and comes to visit him as often as she can. We may also notice the reference to 'prophetic songs' which again bears witness to Geoffrey's knowledge of the Myrddin poems. Most of the time Merlin continues to live under the trees, but in winter retreats inside to watch the stars and to prophesise. Soon after this he is joined by the bard Taliesin and the two wise men fall to talking of the mysteries of wind, weather, and the secrets of Creation. Taliesin, whom we remember is listed alongside Merlin in the *Triads*, is himself an important character, who shares many of Merlin's characteristics, including those of the shaman. A more detailed examination of his story shows the common heritage shared by them both.

Taliesin the Bard

Most of what we know about Taliesin comes from two sources: a sixteenth-century text called the *Hanes* or 'Life' of Taliesin; and seventy poems contained in another of the *Four Ancient Books of Wales*, a fourteenth-century volume known as *The Book of Taliesin*. Apart from these there are several mentions in the great collection of Welsh myths known as the *Mabinogion*, the reference in the *Triads* already noted, and a list of famous bards contained in the *Historia Brittonum* of Nennius, which mentions Taliesin as being among the greatest in Britain.[18]

Despite the lateness of some of this material, it enables us date Taliesin more or less to the fifth or sixth centuries – and to the time of Merlin. This is further supported by internal references in the poems themselves. However, although the fact of Taliesin's historical existence is fascinating, there is another Taliesin – an almost mythical figure who emerges from a ragbag of references and memories of events far earlier than the sixth century, and which refer us back to a time when the links between the earth and the people who lived upon it were more profound than at any time since, when the shaman played the part of magician, priest, lawgiver and physician.

This is not a precise historical time zone, but more of a semi-mythical period when magic and wonder were everywhere present. The historical Taliesin may not have lived then, any more than we can say that Merlin was definitely alive in the sixth century, but both inherited a set of beliefs which were a focus for memories still locked in the minds of people then living.

The *Hanes Taliesin* tells the story of the boy Gwion, taken from his home by the wise-woman Ceridwen and put to watch over a cauldron in which she is brewing a drink of wisdom to make her ugly son Afagddu (who, as we have seen, is also known as Morfran) wise. Gwion accidentally imbibes three drops of this wisdom and when pursued by an angry Ceridwen, runs through a whole range of transformations, into animal, bird and fish – finally being swallowed as a grain of wheat by Ceridwen in the shape of a hen – and subsequently reborn from her womb as a child. Unable to bring herself to kill him, Ceridwen casts the infant adrift on the sea in a leather bag which reaches a salmon weir owned by a lord named Gwyddno Garanhir. There Gwion is found by Gwyddno's hapless son Elphin, famed for his bad luck. On opening the bag and discovering a child within, he comments on the light issuing from its brow. '*Tal-iesin* (i.e. Radiant Brow) shall I be called!' states the infant and goes on to deliver a series of strange riddling poems. Elphin takes him home and raises him. In time he becomes the greatest bard ever known among the Celts.

Later, in one of the poems attributed to him, Taliesin recalls this strange rebirth, as well as the many other aspects of the natural world through which he has passed:

A second time I was formed
I have been a blue salmon.
I have been a dog;
I have been a stag;
I have been a roebuck on the mountain…
I have been a grain discovered…
I have been dead; I have been alive…
I am Taliesin.

These 'boasts', as they are known, echo throughout much of the poetry attributed to Taliesin. We may view them as elliptical references to an inner knowledge, the product of shamanic initiation and training. Like shamans everywhere, Taliesin had access to the kind of knowledge that enabled him to travel and return from the Otherworld in vision. In this way he experiences self-induced trances which give him insight into events both past and future. In later stories he becomes King Arthur's bard and may even be seen to replace Merlin after he withdraws from the world of men.

The Shaman's Dream

Behind this story, and the poetry attributed to Taliesin, lies a vast legacy of initiation lore and wisdom, much of it now lost. But enough has survived to convey much of the spirit and tradition of the Celts, as well as the practice of shamanism among them. The sequence of Taliesin's changes, his drinking of the magical brew of inspiration, echoes the accounts of shamanic practice from other cultures around the world and firmly establishes him as a living repository of an ancient shamanic tradition among the Celts, which is only today being rediscovered. A brief glance at this will help to show how much is shared by Taliesin, and to a lesser degree Merlin, who are seen the inheritors of this tradition, which shows through again and again in the descriptions of their magical and prophetic skills.

Shamanism is the oldest known form of spiritual practice in the world. Its outward symbols have been discovered in Australia, the Americas, Africa, the Far East, Siberia and much of Europe, dating back to the dawn of recorded history. Rock paintings, ancient carved stones, painted shells and antique personal adornments, originating from sites as far apart as Scotland, France, South and North America, the Arctic Circle and the Australian bush, have given intriguing glimpses into the life and practice of the shaman.[19]

In many parts of the world these ancient disciplines are still practised and taught, and through the living carriers of this tradition we have learned to add dimension to the artefacts. The world thus revealed, for all its constant overlapping with the realms of the spirit, is at times an overwhelmingly substantial one, possessing a powerful universality, much as that discussed in the *Vita Merlini* in a dialogue between Merlin and Taliesin.

Because it is not a religion as such, but rather a spiritual practice, shamanism cuts across all faiths and creeds, reaching the bedrock of ancestral memory. As a primal belief system, which precedes religion, it has its own universal symbolism and cosmology, inhabited by beings, gods and spiritual allies that show manifestly similar characteristics though they appear in localised forms depending on their place of origin.

The word 'shaman' comes from the Tungusic language of Siberia and its etymology is debated. Some say it means 'to be consumed with fire' [of inspiration], others suggest it means 'he or she who knows'. If we take the first of these two ideas, it is easy to see how the *Awen,* or inspiration, referred to throughout much Early Celtic poetry and story, refers to just this. It is clear from a careful examination of the poems of Taliesin and Merlin that both were inheritors and, in all probability, actual practitioners of the shaman's path.

Definitions of shamanism vary from culture to culture and tradition to tradition, but most agree on certain common principles, such as soul-flight, the journey out of the body into different states of being, and the ability to heal sickness in collaboration with spiritual allies. Anthropology terms shamanism animistic, founded on the belief that all things have spirit, but practical shamanism is much more – it is a servant of all spiritual traditions, able to draw upon the deep primordial life of the universe, preceding all of our received regions as wisdom inherited by all. It is a transcendent system which puts the practitioner in touch with every level of creation, both inside and outside what is generally accepted as reality. Above all it is supremely practical and requires a pragmatic, down-to-earth respect for truth, nature and knowledge: the three candles that no darkness can extinguish. Thus, Taliesin is able to state that he has 'been' many different things – a reference to the ability of the shaman to become at one with any created thing whether a tree of an animal. In his visionary transformation via the drink prepared by Ceridwen, Taliesin is able to 'become' the creatures into which the story tells us he was transformed. We may remember too, how Myrddin addresses his visionary poems to creatures – pigs and wolves or living things such as trees – during his time in the forest.

The ability to work with spirit helpers is a well-known aspect of shamanic ability, and when allowed to comment for himself Merlin states clearly (both in Geoffrey of Monmouth's account and that of the Norman poet Wace, who translated Geoffrey's text into French verse) that he has contact with a spirit, and that it is by this means that he is able to see the future. Thus, when asked to prophecy by Aurelius, the first of the leaders he serves, he responds:

> Such mysteries should only be revealed in times of dire necessity. If I prophesied for entertainment or without purpose, the spirit that instructs me would fall silent and abandon me when I needed it.[20]

Wace makes this even clearer, when in his *Roman de Brut* (written c.1115–55) he says 'If I spoke boastfully, in jest, or arrogantly, the spirit I possess, from whom I know what in know, would leave my mouth and take my knowledge with him...'[21]

The shaman has many roles – he or she can be a spirit doctor, healer, diviner, seer, prophet, negotiator, ancestral intermediary and ritualist, among other roles. Shamanism itself is the practice of bringing healing, wholeness and harmony to body, mind and soul. Where ancestral laws or environmental boundaries have been violated the shaman will seek a ritual to re-harmonise the relations between people and land, or with tribal ancestors. Shamans continually ply between the otherworld of dream and vision, and the everyday world of waking consciousness. These two worlds are seen as comprising a single reality. Shamans keep open the ways between the worlds in order to maintain a unified vision of creation. No one and nothing is left out of this unity.

Ancient Wisdom

As we observe Merlin and Taliesin discussing the wonders of creation in the *Vita Merlini*, they are concerned primarily with natural phenomena. Geoffrey clearly had access to a number of straightforward medieval accounts of Creation, such as Bede's *De Natura Rerum* or the *Cosmographia* of Bernard Sylvestris.[22] However, much of his information seems to have come from the writings of Isidore of Seville (AD 560–636), a Spanish monk who was, in fact, roughly contemporary with Taliesin.[23] Various arguments have been produced to prove that his works were, or were not, available as early as the late-sixth or early-seventh centuries in Britain and Ireland, and certainly there are fragmentary manuscripts which seem to support this claim. Isidore was really an encyclopaedist who collated a vast range of material from every possible source in a completely unsystematic way. He was also totally credulous, which means that much of what he wrote borders on the fantastic. There is little doubt that he was a major influence on the Celtic cosmographers, and that many of his ideas are reflected in the ideas attached to both Taliesin and Merlin.

Taliesin reports that he had recently come from Brittany, where he had learned 'sweet philosophy' from Gildas the Wise. This is an interesting point because we know that Gildas did indeed settle in Brittany and that he lived contemporaneously with Taliesin and (in Geoffrey's timescale) with Merlin. The two wise men quickly settle down to a long cosmological discussion, Taliesin expounding at length on the creation and the formation of matter 'Under the guidance of Minerva.'

Out of nothing the Creator of the world produced four [elements] that they might be the prior cause as well as the material for creating all things when they were joined together in harmony: the heaven which He adorned with stars and which stands on high and embraces everything like the shell surrounding a nut; then He made the air, for forming sounds, through the medium of which day and night present the stars; the sea which girds the land in four circles, and with its mighty refluence so strikes the air as to generate the winds which are said to be four in number; as a foundation He placed the earth, standing by its own strength and not lightly moved, which is divided into five parts [*sic*], whereof the middle one is not habitable because of the heat and the two furthest are shunned because of their cold. To the last two He gave a moderate temperature, and these are inhabited by men and birds and herds of wild beasts. He added clouds to the sky so that they might furnish sudden showers to make the fruits of the trees and of the ground grow with their gentle sprinkling. With the help of the season these are filled like water skins from the rivers by a hidden law, and then, rising through the upper air, they pour out the water they have taken up, driven by the force of the winds.[24]

Taliesin continues at length, describing the types of the four winds, the outer realm of the fixed stars, the moon and sun, and the spaces between which are filled with spirits, both good and evil – including, of course, the succubae, one of whom had supposedly given birth to Merlin. He then discoursed upon the biology of the seas which, like the land itself, have hot streams leading down to the Underworld and cold streams nourished by the rays of the planet Venus. Next he introduced more details relating to the Earth, with an account of certain islands, of which Britain is said to be the fairest,

... for it bears crops which throughout the year give the noble gifts of fragrance for the use of man, and it has woods and glades with honey dripping in them, and lofty mountains and broad green fields, fountains and rivers, fishes and cattle and wild beasts, fruit trees, gems, precious metals, and whatever creative nature is in the habit of furnishing. Besides all these it has fountains healthful because of their hot waters which nourish the sick and provide pleasing baths, which quickly send people away cured with their sickness driven out. (Ibid)

This is obviously a description of a kind of earthly paradise rather than an actual account of Britain, and from this Taliesin goes on to describe the otherworldly realm of the Fortunate Isles, demonstrating exactly the kind of totally integrated cosmological vision of the shaman.

In addition, Taliesin recalls how together he and Merlin carried the wounded Arthur from the Battle of Camlann and with the help of the ferryman took him to the Island of Apples, ruled over by a nine-fold sisterhood, of whom the first and most famous is named Morgen. This character will later metamorphose into the familiar Morgan le Fay, Arthur's half-sister and arch enemy in the great medieval Arthurian epics of the thirteenth to fifteenth centuries. Here she is represented as goddess-like figure well versed in the healing arts, once again proving Geoffrey's familiarity with more ancient folklore and myth, in which Morgen (under the guise of the Morrígan) appears as a goddess of war. This remains one of the oldest sources which connect Arthur, Morgen and Avalon, and here for the first time we learn more of the fateful Battle of Camlann and of Arthur's eventual end.

These memories prompt Merlin to begin a further strand of prophecies about the leaders who will follow Arthur. But while the two seers are thus engaged, word comes of a new spring that has broken forth from the ground nearby. They go to view this and when Merlin drinks from it his mind is at last restored. Word of this reaches Ganeida and the rest of the court and people begin to make their way into the woods to ask Merlin to lead them again. But he refuses, pleading old age and a desire to retire from the world and to continue his starry observance from within his house. Taliesin decides to remain also, and they are shortly after joined by a man named Maeldin who is discovered wandering mad in the forest just as Merlin had lately done. He too is cured by drinking from the spring and elects to join Merlin and Taliesin in their observatory. Soon after this, Ganeida also comes to join them and the four remain together. Ganeida herself now finally begins to express her own prophetic gifts, the powers he has shared with Merlin but chosen to lay aside in her role as Queen and mother to her children.

The madman Maeldin seems almost like a double for Merlin himself, the similarity of their names, the parallel madness cured by the pure waters of the spring all suggest this. However, there are differences. Geoffrey tells us that this Maeldin had been a friend of Merlin's in their youth, and that his madness was a result of eating poisoned apples given to him by Merlin's ex-mistress. It is hard not to see here references which point us back to 'the lovely, eager girl' who used to bring Merlin food as he lay beneath the apple trees. Perhaps this is the real woman who ceased to visit him after the death of her son? If so, we know nothing more of this story beyond speculation. However, the episode seems to share some of the sources on which Geoffrey drew for his book.

Lailoken the Mad

A curious story found in the *Life* of the sixth century Scottish St Kentigern (also known as Mungo) describes the saint's encounter with a wild madman known as *Lailoken* – however 'some say he was Merlyn [*sic*] who was an extraordinary prophet of the British.' There are two variant versions of the saint's life, the first, known as the *Herbertian Life* (after Bishop Herbert who commissioned it) in *c.*1150, exists only in a fragment, and was followed, in *c.*1175, by a full length biography written by a monk named Joscelyn of Furness.[25] Both are therefore written after the *Vita Merlini* but seem to refer back to a far older set of themes. The earlier text includes a slightly fuller version of the story of Lailoken, which Joscelyn clearly purged as being too pagan.

The account tells of the birth of Kentigern to a lady named Teneu, daughter of King Leudonus (unknown to history) who is loved by Owein, son of Urien of Rheged – both familiar characters from later Arthurian romance. Teneu refused the advances of her noble suitor, who then disguised himself as a girl in order to be received into her chamber. He then seduces her and gets her pregnant. Her father, outraged by this, and assuming she was guilty of lust, condemned his daughter to death. She is thrown from the summit of the rocky outcrop of Traprain Law but miraculously survives the fall. She is then cast adrift in the Firth of Forth in a small boat without oars or sail, in the expectation that the craft will drift out to sea and she will drown. But, caught by the tide, the craft comes ashore in the far side of the Firth at Culross, where Teneu gives birth to the future saint. She is then rescued by another holy man, St Servanus (or Serf), who beings up the child and trains him to become a priest.

Here we already have a parallel between the later story of Merlin's birth, in which his mother is visited by an unknown man – by some described as a demon but actually more resembling a faery lover of the kind widely known in Scotland and northern Britain at the time – who gets her with child: the future Merlin. Then, in the two attempts to kill her, we may see a glimpse of the Threefold Death.

But this is not the end of the story. At the end of his Life of Kentigern Joscelyn adds a story of events that followed the death of the saint. This involves King Ryderch, whom we uncounted earlier in the poems attributed to Myrddin and the account of the battle of Arderydd. Among the king's retinue was a fool named Laloecen, who became so upset by the passing of Kentigern that he was inconsolable, driven mad by grief. In this state he made two prophecies – that both king Ryderch and another lord name Morthec, would both die before the year was out. Both prophecies came true, but Joscelyn says nothing more of the mysterious 'madman' Laloecen.

At this point we may recall the use of the word *llallogan* (usually translated as twin) in the 'Dialogue between Merlin and his Sister Gwenddydd'. Some scholars have suggested that this was a personal name, or even a pet name for Merlin, but it seems more like the name of the mad fool Laloecen from the *Vita Kentigern*. For a full account of the story recorded by Joselyn, which gives us a far clearer outline of the connection between the stories of Merlin's madness and that of the wild man, we have to turn to a fifteenth-century text known as the *Vita Merlini Silvestris*, or 'The Life of Merlin of the Forest'.[26] Significantly, this is bound in with both a copy of the oldest Life of Kentigern and a summary of Joselyn's longer text.

The story told here is much more fleshed out than the earlier versions and may have borrowed from Geoffrey's tale. It describes how Kentigern is praying alone in the forest when he is surprised by a naked and hairy man who comes at him screaming and raging 'like a beast'. The saint manages to calm him down and discovers that his name is Lailoken – which can we clearly see is derived from both the word *llallogan* found in the poem about Merlin and his sister, and the name Laloecen in the *Vita Kentigern*.

The text then goes on to relate the madman's tale of how, during a battle which is described as taking place 'between Liddel and

Carwannock', generally identified with the battle of Arderydd. The text continues:

> The madman stopped running and replied: I am Christian, though guilty of a crime so great that I am forced to suffer in this wilderness the fate destined to me, to live with beasts... I caused the slaughter of those who were killed in a battle well-known to the inhabitants of this country... In this battle... the sky opened above my head and I heard a voice like the sound of thunder ... and when I directed my gaze towards the sound of the voice, I saw a brightness greater than human nature could endure. And I saw also innumerable battalions of a great airborne army, holding fiery spears that flashed like lightning and terrible weapons which they brandished towards me. Then I was beside myself, and in that moment a malignant spirit seized hold of me and gave me unto the keeping of wild beasts, as you may see.[27]

Kentigern eventually heals the madman, but not before we have been treated to a close parallel of the triple death prophecy. This time it is applied to Lailoken himself, who begs for the sacraments to be given him before he dies, and when he is at first refused, gives a succession of monks sent by Kentigern three different ways by which he will die – by being beaten with cudgels, pierced by a sharp stake, and drowning. All three methods are shown to be true when the unfortunate man – having confessed his sins to Kentigern and described his visions as coming from Christ himself – is chased and beaten by shepherds in the service of King Meldred, who in this version stands in for Rodarchus in the unfaithful wife story.

The text ends with a mysterious couplet:

Sude perfossus, lapidem perpessus, et undam,
Merlinus triplicem fertur inisse necem.

Which translates as:

> Pierced by a stake and having endured stoning and drowning,
> Merlin is said to have undergone a threefold death.

This makes it clear that Lailoken is either a substitute for Merlin or the original hero of the tale told by Geoffrey of Monmouth and applied to the figure who was becoming more famous with every retelling of his tale. All three figures, Laloecen, Lailoken and Merlin, are wild men living in the woods; all are prophets and madmen, and all display signs that mark them out as possessed of the same qualities as the shamans of earlier times.

A fourth figure, borrowed from early Irish tradition, seems to have strayed into the Merlin story, displaying the same aspects of his character and actions. This is Suibhne Gelt (the Wild) whose story is told in a twelfth-century text called *Buile Shuibhne* 'The Frenzy of Shuibhne', which contains material from a far earlier time. In this story the wandering seer Shuibhne crosses the sea to Britain where he encounters a wild man (*gelt Bhreathnach*) called Alladhan, also known as *Fer Caille*, 'Man of the Wood'. This man describes having fought in a great battle and being cursed by his opponents' men. This reminds Shuibhne of an episode in his own life, where he had been cursed by a saint during battle, which has set him off on a wandering path. At this point both men predict each other's deaths, which later prove true after Shuibhne has spent a year with his new friend in the woods. The name Alladhan has been linked the word *allaidh* 'wild' which would certainly explain the characters' nature, but it may equally be an attempt to render the name Lailoken into Gaelic.

It seems likely that Geoffrey knew these stories and having heard or read the poems from *The Black Book of Carmarthen*, decided to weave them into a new tale of the increasingly popular figure of Merlin. Kentigern was the original founder of the community of St Asaph, where Geoffrey was later bishop, so he would almost certainly have been familiar with the stories surrounding the saint. A later account of the events described in the *Vita Kentigern* and the *Merlin Sylvestris* texts is found in the *Scottichronicon,* a huge work begun by John of Fordun in the fourteenth century and vastly extended by Walter Bower in the fifteenth. Bower included the story of Merlin's madness in a section headed 'Of the Penitential Marvels of the Prophet Merlin' in which he retold a shortened version of the story, ending with an explanation of why Merlin and St Kentigern are said to have died in the same year, while being apparently separated by a hundred years.[28] Some say that 'it was not the prophet of Vortigern's time called Merlin, but another miraculous prophet of the Scots called Lailoken, who because he was a miraculous prophet was called a second Merlin.' This, as we shall see, is an argument that will be repeated frequently down the centuries as the figure of Merlin evolved.

In the book written around 1146 by Gerald of Wales, describing his journey through the country, we find the following, enigmatic statement:

> That night, which was the Eve of Palm Sunday, we slept at Nefyn. There I myself, Archdeacon of St. David's, discovered the works of Merlin Sylvester, which I had long been looking for, or so I would like you to think. (*Itinerary Through Wales.* Trans L. Thorpe).

We cannot be sure what Gerald meant by this, or what works he refers to (the likelihood is that it is the Myrddin poems), and his phrasing is unclear, but it is interesting to speculate that this redoubtable traveller may have stumbled across an account of the seer which he later filtered through into other works.

The events in the texts concerning Lailoken, especially those concerning the wild man of the woods and his prophetic gifts, strike a shamanic note. As we saw, among traditional shamanic figures seership comes after a period of sickness or seeming madness. In common also with such people Merlin lives separate from his fellow men in the forest, eating grasses and roots. He talks with animals, watches the stars and makes prognostications from events he has observed. Like shamans from the dawn of time people come to consult him and he responds with revelatory visions. Virtually every aspect of his character as described, both in the Myrddin poems and in the *Vita Merlini*, depict him in such a way as to make it hard to imagine that his origin does not spring from memories, buried beneath the surface of nominally Christian Welsh literature and tradition, of the shamans who had once served them as guides and interpreters of the mysterious world around them.

Geoffrey gives us an unforgettable portrait of Merlin: intensely human, crushed by the horror of war, yet as crafty and cunning as any shaman of the old world. His Merlin is a lover also, capable of experiencing jealousy as in the instance of Guendolena's proposed remarriage, yet he harbours an awesome power – the gift of prophecy and seership which enables him to foretell the future and see the truth hidden beneath everyday events. By presenting him in this way Geoffrey established a basic pattern for the characterisation of Merlin which would be reworked again and again through the ages.

Some aspects of Merlin's life, such as his madness, were neglected after Geoffrey's time, though they remained just below the surface as his character underwent further metamorphoses into Prophet, Magician and Sage. However, along with the poems, the brief mentions in the *Triads* and the inclusion of Gwenddolau, Rhydderch and Gwenddydd, the *Vita Merlini* preserved the oldest and most authentic narrative of Merlin's life. Looking at them we see a picture of a fifth- or sixth-century prince, who fought at the historical Battle of Arderydd and was driven mad by the horrific carnage. Afterwards he seems to have run away and lived in the wilderness of the forest, with only animals for company. His experiences there changed him, giving him the gifts of prophecy and seership. From this moment on there would be two distinct Merlin characters. One, the wild man of the *Vita* and the *Myrddin Poems,* would be known as Myrddin Wyllt (the Wild), or in the style of later writers as Merlin Sylvestris (of the woods). The other, whose star gradually ascended until it all but blotted out the shape of older figure, would be Merlinus or Merlin, the son of a devil who possessed great knowledge and wisdom but who was only half human. According to which version was known to the authors who wrote about him the story would take a different course.

Like the ancient shamans in whose footsteps he treads, Merlin Wyllt is an elemental figure, who may remind us of the Green Man, a powerful nature spirit of ancient and world-wide tradition who represented the very essence of the natural world. But when he withdraws into the forest again, as he does at the end of Geoffrey's tale, to live not in the wilderness but in an observatory from which he studies the pathways of the stars, he has already begun to transform into another Merlin. This being is not only a prophet but a magician also – despite the fact that such a title was not to be conferred upon him for several decades after this – it is at these incarnations that we need to look at next.

MERLIN THE PROPHET

Because I am dark, and always shall be, let my book
be dark and mysterious in those places where I will
not show myself.

The Didot Perceval

The Prophetic Child

Merlin's next distinct incarnations are as a prophet and seer, roles
that were already emerging in the poems from *The Black Book
of Carmarthen*, but which gradually became more emphasised as
his character grew and developed. It is probably from this aspect
of his history that a belief arose that Merlin was a Druid, since
the Druids were known to practice the arts of prophecy. One of
the oldest sources for the name Merlin, as ready mentioned, is a
poem dating from the ninth century called the '*Armes Prydein*',
or 'Prophecy of Britain', in which the refrain 'Merlin (Myrddin)
foretells...' is used repeatedly.[1] It is entirely possible that the name
was inserted sometime after the original composition, as there are
also references in the poem to 'the Awen [inspiration] foretells...'
and even to 'the Great Son of Mary declares...' Even if this is the

case, the author of the poem clearly knew of Merlin as a seer and included his name in the ranks of the prophets as a matter of course.

But it is to Geoffrey of Monmouth that we owe the character of Merlin as he is most often represented throughout the Middle Ages and in some instances up to the present. As noted earlier we are used to seeing the terms 'magician', 'enchanter', and 'wizard' casually used to describe Merlin; yet in almost every one of the early medieval writings in which he appears he is never called any of these things. Rather, he is seen as a wise man, a prophet and a seer, and by many of the more religious writers of the time, as a demon – or at least the son of a demon. In reality he was, of course, no more a devil than he was a Christian. But as we saw, this idea seems to have emerged quite naturally from the older legends concerning a wild man living alone in the woods and born to a woman who is visited at night by a mysterious being who became recognised as a demon only in the medieval period.

Geoffrey set out to create a figure who possessed the mystery and stature of the older visionary, figure of Myrddin, into an almost Classical idea of a seer and prophet when he published a collection of the best part of one hundred prophecies attributed to Merlin. The *Historia Regum Brittaniae* (c.1138)[2] incorporated the earlier work and set it within the framework of an older tale which, as we saw in Chapter 1, Geoffrey found in the *Historia Brittonum*, a collection of historical scraps attributed to a ninth-century monk named Nennius – who also gave us some of the oldest glimpses of the figure of the sixth-century Arthur.[3]

In the *Historia* Geoffrey had already begun to establish Merlin in his soon to be familiar role as Arthur's magical counsellor. Later, in c.1150, he turned again to the older figure of Merlin, in a long poem entitled '*Vita Merlin*' ('Life of Merlin'), clearly influenced by the Myrddin poems.[4] It is to Geoffrey's writings, and in particular his collections of Merlin's prophetic utterances, that we owe this aspect of

Merlin's character. While Myrddin was clearly known and established as such within Britain – especially Wales – Geoffrey's books pushed the mysterious prophet out into the wider world and made him a household name among the educated Norman rulers of England.

Geoffrey probably became familiar with folk tales about Merlin during his childhood in Monmouth and later, as Bishop of St Asaph in North Wales, though he rarely visited there, if at all. However, he seems to have fallen under the spell of the mysterious visionary, giving him an important role in the *History of the Kings of Britain*, regarded as one of the most important and influential works of the Middle Ages. Despite the fact that some of his own contemporaries regarded him as a 'fabulator' rather than a bona fide historian, there were enough who believed his account of the early history of Britain as true. The legends of the founding of New Troy by Brutus, grandson of the Trojan hero Aeneas, the story of King Leir and his daughters, and of course the saga of Arthur made the *Historia* a hit on almost every level. As the historian T.D. Kendrick remarked in his book *British Antiquity:*

> Within fifteen years of its publication not to have read it was a matter of reproach; it became a respected textbook of the Middle Ages; it was incorporated in chronicle after chronicle; it was turned into poetry; it swept away opposition with the ruthless force of a great epic; its precedents were quoted in parliament …. [and] even in the eighteenth century there were antiquaries who believed it to be truthful history.[5]

In Geoffrey's account, Merlin's first great prophetic outburst forms a dramatic centrepiece to first half of the *Historia*. The episode brings the narrative to a halt with the prophecies uttered by Merlin to Vortigern, a minor king who makes a bid for power by bringing in Saxon mercenaries to fight the Picts in the North and his own enemies elsewhere. He is briefly popular, but his star soon wanes as more and more Saxons arrive and begin acquiring more extensive areas of land. Finally, the exiled sons of the former High King of Britain (whom Vortigern ordered killed) return at the head of an army and Vortigern flees to Wales, where he intends to build a stronghold from where he can mount a counteroffensive.

Having chosen a site, he sets his builders to work; but every night the progress they have made is undone by a mysterious agency. Vortigern consults his Druids and learns that only the blood of a fatherless child, spilled on the stones, will ensure the completion of the fortress. Sent out to search for such a child, Vortigern's soldiers discover Merlin at Carmarthen. He is the son of a Welsh Princess, but no one knows his father. The woman and her son are brought before Vortigern, and Merlin's mother explains that she has led a devout and pure life, but that she was visited in her chamber by a mysterious being who fathered the child upon her. This of course echoes the story of the conception and birth of Lailoken whom, as we saw, presents many similarities to Merlin's early character.

Vortigern is tempted to disbelieve the account, but Merlin himself speaks out in defence of his mother, and challenges Vortigern and his Druids to explain the real reason why the tower will not stand. He tells them that there is a pool beneath the hill top, and that within it is a stone coffer containing two dragons, one red and the other white, who battle mightily every night, thus causing the ground to shake and the work of the king's masons to fall. Vortigern orders his men to dig and finds that all is as Merlin had foretold. The wise child then explains that the Red Dragon symbolises Britain and the White Dragon the Saxons, and prophesies that after a time the White will overcome the Red. He then goes into a trance and for the next fourteen pages in Geoffrey's book proceeds to expound the future of the race to the very end of time.

In the process he predicts the coming of Arthur 'the Boar of Cornwall', which will 'bring relief from these invaders, for it will trample their necks beneath its feet' and warns Vortigern of his own forthcoming death. The end of this extraordinary outburst is apocalyptic, with references to riot among the planetary houses and the fall of deadly rain. Finally, 'In the twinkling of an eye the seas shall rise up and the arena of the winds shall be opened once again. The Winds shall do battle together with a blast of ill omen, making their din reverberate from one constellation to another.'[6]

* * *

The whole structure and content of the prophecies, especially in Geoffrey's book, show a remarkable grasp of the tides which control the fate of the world, and Merlin's vision of the future is as terrifying as anything foretold by Nostradamus several hundred years later. Wherever Geoffrey found the material for this part of his book (some is now recognised as being from the *Pharsalia*, a work by the first-century Roman poet Lucan)[7] it was clearly not from his own mind, indicating, as already stated, that he was in some way the recipient of a body of traditional lore associated with Merlin. The earlier collection of prophetic materials, published separately as belonging to Merlin, before the appearance of the *Historia* or the *Vita Merlini*, have long been dismissed as a ragbag collection of materials stolen from older sources – but since these sources are no longer available, we cannot be certain what they were. Geoffrey's *Historia* has been the cause of scholarly debate for generations, and while many earlier critics dismissed him as a flagrant forger, a more recent attitude tends to emphasise his value as a recorder of traditional tales and native folklore. It is now widely accepted that Geoffrey had access to older material which recorded Merlin's inspired utterances – although whether these were entirely genuine, or represented a Merlin tradition, has still to be completely established.

Another medieval historian, William of Newburgh (1136–1198) writing later in the same century, says of Geoffrey that he added considerably to the original prophecies while he was translating them into Latin. Geoffrey himself claimed that he was merely translating 'a certain very ancient book written in the British language', lent to him by Archdeacon Walter of Oxford, and that this was the source of all that he wrote. No trace of this book has ever come to light and it has generally been considered to be an invention of Geoffrey's to add veracity to his fanciful history. While there is no reason why there should not have been such a book, it is evident that Geoffrey considerably embellished his sources.

The source of the story of Merlin's confrontation of Vortigern and the Druids is found in the writings of the ninth-century monk Nennius, whom, as we have seen, contributed one of the few possibly authentic records of the Arthurian era. His youthful prophet was named Emrys (or Ambrosius in Latin) and it seems that in order not to confuse him with Ambrosius the son of Constantine, who overthrew Vortigern, Geoffrey borrowed the name and some of the characteristics of Merlin from the older traditional figure of whom he was already aware.

Overall Geoffrey presents the character of Merlin as ambiguous – he is, at one and the same time, the product of a union between a human woman and a demon (admittedly a minor one) – despite this, Merlin is able to do good, his knowledge of the future and his prophetic utterances being generally seen as beneficial. However, Merlin was not always seen as a positive force. Several of Geoffrey of Monmouth's contemporaries criticised him for writing about a demonic character, belief in whom might be considered heretical. William of Newburgh in particular took him to task for allowing that prophecy was either correct or permissible in Christian terms. In his *Historia Rerum Anglicarum* (The History of English Affairs, *c*.1196) he wrote:

> His [i.e. Geoffrey's] story is that Merlin was born of a woman and sired by a demonic incubus; accordingly, he ascribes to him a most outstanding and extensive foreknowledge of the future, on the grounds that he took after his father. In fact, we are instructed by both true reason and the sacred writings that demons are shut out of God's light and are wholly unable to have prior knowledge of the future.... In short, they [the demons] are often deceived and deceive by their guesses, though these are quite sophisticated, but by means of trickery in their predictions they lay claim amongst naïve people a foreknowledge of the future which they do not at all possess.[8]

Books of Prophecy

Another writer, roughly contemporary with Geoffrey of Monmouth and sometimes considered as only slightly more reliable, is the twelfth-century historian and traveller Giraldus Cambrensis, whose book, *Expugnatio Hibernica* (The Exploration of Scotland) adds to our understanding of native prophecy. His intention was to include the prophecies of Merlin in his book, and though unfortunately no trace of this has survived, his comments on the native prophetic literature of the Celts is of considerable interest.[9]

He refers to them as *Liber Vaticiniorum* (Books of Prophecy) and talks of translating them from 'the barbarous garb of the British tongue', suggesting that he was referring to actual written works. However, he goes on to say that the prophecies were orally retained by many British bards, and that very few were actually committed to writing. Their publication, he adds, was much desired by King Henry II. Giraldus himself, being insufficiently skilled in the Welsh language, was assisted in his translations by native speakers. Despite the seeming contradiction of this statement, Giraldus' next comment is more illuminating. These prophecies are, he says, much adulterated by modern additions added by the bards, all of which he intended to exclude, keeping only what seemed true to their rudeness and simplicity! This is significant, recognising as it does not only the existence of such primitive material, but also the tendency in medieval bards to augment the original material with current prophecies (and doubtless more besides).

Further evidence for the survival of original materials comes from a collection of Merlin prophecies collected by John of Cornwall, a little after those of Geoffrey, in *c.*1140. John also claimed to have 'translated' them from the British language, by which he may mean either Cornish, Welsh or Breton. In any case they were written (by John) in Latin, apparently at the request of the Bishop of Exeter, so that more educated people would be able to understand them. The prophecies have been subtly updated and John's own notes offer interpretations slanted towards current events. In places the wording echoes the poems from *The Black Book of Carmarthen*.

John of Cornwall (fl. mid to late twelfth century) claimed that his book was a translation of an authentic work of vaticination, which he attributed to Merlin. His work is clearly political in its anti-Norman, pro-British stance. When compared to Geoffrey's work it shows just how sympathetic to the Normans the latter was, and how he strove to substantiate Norman claims to the British throne while extoling the virtues of their nobility. The editor of the only extant manuscripts of John's prophecies, Michael Curley, suggests – on the strength that less than a tenth of the total prophecies are the same as Geoffrey's – that both men were working from an independent source – in this instance almost certainly Celtic in origin – probably Cornish, and that he was familiar with the older Myrddin poems, which he drew upon.[10]

John makes his own political stance clear in the final prophecy of his book, when he called for an alliance between Cornwall and

Brittany to drive out both the Saxon and Norman invaders. The ultimate source for this would seem to be the tenth-century poem 'Armes Prydain Fawr' ('The Prophecy of Britain') which is found in *The Book of Taliesin*. In linking two great historical heroes, Conan (Cynan) of Cornwall and Cadwaladyr of Wales, John must have known this work, which states:

> As for Cynan and Cadwaladr, mighty in arms,
> Their fate will be celebrated forever.
> Two wise and steadfast rulers,
> Trampling down the English in God's name,
> Two generous men, gift-giving cattle-raiders,
> Two brave, eager men, of a single faith and fate.
> Two guardians of Britain with mighty armies
> Two bears that daily battle cannot thrive …[11]

It is possible that this anti-Norman approach accounts for the single remaining manuscript – the others perhaps being destroyed to prevent an uprising among the Celtic population of Britain.

Michael Feletra, in his closely argued paper 'Merlin in Cornwall',[12] produces considerable evidence in favour of the original source for both John of Cornwall and Geoffrey of Monmouth being a native Cornish text. If he is correct this shows an established lineage for Merlin's prophecies for a period older than either surviving text. It seems likely in any case that John's work may have been an intermediary between the older Myrddin poems and Geoffrey's compilation.

The sources – actual or proposed – for Geoffrey's selection of prophecies, continues to be debated. The most likely scenario is that Geoffrey knew the prophecies attributed to the Welsh Merlin, and that he copied these, adapting them as he went, and adding references to actual events that took place in his own lifetime. By 'backdating' the texts to a distant past, he is able to present Merlin as a significant prophet. The other possibility is that Geoffrey's own statement at the beginning of the *Historia*, – that his source was a certain 'ancient British book', given to him by his colleague Walter, Archdeacon of Oxford, is also the source of the prophecies. As the text of this book has never been discovered, doubt has been cast on its existence. Certainly, many medieval writers regularly claimed antique sources for their work in order to give them veracity; however, there is no reason to suppose that Geoffrey's book did not exist. One contender is a work known as *The Deeds of Arthur*, which was in the library of John Dee during the reign of Elizabeth I, but which has subsequently vanished. Again, we have no certain evidence one way or the other.

Visionary Disciplines

Prophecy was very much part of the lifeblood of the Celts. Indeed, the role of the seer was regarded as crucial to the spiritual well-being of the people – to the extent that distinct groups whose task it was to explore the prophetic arts existed throughout the Celtic world.[13] Among the Druids, who were the official priesthood of the Celts, their seers, called Ovates (a term borrowed from the Latin *vates*, seer, which shows a late influence on the way we see them today) were particularly important. The Ovates specialised in prophecy and divination, using a variety of methods including observation from nature, incantation, and dream. Merlin himself is referred to throughout Geoffrey's book as a prophet.

After the suppression of the Druids by the Romans in AD 64, the role of the Ovate was virtually lost in Britain. The newly established Christian religion had no use for pagan prophecy, although seers like the *Awenyddion*, who gave oracular advice to questioners by going into a deep trance, remained active in Wales into medieval times. Instead, the role of seer was largely incorporated into that of the poet in both Britain and Ireland, where they continued to influence society in ways similar to their lineal forebears. Many seers continued to work underground, offering hope to a conquered people, spreading tales of the immanent return of the heroic Arthur from the otherworld. The same is true of Merlin's time, where many of the surviving prophecies attributed to him are aimed at the defeat of the Saxons and the restoration of the British nation.

The native inhabitants of Britain never regained their primacy. After the Romans left, the Saxons settled the bulk of the South and Midlands and the surviving British Celtic kingdoms, particularly the Cymry (whom the Saxons called 'Welsh' or 'foreigners,') were pushed to the Western margins. During the medieval period the Welsh sought solace against this through prophecy, which strengthened them in their struggle against the Normans. Ironically, since this latest wave of incomers sought amid the relics of the Arthurian lineage for connections to the land they had conquered, the Welsh were just as assiduously seeking signs that foretold the eminent doom of their new masters!

The element of prophecy within Merlin's history is so important that it requires some investigation here. We are fortunate to know of several methods used by Celtic seers to obtain prophetic insight or to access inner wisdom, notably three techniques, known as *Imbas Forosnai, Teinm Laegda,* and *Dichetal do Chennaib.* There are numerous references to these disciplines in Irish mythology and literature, but for a definition of sorts we have to turn to a huge collection of texts compiled in the twelfth century and known as *The Ancient Laws of Ireland.*[14] There we find all three techniques listed among the skills required of the poet. *Teinm Laegda* is described as the means by which the poet receives wisdom through the words he chooses – or, to put it simply, that he experiences inspiration. *Imbas Forosnai* is described as wisdom imbibed directly from master to pupil, 'by word of mouth'. *Dichetal do Chennaib*, which literally means 'invocation by the ends of the fingers', concerns the acquiring of wisdom directly and without contemplation, perhaps through touch. All three are concerned with inspired knowledge.

Another early text, the ninth century *Cormac's Glossary*, reiterates the catalogue of the *Ancient Irish Laws* with significant additions:

> *Imbas Forosna* 'Manifestation that Enlightens': discovers whatever the poet likes and which he desires to reveal... The poet chews a piece of the red [raw] flesh of a pig, or a dog, or a cat, and puts it then on a flagstone behind the door-valve, and chants an incantation over it, and offers it to his gods, and calls them to him, and leaves them not on the morrow, and then chants over his two palms, and calls again gods to him, that his sleep may not be disturbed. Then he puts his two palms on his cheeks and sleeps. And men are watching him that he may not turn over and that no one may disturb him. And then it is revealed to him that for which he was engaged till the end of a *nomad* [three days and nights] ... And therefore, it is called *Imm-bas*, to whit, a palm (*bas*) on this side and a palm on that around his head. [St] Patrick banished that [along with] the *Tenmn Laida* 'illumination of song' and declared that no one shall belong to heaven or earth [that practices it], for it is a denial of baptism. *Dichetal do Chennaib* 'extempore incantation' however, *that* was left, in right of art, for it is science that causes it, and no offering to devils is necessary, but merely a declaration from the ends of his bones...[15]

This description, on the face of it, seems clear enough – though yet again we see an attempt to banish all such practices as demonic. The person seeking enlightenment, on any subject he wishes, through *Imbas Forosna*, first chews a piece of raw meat, then places it on a doorstep and invokes the gods. He then apparently puts his hands over his face and sleeps for two or three days and nights, during which time he is watched over to see that he does not turn over and is not disturbed by anyone. This form of trance state was common among classical shamans the world over; as someone versed in the shamanic arts, Merlin would certainly have been aware of the technique.

The consumption of food from the land in order to gain answers was also a part of Druid practice, as the following account makes clear. It concerns a Druid named Bicne, who

> ... whenever he could not decide on some dark-meaning question which the men of Ireland posed him he should consume some of its fruit, corn, fish, milk or chestnuts.'[16]

Food offerings of this kind remained the chief method of sacrificing to spirits throughout Europe even after the spread of Christianity. The slaughter of large animals such as oxen, yielding meat to feed a whole community, was usually performed in a manner reminiscent of ancient sacrificial rites where both people and spirits partook of the meat. Throughout Europe, such communal festivities continued with full pagan fervour, only marginally allowed and sometimes Christianised by its unofficial canonisation as a saint's day.

The placing of the two palms over the cheeks, mentioned in the *Glossary* suggests the covering of the eyes. This echoes references to the darkened chamber in which poets were said to seek inspiration – or indeed to a meditational habit in which the outer world is excluded as far as possible. Another method, known as the *Tarb Feis* or Bull Feast, emphasises this same importance of darkness and enchanted sleep. The Irish story of 'The Destruction of De Derga's Hostel' describes this practice in vivid terms.

> A bull feast was prepared by the men of Erin in order to determine their future king; that is, a bull was killed by them and thereof

one man ate his fill and drank its broth, and a spell of truth was chanted over him in his bed. Whomsoever he would see in his sleep would be king, and the sleeper would perish if he uttered a false word.[17]

It is worth noting that the three animals mentioned in the *Glossary*, the pig, the dog and the cat, were significant animals among the Celts, each with its own spiritual focus. Also, that Merlin offered his own verses to a pig. The text does not say that the subject *ate* the meat, only that he 'chewed' it, and afterwards laid it behind the door. This almost certainly refers to the ancient sanctity of the threshold, across which one could not pass unless invited, and to a possible altar stone set up near the door for offerings to the household gods. The act of chewing is known to release endorphins which produce a feeling of heightened awareness.

Cracking Open the Meaning

The second of the three divinatory methods, *Teinm Laegda* or 'Illumination by Song', is aptly described by the fifth-century Irish poet Cruitíne, who when he speaks of the process of writing a poem, says:

> One must crack open
> its secret narrative.[18]

This secret narrative or subtext is not about literary meaning but about the hidden or otherworldly truths hidden within a subject. Poetry is literally seen a means of discovering a visionary truth. The Irish hero, Fionn Mac Cumhail, has frequent recourse to this method of divination. On one occasion he uses it to discover not only the reason for a nocturnal attack on his encampment, but to learn the identity of a headless body which has been discovered nearby. Putting his thumb into his mouth, he speaks through the power of *Teinm Laegda*:

> He has not been killed by people –
> He has not been killed by the people of Laighné –
> He has not been killed by a wild boar –
> He has not been killed by a fall –
> He has not died on his bed – Lomna![19]

Fionn then goes on to discover that Lomna has been murdered by his fool. What is so interesting about this is the way it echoes Merlin's perception of the youth disguised by his sister, for whom he predicts a different death on each occasion.

We see here that the poet uses oracular skills to crack open the conundrum, and that Fionn's 'magical thumb' is employed. According to various stories, his thumb is imbued with otherworldly wisdom since he touched the Salmon of Knowledge caught by his master Finneces with this digit or, alternatively, had it trapped in the door of a faery hill.

The fingers or thumb seem to figure prominently in the lore of seers, and it is not surprising to find that the last of the three methods listed in *Cormac's Glossary* uses them in a specific way. *Dichetal do Chennaib*, 'Extemporary Invocation' or, as it is sometimes translated 'Invocation from the Finger-Ends' is described thus:

> When the poet sees the person or thing before him, he makes a verse at once with the ends of his fingers, or in his mind without studying, and he composes and repeats at the same time.[20]

It is interesting to note that in present day Ireland the whorls on the ends of the fingers are called *suil mé ire*, 'the eyes of the fingers'.

'Seeing with the fingers' is a good description of the visionary touch, a kind of psychometric sensing which yields information.

Before St Patrick brought Christianity to Ireland, there was an older method of practicing *Dichetal do Chennaib*. In this 'the poet placed his staff upon a person's body or upon his head, and found out his name, and the name of his father and mother, and discovered every unknown thing that was proposed to him, in a minute or two or three...' *Dichetal do Chennaib* was the only authorised method of divination allowed by St Patrick since, 'he did not leave them after this any rite in which offering should be made to the devil.' The Christianised rite does not allow for touching the subject nor for invocation of spirits; 'Invocation from the Finger-Ends' is thus robbed of its tactile and spiritually inspired method.

These methods of prognostication did not endure in their original forms, but the incubatory aspects of *Imbas Forosna* were still in use by bardic students in Ireland and Scotland as late as the eighteenth century. They were given poetic subjects for composition and then secluded in 'houses of darkness' where they would lie, totally covered by a blanket, often with a stone on their chests to prevent drowsiness, and other stones to secure the their covering, to pursue their metaphors in the close darkness. This method of poetic incubation recalls aspects of *Imbas Forosna* and the *tarbh-feis*. In the houses of darkness, the answer sought is a poem, its metaphors relentlessly pursued down the pathways of song to the regions of the otherworld. The seers sought answers to problems in much the same way.

The Spirit of Inspiration

In each instance of these methods, whether they are used to uncover poetic insight or to access the hidden wisdom of the otherworld, we see that the role of the poet and the seer were considered as interdisciplinary. Poets were also seers; seers were poets. Merlin, in his earliest incarnation, is both.

In the light of this it is not surprising that the Celtic prophetic tradition, of which Merlin is very much a part, is primarily fuelled by the search for poetic inspiration. Stories about finding *imbas* (Irish) or *awen* (Welsh) – both words for inspiration – are at the heart of this tradition. *Imbas* is said to reside in the Salmon of Knowledge which swims elusively through the training of the visionary poets of Ireland; *awen* is sought in the inspirational draught of many British cauldrons, from the Welsh Ceridwen's initiatory cauldron to the regenerative cup of the Holy Grail.[21]

Inspiration is perceived as a spirit which is sought by the practitioner, courted under a variety of bewildering metaphors as a fish, a swiftly rushing river, hazelnuts, a spiral tower, a net of stars, a faery woman – to name only a few. The results of the union between inspiration and the practitioner are described in a variety of metaphors – as abundance, overwhelming waters, vigorous energy, or vortices of penetrative light.

The text known as *The Three Cauldrons*, a teaching manual intended for poetic students, provides a typical example in its description of the poetic reception of inspiration, received from the sacred Well of Segais which rises from the land of the Sidhe (the faery people):

> Joy at the approach of *imbas*
> amassed by the nine hazels of fair fruitfulness
> in Segais of the *sidhe*,
> which hurtles upstream along the Boyne
> in a ram's head bore,
> swifter than a three-year-old at the racetrack,
> in the middle of June each seventh year.[22]

If we turn to British tradition, we find the art of the *awenydd* or 'inspired one' (pl. *awenyddion*), is also concerned with oracular vision and inspiration. An account related by the twelfth-century chronicler Gerald of Wales, and is strongly reminiscent of Merlin's trance-like state described in Geoffrey's *Historia:*

> When you consult them [seers] about some problem, they immediately go into a trance and lose control of their senses, as if they are possessed.
>
> They do not answer the question put to them in any logical way. Words stream from their mouths, incoherently and apparently meaningless and without any sense at all, but all the same well expressed; and if you listen carefully to what they say you will receive the solution to your problem. When it is all over, they will recover from their trance, as if they were ordinary people waking from a heavy sleep, but you have to give them a good shake before they regain control of themselves... They seem to receive this gift of divination through visions which they see in their dreams.[23]

Gerald goes on: 'You will object that the prophets were not possessed when they prophesied, whereas we read that when Merlin Sylvester made his prophecies he was in a frenzy, and in the same way the other soothsayers about whom I have written ... seem to be possessed.'[24]

The British *awenyddion* are literally filled with *awen,* just as the Irish poets are filled with *imbas.* Both are possessed by the spirit of inspiration. The poet pours himself into the augury, journeying through the channels provided by the unfolding metaphor like a salmon thrashing upstream to its spawning ground. This metaphor itself is often used by poets to describe the process, and two major exponents of the poetic tradition – Taliesin, who as we know was Merlin's friend or even successor, along with the Irish poet and warrior Fionn Mac Cumhail – have myths in which they are closely associated with the salmon. To possess the Salmon of Knowledge is to possess wisdom in the beliefs of the ancient Celtic world.

The myth of Taliesin and his transmogrification into animal, bird, fish and seed is, as we have seen, a major example of the initiation experienced by the poet and the seer alike. In Irish tradition, the story of Fionn is equally important for the glimpse it gives into a forgotten world of visionary experience.

Taliesin imbibes the wisdom of the Cauldron when he places his burned thumb into his mouth. The other character who shares this unusual mode of magical transmission is Fionn, who possessed wisdom equal to that of Taliesin – though never so totally expressed in the records that have survived. The story of Fionn's childhood, and his acquiring of wisdom, is told in an Irish text *The Boyhood Exploits of Fionn* which has been dated to as early as the tenth century and, as ever, contains even older material.[25]

As a youth Fionn was at a place called Moy Liffey, in Kildare, when he spied some youths playing hurly, and joining in, defeated them all. When they complained to their lord, he told them to kill the stranger, but they declared that they would be unable to do so because of his strength. Asked to describe the youth they said that he was 'A shapely fair youth'. The lord said he should henceforth be called Fionn (Finn 'the fair') and the name stuck to him. This story, though not exactly the same, recalls that of Merlin, who when discovered by Vortigern's men, was playing football with a group of youths who mocked him for having no father. As we saw, this led to Merlin's first prophetic outburst; Fionn himself goes to learn poetry from Finneces (White Wisdom), who lives on the shores of the magical River Boyne, and who had been seeking the Salmon of Wisdom which swam in Fec's Pool for seven years, since it had been prophesied that he would find it, eat it and know everything. However, when it was found, Finneces entrusted its cooking to Fionn who, though cautioned to eat nothing of the fish, nevertheless thrust his burnt thumb into his mouth when it was splashed by some of the liquor in which the salmon was cooked. So, it is the boy, not Finneces, who receives the wisdom of the salmon. The old poet immediately recognises the boy as Fionn, naming him as the prophesied receiver of wisdom. After this, Fionn had only to put his thumb into his mouth to have prophetic knowledge.

> It is that which gave the knowledge to Finn, to whit, whenever he put his thumb into his mouth, and sang through *teinm laida*, then whatever he had been ignorant of would be revealed to him.[26]

It is interesting to notice that as well as receiving the wisdom of the salmon Fionn is already a poet, which he becomes through falling ill. It is well known that in many instances shamanic abilities manifest themselves after illness, so that Fionn may be seen as both a poet and a shaman, just as are both Taliesin and Merlin. Although there is no story attached to Merlin which actually followed these lines, the poems attributed to the seer, in both early and later sources, provide enough similarities to suggest that the story of Merlin's madness parallels the 'poetic inspiration' of his fellow visionary poets and prophets, Taliesin and Fionn.

Messages from the Land

Physical contact with the earth is another important part of the transmission of both seership and oracular skill. The land held information like a great book, which could be accessed by those with the skill to see or hear them. The most subtle methods of prophetic tradition in these islands seem always to have been available to those who live within the spiritual continuum of the land, and this, we have seen, is a central aspect of Merlin's life in the wilderness. The ancient gifts of the seer poets were not fuelled merely by clairvoyance or poetic sensibility, but by resonance, touch, connection. Their ability to root into any object, place or person and discover identity, quality and answers to questions concerning these is part of this symbiotic continuum. Thus Taliesin speaks constantly of 'becoming' certain objects – a tree, a staff, a stone or a lantern – as well as being able to slip between the cracks of time to predict future events.

In a story curiously reminiscent of the building of Vortigern's Tower, we again hear how contact with the earth could manifest revelations. The incident happens during the creation of the monastic community on the island of Iona. The buildings intended for the community would not stand, and seeking advice through prayer its founder St Columba received a disturbing instruction: one of the monks must be buried alive. A man named Odhran volunteered for this very pagan sounding sacrifice in order that the monastic settlement may proceed. However, when Columba unearths him in a fit of unease after twenty days, Odhran sits up and cheerfully announces that: 'hell is not as it has been reported...' Columba at once orders the grave to be closed again, lest Odhran give voice to any more unsettling revelations this kind! Here, yet again, the earth itself seems to bring visions.[27]

Given this, it is perhaps not surprising that among the tasks undertaken by the Druids and poets of the ancient Celtic world, the chief of these was the preservation of the land from harm. British bardic tradition speaks of 'perpetual choirs of song' which hold the land in unity and spiritual health, while the central theme throughout the many versions of Merlin's history is his single-minded devotion to the kings he serves, of course including Arthur, and to the land over which they rule,

The Prophetic Line
Apart from the accounts of divination and seership examined above, there also exists a vast body of prophetic literature which, though it offers little by way of clues to the methods used, does reflect the state of mind and the situation of the people who

referred to it. Along with the prophecies ascribed to Merlin himself we may list the extraordinary outpourings of Shuibhne Gelt, whose dialogues with a circle of unseen figures reflect the innermost journeys of the ancient shamans and whose story, as we saw, blends with that of Merlin and Taliesin. Additionally, there are the prophetic utterances, extending to hundreds of pages, made by the twelfth-century prophet Thomas the Rhymer, who lived on the borders of Scotland and is still believed to lie in enchanted sleep beneath the Eildon hills. Later came Coinneach Odhar, named 'the Brahan Seer', whose prophetic curse against the family responsible for his murder are among the most remarkable instances of prophetic accuracy to have survived.

The tradition of seership among the Celts has continued into our own time, when the prophecies of Merlin are again being considered and discussed, weighed and measured to establish their degree of accuracy. When the coming of Christianity forced the old poets and seers to go into hiding, they took the traditions of seership with them, where they became part of the folklore of a conquered people. But such skills never really ceased to be practised, and even when this was not openly admitted, for fear of angering the churchmen of the time, the number of people possessing 'second sight' continued undiminished, especially among the highlands and islands of Scotland. Thus, it has continued to the present, when a new generation of seers, mostly unbeknown outside their own immediate families, keep the traditions of seership alive. At the other end of the spectrum, in the revival of interest in the practice of Druidry in our own time, the ancient prophetic arts are as important as ever.

We have no means of knowing whether Merlin used any of the techniques discussed above to make his prophecies; what we can say, without question, is that he belonged to an ancient lineage of seers and prophets, who were more closely in tune with the natural world and far more instinctual in the practice of their art.

Merlin is often described as falling into a trance, in which state he is able to discover the truth about events that have already happened elsewhere, or are yet to be. This is wholly in keeping with his depiction as a shaman, a bard and a prophet, as well as with the procedures of the *Awenyddion* in Wales. It explains to a large extent why the early authors who told his story chose to depict Merlin as having direct access to inner wisdom rather than as practicing any specific techniques.

Merlin's Dark Vision

If we look at the actual prophecies attributed to Merlin, especially the older ones, we see several distinct themes. All are linked, not surprisingly, with the future well-being of his people. We have already examined two of the poems from *The Black Book of Carmarthen,* which gave us some idea of Merlin's life. Others, from the same source, offer a selection of prophetic statements that refer both to events believed to have taken place during the Dark Age period, and others which relate to later events.

As we saw in Merlin's dialogue with his sister, where he is repeatedly prompted to name the successive kings who will rule over the Cymry (Welsh), he offers a number of names. Some of these are known individuals, such as Cadwaladyr, who ruled over part of Wales in the seventh-century, or Owain Gwynedd (1100–1170) who fought against the Normans in the twelfth century. In a more extended passage Myrddin expounds further, suggesting even that the events to come might be so terrible as to announce the end of the world:

> I will declare to you, Gwenddydd,
> Predicting from age to age –
> After Cadwaladr, Cynda.
> A hand on the cross of every sword,

Let all take care for their lives –
No reconciling with Cynda.
I foretell that a prince will come,
After much affliction – a prince of Gwynedd,
Who will overcome all opposition...
From that time the Cymry will suffer...
Impossible to say who will rule...
Lament, wretched Cymry!
When killing becomes the first duty
From sea to sea and across the land –
Surely the world is at an end ...?

The end of the Arthurian era seems to have signalled an end to organised resistance on the part of the Britons against their Saxon invaders, though individual chieftains continued to carry out sporadic raids on the enemy, and enclaves of native resistance existed across the country. Arthur's period as leader of the resistance had, in any case, blunted the force of the invasion to the extent that it became a semi-peaceful settlement. Added to this was the belief, which came into operation within months of his passing, that Arthur would one day return to lead his people to victory.

This situation created the need for a continuing bardic tradition, which included the art of prophecy, and would ensure that such beliefs never died. Myrddin, Taliesin and Gwenddydd all prophesied the return of Arthur; in later times these prophecies were taken up, elaborated and added to, giving rise to a vast body of prophetic literature – much of it forged – which began to be applied to later political events.

The Britons never really ceased to fight the Saeson (English) and to hope for the appearance of a deliverer – whether in the shape of Arthur, Owein Gwynedd or Cadwaladyr, or numerous lesser figures. The prophetic literature of the period between

600 and 1500 abounds in references to the strength of the Britons and their expected triumphs, to battles they have fought or will fight. The importance of such writings was recognised in a statute issued during the reign of Edward I, prohibiting 'Bards, Rhymers and others, idlers and vagabonds ... lest by their invectives and lies they lead the people to mischief and burden the common people with their impositions.' Henry IV was later even more specific in his condemnation of wandering minstrels who by their 'divinations and lies were the cause of insurrection and rebellion in Wales.'

Destiny's Door

One of the most difficult of Merlin's prophetic works is a poem called the *'Peiryan Vaban'* 'Commanding Youth'. It gives us further clues to Myrddin's story and shows him acting as a seer predicting events in to his own time, rather than as opening the door into the future destiny of Britain. This is such a difficult poem that it has hardly ever been attempted in English. Caitlín Matthews' new translation – a full version of which is to be found in the appendix to this book – opens the door onto a strange and wondrous world.

The narrator of the poem is Merlin himself, who seeks to console the unnamed youth in the face of the Irish assaults, led by Aedan mac Gabhran, King of Scottish Dalriada, against Rhydderch of Strathclyde whom, as we know from the Myrddin poems and Geoffrey's *Vita Merlini,* was married to Merlin's sister. The work is found in a fifteenth century source, sandwiched between two of the poems attributed to Merlin in his madness. As so often in these poems he mourns for the loss of Gwenddolau, and addresses Gwenddydd, together with a character who seems be Rhydderch's champion, Gwasawg. As the enemy closes on Dumbarton (Alcluid) he seeks to console the Commanding Youth – who may be either an actual young man caught up in the maelstrom of war, or Merlin himself, since he seems to refer to himself in the third person towards the end of this verse:

> Commanding Youth – cease your sighing!
> Aedan will come across the spreading sea,
> But the Youth shall not be caught by thunder nor lightning.
> Many forays and tramplings, many weapon-holders in Aedan's pay,
> Many long-headed lances, many tall spears,
> Come to seize the land. Gafran increases.
> Many breastplates, many helmets on heads, intent on cattle;
> Many red swords, many gruff squires bent on warrior slaughter,
> Many lively steeds, many light, broad shields shining.
> And he says to Gwenddydd, when daylight dawns, then the
>   prophecy will unfold,
> And he says to Gwasawg, that he respects neither shelter, fold nor
>   church.

As ever, the meaning is elusive. However, Merlin seems to be referring to an older prophecy, perhaps of his own making or possibly by another, which refers to events then unfolding. It is even possible that the words *Peiryan Vaban*, which can be translated as meaning 'Cauldron Boy', might refer to Taliesin, who according to tradition received the gifts of vision and poetry from a brew distilled in the Cauldron of Ceridwen, the Celtic goddess of inspiration. In this poem the prophetic voice is more intimate, as though Merlin were still freshly come into his state of madness and wonder.

New Masters

Another poem from *The Black Book* illustrates the way Merlin's prophecies could be shown to reflect events which took place long after his own time. 'A Fugitive Poem of Myrddin in His Grave' presents a bleak future for the Welsh and may well reflect the harsh rule of the Normans from the eleventh century onwards. Certainly, the vision reflects the feelings of a conquered people.

When the black wheel of oppression
Comes to destroy exhausted Llogres [Britain]
Defence will be bitter and sustained.
The White Mount [London] will see sorrow
A long regret to the people of the Cymry...

When the red Norman comes
And a castle is built at Aber Hodni. [Brecon St John the Evangelist]
Greatly taxed will be the Llogrians –
Even predictions will be costly...

When Henri comes to claim
Mur Castell on Eryri's border [Tomen -Y-Mur]
Trouble across the sea will call him.

A time will follow, towards the end of the age,
When the young will fail from adversity
And cuckoos die in Maytime...

There will be a time when everyone delights in fine clothing
When the lord's counsellors become vagrants;
Bards go empty handed – through priests will be happy;
Men will be despised, and frequently refused.

There will be a time of days without wind or rain,
With little ploughing and less food,
One acre of land worth nine.

Men will be weak and unmanly
And corn grown under trees –
Though feasts will still occur.

Such references to the coming of the Normans were almost
certainly added after the event, and it is all too easy to dismiss
Merlin's prophetic utterances for this reason. However, what is
important is not so much the nature, or for that matter the accuracy
of the statements, but the fact that Merlin is remembered first as
a seer and prophet, rather than as the magical wonderworker of
later times.

A Continuing Tradition

Throughout the Middle Ages and beyond, the traditions of
Merlin's prophetic writings continued to flourish, each successive
age shamelessly updating them to suit their own ends. Manuscripts
copied during the early part of the Middle Ages continued to
circulate even as late as the seventeenth century, when books and
almanacs attributed to Merlin were still in circulation, substantially
embroidered by successive transcribers and those studying the
ancient history and lore of Britain.

One of the most detailed examples of these later versions of
the prophecies which kept alive the traditional view of Merlin as
prophet, is a book entitled *The Life of Merlin, With His Strange
Prophecies or Chronographical History* by Thomas Heywood,
published in the reign of Charles I.[28] This is, in essence, a reworking
of the writings of Geoffrey of Monmouth, with additions from
the fifteenth century *Holinshed Chronicles* (a major source for
Shakespeare's historical plays) and others. Despite the title, it is not
actually a biography of Merlin at all but more of a commentary on
the prophecies.[29] Much of the actual prophetic writing is certainly
Heywood's own. The original preface makes his intention clear.

Courteous & considerate reader. I have here exposed to thy especial perusal The Life and Prophecies of our famous Predictor Merlinus surnamed Ambrosius; who though he lived in the time of profane paganism, was a professed Christian, and therefore, his auguries the better to be approved and allowed, which thou hast, with all their exposition and explanation, making plain and evident how genuinely and properly they comply with the truth of our chronology. In which you shall find (adding the supplement of the history from Brute, who laid the first foundation of our British Colony, to the time of king Vortigernus or Vortigern, the usurper of the crown, under whose reign Merlin first flourished) a true catalogue of all the kings of this island with a summary of all passages of state, ecclesiastical or temporal, of any remark or moment, during their principalities and dominions, insomuch that scarce anything shall be here wanting to the best wishes, if thou art desirous to be instructed and faithfully informed in the knowledge of our English annals.[30]

This weighty claim is followed by the familiar story of Merlin's prophetic outburst before Vortigern, and thereafter by lengthy interpretations of the prophecies found in the writings of Geoffrey of Monmouth, much augmented, so that they are seen to refer to successive monarchs up to Heywood's own time. Interestingly, there is a portrait of Merlin at the front of the book which shows him in the garb and tonsure of a monk – yet in the background, roaming across a fantastic landscape, are numerous wild beasts – suggesting that Heywood was familiar with the older figure of Merlin and his time in the wilderness (see plate section, page 7).

This was by no means the last time Merlin's name would be attached to prophetic statements actually penned by later hands. In 1610, the great dramatist Ben Johnson wrote an elaborate masque: *The Speeches at Prince Henry's Barriers*, which was performed at the investiture of James I's fifteen-year-old son Henry as Prince of Wales.[31] In it, Merlin celebrates all the great monarchs of Britain from Arthur to James himself, who claimed descent from Arthur, just as so many other kings had done throughout the Middle Ages. Merlin then paints a flattering portrait of the king which leaves us in no doubt of its author's desire to compare James with the great British hero.

> ... all these spurs to virtue, seeds of praise
> Must yield to this that comes. Here's one will raise
> Your glories more, and so above the rest,
> As if the acts of all mankind were prest
> In his example. Here are kingdoms mixt
> And nations joined, a strength of empire fixt
> Conterminate with heaven; the golden vine
> Of Saturn's age is here broke out again...
> For noble use, prefer it afore them:
> Royal and mighty James, whose name shall set
> A goal for all posterity to sweat
> In running at, by actions hard and high:
> This is the height at which your thoughts must fly.
> He knows both how to govern, how to save,
> What subjects, what their contraries should have,
> What can be done by power, what by love,
> What should to mercy, what to justice move.
> All arts he can, and from the hand of fate
> He hath enforced the making of his own date.[32]

After this, most of the prophetic writings attributed to Merlin were very clearly concocted by others to further political ends. William Lilly (1602–1681), the court astrologer to Charles I, issued his *England's Prophetical Merline* in 1644 and this was so popular that it went into several further editions over the next decade.³³ No lesser writer than Jonathan Swift, best known for his polemical writings and for the great satire of *Gulliver's Travels,* was prompted to make fun of such works by producing one of his own. *A Famous Prediction of Merlin, The British Wizard, Written Above a Thousand Years Ago, and Relating to This Present Year [1709], with Explanatory Notes by T.N. Philomath*³⁴ was, according to Swift, discovered by him in 'an old edition of Merlin's prophecies, imprinted at London by Johan Haukens in the year 1530.' He gives the text 'in its original orthography' as follows:

Seven and Ten added to Nine,
Of France her Woe this is the Sign,
Thames River t'was frozen,
Walk sans wetting Shoes nor Hosen.
Then cometh forth, I understand,
From Toune of Stoffe to fatten Londe,
An hardy Chieftain, woe the Morne
To France, that ever he was born.
Then shall the Fish bewail his Boss;
Nor shall Grin Berrys make up the Loss.
Young Symmnel shall again miscarry:
And Norway's Pride again shall marry.
And from the Tree where Blossoms fell,
Ripe Fruit shall come, and all is well.
Realms shall dance hand in hand,
And it shall be merry in old England.
Then old England shall be no more,
And no Man shall be sorry therefore.
Geryon shall have three Heads again,
Till Hapsburg maketh them but twayne.³⁵

A glance at the explanatory notes which accompany this 'ancient' prophecy shows how Swift was able to interpret every line to make the text say exactly what he wanted while suggesting its antiquity:

> The Fish, etc. By the Fish is understood the Dauphin of France, as the King's eldest sons are called:
>
> It is here said, he shall lament the loss of the Duke of Burgundy, called the Boss, which is an old English word for Hump-shoulder or Crookback, as that duke is known to be:
>
> And the prophecy seems to mean, that he should be slain.
>
> By the 'Grin Berrys', in the next line, is meant the young Duke of Berry the dauphin's third son, who shall not have valor or fortune enough to supply the loss of his eldest brother.[36]

Prophetic Truths

By this time, it was easy to poke fun at the ancient prophets, but were any of those made by Merlin actually genuine? As with all such writings, it is easy to see truths when they are viewed with hindsight; and as we have already noted, references were added in later times to bring the prophecies up to date. Commentaries on the original *Prophecies of Merlin* began to appear from the Middle Ages onwards, in which the words were twisted and turned in order to extract new, generally political, meanings from them.

One such commentary, which appeared in the fifteenth century, systematically adds details by the simple device of remarking: 'And Merlin also said...', all intended to make the prophecies live again for that time. However, if we turn back for a moment to the prophecies collected by Geoffrey of Monmouth and included in the *Historia Regum Britannia*, we find that certain details possess a surprising resonance for our own time. For example, Merlin is quoted as saying:

The river Thames shall encompass London, and the fame of this
work shall pass beyond the Alps. The Hedgehog shall hide his
apples within it – and shall make subterranean passages.[37]

It is possible to see in this a reference to the Thames Barrier, erected
to control the river's tidal flow in 1998 to prevent the river from
actually encompassing the city. In addition, the Hedgehog's apples
may refer to the riches of London which are, as they have ever
been, hidden beneath the city in subterranean vaults.

Later, when Merlin says of the sacred hot springs of Bath that
they will 'grow cold' and that their waters will be found to be
poisonous, he could well be referring to the closure of the Roman
baths in this city from 1979 onwards after the discovery of an
amoeba thought to be responsible for meningitis.

Details of this kind may be considered in the same light as the
fevered investigation into the writings of the Renaissance seer
Michel de Nostradame (better known as Nostradamus), whose
visions have undergone regular reinterpretation in the light of
evolving events. Thus, he is seen to have predicted the assassination
of President Kennedy and even the disaster of the terrorist attack
on New York in 2001. Nothing quite so epic can be attributed to
Merlin (unless one counts the apocalyptic visions at the end of his
Prophecies) but this is in keeping with a native seer whose concerns
were with his own people and land rather than the greater world.

In the end, as with all such prognostications, it is a matter for
the individual what they see and choose to believe when they read
such statements as:

The roaring whelps shall watch, and leaving the woods shall hunt
within the walls of the cities! They shall make great slaughter of
those that oppose them and shall cut off the tongues of bulls! They
shall load the necks of roaring lions with chains and restore the
times of their ancestors.[38]

The view of many scholars who have studied the prophecies – both those attributed to Myrddin, as well as those compiled by Geoffrey of Monmouth and John of Cornwall – is that they were at least partly intended for the amusement of the educated intelligentsia, who enjoyed playing the game of interpreting what they read. Certainly, the number of commentaries, dating from the twelfth to the fifteenth centuries, suggest this. Extending the original compilation more than fifty times its original length, these are a source of study in themselves.

The most recent and valuable interpretation of the Prophecies is that undertaken by R.J. Stewart in his 1986 book *The Prophetic Vision of Merlin*.[39] He sees the above passage as referring to the rebellion against Henry II by his three sons (the roaring whelps) in 1174. And, since these events took place after the lifetime of Geoffrey of Monmouth, but still before the prophetic industry of reprinting and doctoring Merlin's prophecies had really begun, it is unlikely that these details were added later.

The passage in question is followed by an even more remarkable one, in which Merlin says:

> ... then from the first to the fourth, from the fourth to the third, from the third to the second, the thumb shall roll in oil.

Stewart has rightly pointed out that this reflects the historical sequence of kings from Richard I to Henry IV to Richard III to James II, suggesting that Merlin's prophetic vision here stretches into the seventeenth century! The reference to the rolling in oil probably refers to the method of anointing kings at their coronations with sacred chrysm, applied to the brow, hands and feet by the presiding archbishop, who uses his thumb to do so.

Such remarkable statements suggest that Merlin's reputation as a seer was justified. Those who read the prophecies in the

Middle Ages saw what they wanted to see; but there is another level of perception, familiar to the ancient Celtic seers, which took them beyond the everyday into a place where they could encompass a greater reality. Merlin clearly had access to this deep well of vision, and just like the ancient shamans in whose lineage he stood, from it he brought back knowledge and understanding that transcended ordinary perception.

Merlin's Cave

By the end of the seventeenth century Merlin's prophetic star was beginning to wane. The eighteenth century was less interested in the legends of Arthur than previous times – though in less than a hundred years this would change forever with the dawn of the Victorian era and the obsession with Arthurian literature fostered by Queen Victoria and Prince Albert. Before this, one of the strangest echoes of Merlin's original role as a prophet took an unlikely form.

In 1732, Queen Caroline, wife of George II, commanded an ornamental building to be constructed in Richmond Gardens in London.[40] It was to be called the Hermitage and included a series of busts of leading scientists and philosophers of the time. Such was the success of this building, which was open to the public, that the Queen gave orders for an additional building to be erected, which was to be called 'Merlin's Cave'. This contained statues of Merlin and his 'secretary' who was depicted taking down new prophecies, and there were in addition tableaux of scenes from the prophet's life. At times actors were appointed to take the parts of Merlin and his copyist, and these may even have drafted 'replies' (for a price) to people asking genuine questions.

The extraordinary architecture of this site, which was a mixture of Gothic, Palladian and Rustic, captured the imagination of the public – though the Queen's political opponents were quick to make fun of it at her expense. The possessor of an extended Arthurian library, the queen was a passionate reader of medieval literature. She commissioned a deluxe edition of Cervantes' novel *Don Quichote*, in Spanish, which at this time was still considered a minor classic.[41] It was thus recognised as a masterpiece in Britain before its author's native Spain. The Queen loved the book because of the way in which Merlin (who appears several times in the novel) predicted the reign of various kings who were perceived as forerunners of the Hanoverian dynasty. The creation of the Cave and the installation of 'Merlin's Library' in the heart of London was clearly designed to celebrate the Matter of Britain, as Arthurian literature was known, and to imply that Caroline's own lineage, together with that of her husband, were allied with the ancient kingdom of Britain: thus offering proof of the Hanoverian right to rule via the prophetic insights of Merlin himself, who was of course famed for legitimising Arthur. The Queen was indeed suggesting, as had so many monarchs before her, a descent from the lineage of the Once and Future King.

Interest in Merlin and Arthur briefly flowered again as a result of the existence of the Cave. It seems likely that it was at this point that the cave which pierces the headland of Tintagel in Cornwall, a place long associated with Arthurian origins, received the name 'Merlin's Cave'. At the same time, a play by William Rowley, *The Birth of Merlin*,[42] originally written in 1626 with lines supposedly contributed by Shakespeare, was revived under the title *Merlin, or the British Enchanter*,[43] and an opera by the playwright John Dryden, with music by Henry Purcell, was also revived. Both works emphasised Merlin as a leading character and focused on his prophetic abilities.

But this fascination with the great seer was soon over, though it never wholly died out, and occasional reprints of the famous prophecies of Merlin were still to be found. Less than thirty years after the ornamental buildings in Richmond Gardens were demolished, another great prophet, William Blake, invoked Merlin in the context of his own revolutionary beliefs – in this instance that Monarchy and Church must be fettered in order that a new freedom of the individual might blossom:

'Merlin's Prophecy'

The harvest shall flourish in wintry weather
When two virginities meet together.
The King and the Priest must be tied in a tether
Before two virgins can meet together.[44]

William Blake:
From a Notebook of 1793

After this, it could be said that Merlin's prophetic voice fell silent for almost 200 years. Not until our own time, with the blossoming of interest in Druidry, Arthurian myths, and the lore and legends of the Celts, was Merlin to be invoked again as a prophet. Towards the end of the twentieth century, books claiming to contain messages received from Merlin were published to wide acclaim, and practitioners of ritual magic and Druidic mysteries took Merlin as their master and role model. However one views such claims, there is no denying that interest in Merlin has undergone a huge resurgence in our time, and that his prophetic voice has been heard again across the world.

But it is his reputation as a practitioner of magic that has probably done more than anything to keep him in the forefront of interest. It is to this aspect of his career that we turn next.

3

MERLIN THE MAGICIAN

Why mother, I can be but half a man at best,
And that is your mortality; the rest
In me is spirit. 'Tis not meat, or time,
That gives me growth and bigness. No, my years
Shall be more strange than yet my birth appears.

'The Birth of Merlin'
Rowley and Shakespeare

As we have already noted, despite possessing the traits of the magician, Merlin is never actually called by this title – any more than he is called Enchanter, Sorcerer, or Wizard. These terms, which are now very familiar, only began to be applied later, mostly from the eighteenth and nineteenth centuries onwards, and increasingly in our own time. For all this, the archetypal figure of the magician looms large in medieval literature, and it is no surprise to find Merlin betraying most of the qualities that designate him as such. For this reason, in order to consider these traits separately from those of shaman and prophet, he is referred to here by this title.

In fact Merlin is something of an anomaly among his fellow medieval magicians, who seem almost limited when compared to their forbears – few emulating the kind of feats attributed to, for example, the Greek Apollonius of Tyanna or the Biblical King Solomon, both of whom were seen as powerful magicians at this time. This was in part due to the influence of the medieval Church in Europe, which governed the physical extent of knowledge – in the form of books, manuscripts and documents – keeping these under its scrutiny, and impressing upon them a wholly Christian view. What remained as accessible, to scholars and story tellers alike, was at the folkloric end of the spectrum, which turned the Roman poet Virgil into a magician.

But the medieval era was also characterised by a sense of curiosity, and it was this which enabled the magician to re-establish a place in the imagination of the world. Medieval scholars wanted to know how the world worked, even if the Church officially forbade them to ask. Alchemy flourished under these difficult conditions and scientific investigation was a force to be reckoned with, despite being curtailed by Rome. One of the most important medieval wizards, Roger Bacon (*c*.1214–*c*.1292) was actually a Franciscan monk, yet he did not exclude magic from his studies, allowing it to contain at least 'some truth'. He managed, in an extraordinary way, to become an almost archetypal magician in his own lifetime while still maintain his spiritual beliefs and avoiding charges of heresy. His Italian brother, Giordano Bruno, suffered a less enlightened reception, and ended up being burned at the stake on 17 February 1600 for daring to believe in magic. He wrote two poems about Merlin, which are included in the Appendix at the back of this book.

The view of Merlin as a magician is very much a product of medieval thinking. He differs in many ways from the character discussed in the previous chapters. Though he retains his role as a prophet, he also becomes an enchanter, the creator of the Round Table, and the guide and guardian not only of Arthur but also of the fellowship of knights who meet at the table. Hidden within these archetypal roles we can still glimpse aspects of earlier, Celtic magic – especially in the figure of the wondrous youth who is born with magical powers which enable him to accomplish miracles and great deeds.

In fact, Merlin's reputation as a wizard was established early in his career. Having confirmed him as a prophet of great stature in the *Historia Regum Britanniae*, Geoffrey of Monmouth went on to show that Merlin's powers did not end there. After the Vortigern's tower episode, we next meet Merlin when he is sought out by the rightful heirs to the British throne, Ambrosius and Uther, whose triumphant return from exile had been foretold by the young prophet. Having heard of his remarkable debut on Dinas Emrys, a hillock near Beddgelert in Gwynedd, north-west Wales, they call upon him to create a monument for those who had fallen in battle against the Saxons.

Discovered at the Fountain of Galbes, where he is said to go often 'to recreate himself', Merlin is brought before the newly crowned King Aurelius, who greets him lightly and immediately asks to know about future events. Merlin's response is direct and to the point: 'Mysteries of that sort cannot be revealed ... except where there is the most urgent need for them.'

The poet Wace, who adapted Geoffrey's text for a Norman audience, describes the scene in greater detail. Here Merlin responds as follows:

> I dare not open my lips to speak of such awful matters. Should my tongue be unloosed by greed or lightness, should I be puffed up by vanity, then my familiar spirit – the being by whom I know that which I know – would withdraw his inspiration

from my breath. My knowledge would depart from me, and the words I speak would be no weightier than the idle words on every gossip's lips[1]

His words are significant. Like the many wizards who throng the pages of medieval tales, Merlin is shown to respect the spirits with who he communicates and from whom he receives wisdom and knowledge. He shows that he is no mere wonderworker but someone who possess a deeper connection with the otherworld from whence he derives his power. He also aligns himself with the older shamanic figures who had, by this time, either been forgotten, or like Merlin himself, been transformed into wonderworking magicians.

Suitably abashed by his powerful statement, Aurelius turns to the subject of the monument. Merlin suggests that a circle of giant standing stones, known as the Giant's Dance, should be brought across the sea from Ireland and re-erected near the site of the battle. Aurelius' response is to burst out laughing. 'How can such large stones be moved from so far-distant a country?' he asked. 'It is hardly as if Britain itself is lacking in stones big enough for the job!' Again, Merlin rebukes him:

'Try not to laugh in a foolish way...' answered Merlin. 'What I am suggesting has nothing ludicrous about it. These stones are connected with certain secret religious rites and they have various properties which are medicinally important. Many years ago, the Giants transported them from the remotest confines of Africa...

'Their plan was that, whenever they fell ill, baths should be prepared at the foot of the stones; for they used to pour water over them and to run this water into baths in which their sick were cured... There is not a single stone amongst them which hasn't some medicinal virtue.'[2]

Hearing this, the Britons are convinced, and at once mount an expedition to fetch the stones. This entails a brief struggle with the King of Ireland, but once this opposition has been overcome, they begin considering ways to bring the stones back to Britain. Merlin watches them for a while, then challenges them. 'Try your strength young men … and see whether skill can do more than brute strength!'

Of course, the artificers struggle with ropes and pulleys, but to no avail. Then Merlin laughs and sets to work. Wace's adaptation of Geoffrey's text describes what happens next:

> Merlin … walked warily around the stones. His lips moved without stay, as those of a man about his orisons [prayers], though I cannot tell whether or not he prayed. At length Merlin beckoned to the Britons. 'Enter Boldly!' cried he, 'There is naught to harm. Now you may lift these pebbles from their seat and bare and charge them on your ships.' So, at his word and bidding they wrought as Merlin showed them.[3]

The stones are floated across the sea to Britain, where they are set up on the Plain of Amesbury. Nothing further is said about how this was achieved, but whether Merlin made use of technical skills or magic, the feat established him as a wonderworker from that moment onward.

It is clear from the description of the stones that Geoffrey is actually referring to Stonehenge (he repeatedly confuses Amesbury with both Avebury and Stonehenge – both sites of vast stone circles). At this point no one knew how the stones had been erected, or by whom. Their connection with the Druids did not arise until the seventeenth century, but the air of mystery surrounding them made them a perfect setting for this first great magical act of Merlin.

prophets, or by launching thunders, or causing the
flash in the clouds, or other things to take place by
which we obtain a knowledge of future events.[8]

nteresting about this is the way Geoffrey manipulates
ke it seem less pagan and threatening. His statement
Maugantius) that these beings partake of the aspects of
d angels, is completely absent in Apuleius' text, but since
man poet's writings had been attacked by St Augustin in his
s *Dei* (City of God) Geoffrey could not have used it without
ring the original to make it sound less heretical and thus
e Merlin a sympathetic being who combined both ancient
an and therefore devilish power with that of someone who has
en baptised and shared the visionary aspect of saints rather than
mons. The subtlety of the citation is extraordinary and testifies
o Geoffrey's skill at developing his sources. The whole topic of
he sexual proclivities of nuns was debated widely throughout
the ages, with some surprisingly sympathetic statements ranged
alongside those who thought such women should be burned.[9]

It may that Geoffrey, looking for an origin for his wonder-working
prophet, chose to make him the offspring of a demon, but it is
equally possible that he simply borrowed from a well-established
myth which told of the birth of a wonderful child. The fact that
Merlin's birth was described in this way was to affect the direction
of his history thereafter, as we shall see. It is also in keeping with
stories describing the wondrous births of heroes and saviours
around the world, from Achilles to Christ.

In Celtic tradition this was the framework for a specific myth:
that of the Wondrous Child. Such children were invariably
begotten by an unknown or otherworldly father on an innocent
virgin, who is subsequently rejected by her parents or tribe because
of a prophecy that says that the order of things will be dislocated

Interestingly, as several commentators have pointed out, the route taken by the stones, by sea from the West then overland to their final resting place, is curiously like the probable direction the famous bluestones were brought from the Prescelly Mountains in Wales to Salisbury Plain. Given that the quarry from which the stones were taken is only 20 miles from Carmarthen, which has its own associations with Merlin as we saw earlier, it is hard not to speculate whether the story told by Geoffrey may not be a resonance of the original construction of Stonehenge.

A contemporary authority on the Arthurian Legends, Geoffrey Ashe, has argued plausibly that what we may, in fact, be looking at here is a very ancient memory indeed, of a god-like builder of the great henge, remembered through Druidic and later bardic lore, who somehow became linked to the name Merlin, possibly through the geographic link between Merlin's home town and the site of the Prescelly quarry.[4] Whatever the truth, this single act established Merlin's already impressive credentials as a worker of wonders. From this point onward he was increasingly represented as a magician – despite not being termed that – who could change shape at will and had access to unearthly or occult lore.

The Wondrous Child

One factor which very clearly influenced the evolving portrait of Merlin as a magician was the strange story of his birth. Throughout the Middle Ages it became virtually *de rigour* that a magician should be born under strange circumstances and possibly with non-human parents. Merlin's story correlated with this at almost every point and hid an even greater secret.

We have heard how Vortigern was told to seek a child without a father to sacrifice on the foundation of his tower. This child is, of course, Merlin, and he is only discovered when Vortigern's officers overhear an altercation between Merlin and another boy, who accuses him of having no father. When they make enquiries, Vortigern's men discover that the boy's mother is a princess of Demetia (South Wales) and that after giving birth to her child has retired to the nearby Convent of St Peter, where she lives with the nuns. They go to the convent and take the woman and her child to Vortigern, who questions her as to the birth of her son. Her answer is intriguing:

> I did not have relations with any man to make me bear this child.
>
> I know only this: that when I was in our private apartments with my sister nuns, someone used to come to me in the form of a most handsome young man... Many times, too, when I was sitting alone, he would talk with me, without becoming visible; and when he came to see me in this way he would often make love with me, as a man would do, and in that way he made me pregnant.[5]

The wording here is oblique but suggests that Geoffrey had decided that Merlin's mother was already living with the nuns – maybe had already taken the veil since she refers to them as 'my sister nuns'. Yet curiously there seems to have been no objection to the sudden appearance of the handsome young man in her private rooms. Even more strangely, it is when she is alone that the man appears visibly and makes love to her, when he is apparently invisible at other times. The phrase 'as a man would do', seems to suggest not only that this innocent virgin had a pretty good idea of what a man would 'do', but that the mysterious visitor was not human; but if not, then what was he?

Vortigern, equally mystified, summons one of his advisors, a wise man named Maugantius, and asks him. This man relates that he has heard of a number of people born in thus way and refers to the Roman author Apuleius 'who asserts in *De Deo Socratis* [that] between the moon and the earth hove spirits which we call

incubus demons. They h...
that of angels, and when th...
have intercourse with wome...

It is at this point that Merlin l...
Vortigern's reason for bringing h...
revelation of the red and white dra...
this curious statement regarding in...
found the idea that Merlin was the s...
half-man, half-angel, is impossible to ...
referred to by Vortigern's aide does inde...
passage concerning incubi, though it is c...
than Geoffrey's account and differs in a num...

Apuleius does say that 'daemons' inhabit ...
Earth and the moon, and that they possess ...
human beings. They are 'rational creatures, susce...
in spirit, in body composed of the *aer*, everlasting in...

The passage in question reads:

> ... there are certain divine powers of a middle nature, s...
> this interval of the air, between the highest ether and the...
> below, through whom our aspirations and our deserts...
> conveyed to the Gods. These the Greeks call by name 'daemo...
> and, being placed as messengers between the inhabitants o...
> earth and those of heaven, they carry from the one to the other,
> prayers and bounties, supplications and assistance; being a kind
> of interpreters and message carriers to both. Through these same
> demons, as Plato says in his *Symposium*, all revelations, the various
> miracles of magicians, and all kinds of presages, are carried on.
> For specially appointed individuals of this number, administer
> everything according to the province assigned to each; either
> by framing dreams, or causing ominous fissures in entrails, or
> governing the flights of some birds, or instructing others in song,

if she bears a son. As a result of this, she gives birth to her child either in secrecy or with great difficulty, friendless but for servants or beasts. The child is reared among animals or poor people, who foster him in great danger. The qualities of the child then bring him to the notice of the person of wisdom who agrees to foster and teach him knowledge or skills. The boy is then brought to court, among his own kindred, where he astounds royalty and wise men by his precocity. His mother, who has lost her child or put him from her for safety, receives him again secretly and gives him a name and destiny, arming him with weapons or magical powers.

From this beginning he becomes either a great hero possessing deep wisdom, or else a visionary. He changes the old order of things, brings fresh vigour to the land and overturns evil customs. His opponents challenge but are unable to overcome him: this can only be achieved when he voluntarily accepts his destiny. Before his end, which often means withdrawal from the world, he sleeps with a virgin unknown to him, who will give birth to the next wonder child.

Merlin is very much the inheritor of such ancient traditions, and a true child of wonder. In the sequence of events listed above, he too is born of the union of earthly and unearthly parents, is brought up in secret, is challenged by adversaries whom he easily overcomes, emerges into the world and astounds everyone with his magical and prophetic skills. Later he will change the direction of the world, before withdrawing into a place from which his voice will continue to be heard.

The Devil's Brat

The next writer to deal with the character of Merlin wanted nothing of this. He was a twelfth century Burgundian knight named Robert de Boron. Though little or nothing is known of the life of this author, he is acknowledged in having had as profound effect on the development of the Arthurian tradition. His trilogy of works, of which *The Romance of Merlin* (c.1195)[10] is one, changed the course of the other great theme of the medieval romancers, the Grail, into wholly different waters by being the first to specifically connect it with the chalice of the Last Supper. Obviously a religious man, Robert did something similar with the Merlin story, taking the strange story of the birth of the Wonder Child and spinning around it a web of Christian symbolism and Biblical reference.

According to this account, the devils in hell are so disturbed by the effects of Christ's ministry on Earth, followed by the events of the Crucifixion and Resurrection, and of course the Harrowing of Hell, that they decide to devise a plan to counteract this. One of the devils is dispatched to father a child on an innocent human woman. This child, in a parody of Christ's birth, will receive all the knowledge and powers of hell, enabling him to spread evil throughout the world. The devil selects the family of a well-to-do man, and gradually kills all of them off until there are only three daughters surviving. The eldest is tricked into becoming a prostitute and is killed for it. The second daughter follows in her sister's footsteps and is driven mad. The third daughter remains pure and is taken into the house of a saintly man named Blaise, who reinforces her Christian beliefs. In the end, however, the devil succeeds in gaining access to her room and (the text is somewhat ambiguous about how this is done) in impregnating her while she sleeps. When this becomes evident, there is much consternation and calls for the girl to be burned at the stake. But her guardian succeeds in allowing her at least to have her child before facing judgement, and she is shut in a tower until she gives birth. When the child finally comes forth, he is covered in long, back hair, and the midwife is almost afraid to touch him. But his mother at once requests that he be taken and baptised in the name of Merlin, which was her father's name. This is done and the pelt of black hair falls away. The child is nursed by his mother until he is nine months old, at which time he looks to be more than a year in size, and by the time he is eighteen months he appears more like two-and-a-half years old.

Hearing of this the authorities decide to put the woman on trial. When she comes before the judge and tells her tale – that she had never known a man but became pregnant in her sleep – she is disbelieved, but at this moment the infant Merlin speaks up and accuses the judge himself of having been fathered by a man who was not his father. Astonished and fearful, the judge nonetheless has his mother brought before him, and Merlin shows that he has complete knowledge of her life by revealing that the true father of her child was in fact her priest, with whom she had repeatedly lain at a time when she was estranged from her husband. Finally, she breaks down and admits everything. Merlin then explains that his father was a devil but that because his mother called upon God and the Virgin when she discovered she was with child, his soul had been redeemed and he had received both the knowledge of heaven *and* hell which enables him to see both the past and the future.

Unable to condemn his own mother, the judge sets Merlin's mother free and she and the child return to Blaise, who on hearing all of these wonders decides to set down the story of Merlin in a book. This Merlin encourages, and begins to relate many wonders to the old man, including the story of the Grail. The story now turns to the Vortigern episode, which follows the version told by Geoffrey of Monmouth fairly closely, though instead of prophesying at length, Merlin returns to Blaise – whom he has instructed to go to live in Northumberland – and tells him of the recent events as well as many others things.

Let us pause here to examine this text more fully. No one agrees about Robert's sources. He himself refers to 'a certain high book' in one of his other, connected romances, but as is so often the case in the medieval tales we have no idea what this was. He seems to have known of other Grail romances and he had certainly read Geoffrey of Monmouth. The rest, in particular the overt Christianisation of Merlin, we may assume comes directly from Robert himself. The Devil's plot to confound the influence of Christ in the world by creating what is in fact an Antichrist – a theme beloved of several medieval writers – is ingenious, and enables him to present Merlin as at least half good, as well as neatly explaining how he came by his deep knowledge and magical powers. Robert would also have been aware that prodigious growth and an awareness of arcane matters was a sign of heroic status. The fact that the demon who engendered him was apparently also named Merlin suggests that the final action in the list of requirements undertaken by the Child of Wonder is to cause the birth of another and that this may also be true of Merlin.

The introduction of the old confessor, Blaise, who virtually becomes Merlin's secretary and records all his deeds thereafter, is interesting. Blaise is probably a corruption of the name Bleheris, a semi-fictional Welsh storyteller who is also supposed to have written a Grail story which became the foundation of much later work. Whether he existed or not does not really matter in this context, but it does suggest that Robert may have had access to a book attributed to this writer, which may have told a more detailed version of Merlin's life. It is even possible that this same source was used by Geoffrey of Monmouth, though there is no conclusive proof of this.

In the *Romance of Merlin*, the ancient Celtic theme of a union between a mortal and an immortal in order to produce a Wonder Child has become warped by Christian dualism. Nevertheless, Merlin still triumphs as someone who revels the truth unerringly and vindicates the resourcefulness of human nature through both his natural and unnatural gifts. Such cleverness was distrusted by the medieval mind, which saw such ingenuity as devilish, or inconsistent with surrender to the will of God. This ambivalence was to pursue Merlin into the mainstream Arthurian legends, where his supernatural abilities enable him to procure a mother for Arthur – who will himself be portrayed as a prodigious child whose birth is surrounded in mystery.

The Birth of Arthur

Once Merlin and his magic had been drawn into the sphere of the Arthurian tradition it was inevitable that his role should become that of guardian and guide to the young king. More importantly he is seen as active in the actual process of the future king's conception, as though echoing his own strange birth, to produce another child of wonder.

Again it is Geoffrey of Monmouth, who did so much to shape the Arthurian mythos, who gives us the earliest surviving version of the story. In the *Historia*, after the triumphal return of Aurelius and Uther, the former rules only briefly before being poisoned, after which his brother becomes king. His first victory, over the Saxons, is aided by an alliance with Gorlois, Duke of Cornwall, and at the celebrations which take place after the battle, the duke's wife, Ygerna, is present. As soon as he sees her Uther is

> ... immediately filled with desire for her, with the result that he took no notice of anything else but devoted all his attention to her. To her and to no one else he kept ordering plates of food to be passed to her. Also, he kept sending his own personal attendants with golden goblets of wine... When Ygerna's husband saw what was happening, he was so annoyed that he withdrew from the court without taking his leave.[11]

This makes Uther so angry that he declares war on his former ally and raising a huge army pursues Gorlois back to his lands. Fearing for his life and the safety of his wife, the duke places her in the care of trusted officers in the castle of Tintagel. He himself fortifies the nearby camp at Dimilioc (probably Tregeare Rounds, some 5 miles from Tintagel). Learning of this, Uther attacks both places and is repulsed. Tintagel castle itself is considered virtually impregnable and the knowledge that Ygerna was within drives Uther mad. At the suggestion of his advisors he summons Merlin who was, according to Geoffrey, amazed at the strength of Uther's passion and promised to help him. Interestingly, there is an attempt to avoid Merlin's use of magic to bring about the desired events. Geoffrey's text reads: "'If you are to have your wish [said Merlin] you must make use of methods which are quite new and until now unheard of in your day, By my *drugs* I know how to give you the precise appearance of Gorlois, so that you will resemble him in every respect."' [Italics mine.] He continues by saying that he will also change one of the king's followers into the likeness of Gorlois' captain and himself into another man. Together they will go to the gates of Tintagel and be admitted.

Just what these drugs are that Merlin is supposed to use is never revealed, though in Robert De Boron's *Merlin* he gets Uther to rub his face with a herb which transforms him. Later texts make it clear that he uses magic. But the outcome is that the three men arrive at Tintagel looking like the duke and his men and are admitted. That night Uther lies with Ygerna and begets Arthur upon her. At the same time, Gorlois leads a foray against Uther's army and is killed, thus ensuring by a technicality that the future king Arthur's paternity is assured and leaving the way clear for Uther to marry the widowed Ygerna. The couple live happily together after this and have two children: Arthur and a girl, who is christened Anna.

Arthur's birth, brought about in this way through the disguising of a man by otherworldly means to resemble the husband of the woman he loves, fits the ancient Celtic myth of the Wondrous Child. In addition, it paves the way for Merlin to engineer his next miracle – the Sword in the Stone – which brings with it public recognition of his protégée.

Not long after this Uther falls ill and, from a litter, leads the defence of his kingdom against a resurgent Saxon attack. This weakens him so much that he dies, and is deeply mourned by his followers, who now seek to elect a new leader. As Uther's son, Arthur is an obvious choice, even though he is only fifteen. He is crowned forthwith and begins a triumphant reign. Curiously, however, we hear nothing further of Merlin in Geoffrey's book. Having brought about the founding of a new dynasty, he simply vanishes. It is as though Geoffrey became so interested in Arthur's career that he forgot about the famous prophet.

Other writers were not slow to take up the story however, and in the accounts that followed, Merlin's magical status came more and more to the fore. In Robert's version, as in most that followed, the election of Arthur to king was less of a foregone conclusion. Others contested his parentage and legitimacy and it is up to Merlin to arrange a spectacular event to ensure that the destined king is chosen.

The scene is one of the most famous of the stories of Arthur and has been retold countless times. Merlin arranges for all the various contenders to come together in London to choose a new leader. He then sets up a block of marble with an anvil set into it through which is sunk the blade of a sword. Around the anvil is written, in letters of gold, the following legend:

WHOSO PULLETH THIS SWORD FROM THIS STONE
IS RIGHTWISE KING BORN OF ALL ENGLAND.

When word of this spreads, a group of would-be kings try to free the sword. But of course, Merlin has seen to it that only Arthur can succeed, so that with this single act he establishes himself as the worthiest person to rule.

The sword from the stone is often confused with Arthur's more famous weapon, Excalibur, but in fact the young king does not get this sword until later, when the first one provided by Merlin shatters in battle. In fact, his next great magical act is to provide Arthur with a far more powerful weapon.

Many versions of this episode exist, but by far the best is that composed by Sir Thomas Malory in his great fifteenth-century prose masterpiece *Le Morte D'Arthur*. This book, which is the most famous of the surviving Arthurian texts, has done more to keep the legends of Arthur and Merlin alive than any other. Malory, whose colourful life has been the subject of much speculation in recent years (according to some sources he spent most of his life in prison on charges of rape, murder, and treason) wrote his book between 1469 and 1470, drawing upon a vast thirteenth-century compilation, nowadays known as the *Lancelot-Grail Cycle*,[12] collected by Cistercian scribes at the Abbey of Clairvaux in France. Malory's version is much shorter than the original and shows him consistently compressing his source to make a better and tighter story. His prose is lyrical, fast-paced and savage by turns, according to the needs of the story, and his ear for dialogue is unsurpassed until Shakespeare. His Merlin is shown in the guise of a fully-fledged magician (though still not called that), who shapeshifts, overthrows opponents with the raising of a hand, and finds Arthur his second great sword.

The Gifting of Excalibur

Heroes have always been portrayed with magical swords, which often ensure their recognition as the rightful heir to a kingdom. The Greek hero Theseus earns the right to rule by lifting a huge boulder beneath which lies his father's sword. In Germanic mythology Siegfried proves his worth by pulling out a sword embedded in a tree and there are numerous variations around the world. Arthur is no exception to the pattern. In the earliest versions of his story, told in fragmentary form in the Welsh sources such as the *Mabinogion*, he wields a sword named Caladvwlch, which probably derived its name from Caladbolg (Harsh Lightning) a weapon carried by Irish heroes. Geoffrey calls it Caliburnus, which is a clearly a Latinisation of the older name, and this metamorphosed gradually into 'Excalibur' (usually glossed as 'Cut Steel').

Another possible origin for the name of the sword, which has come to light only recently, focusses on a group of Scythian warriors from the steppe lands, until recently part of modern-day Russia. Some 1,500 of these warriors were stationed in Britain as part of the Roman occupation. A number of parallels exist between these people and the Arthurian knights of the medieval tales, not least the fact that they were led by a Romano-British general name Lucius Artorius Castus. But one of the most remarkable similarities is that these tough warriors worshipped a sword stuck point down, either in a stone or the earth, as a representative of their god of war. As if this was not enough, it has been noted that a sub-group of these people, who were famous smiths, were called the Kalybes, from which we get *chalybus* (steel) and *eburnus* (white) – hence Caliburnus.[13]

In virtually every version of the story, it is Merlin who arranges for Arthur to get the sword, which is in the keeping of the Lady of the Lake, one of the most powerful otherworldly and magical figures alongside Merlin himself. When the sword from the stone breaks, Arthur is bereft of his heroic weapon, but Merlin calms him by saying that he will obtain for him a far better sword. Let Malory take up the tale:

> ... they rode until they came to a lake, the which was a fair water and broad, and in the midst of the lake Arthur was ware of an arm clothed in white samite, that held a fair sword in the hand.

Lo! said Merlin, yonder is that sword that I spake of. With that they saw a damosel going upon the lake. What damosel is that? said Arthur. That is the Lady of the Lake, said Merlin; and within that lake is a rock, and therein is as faire a place as any on earth, and richly beseen; and the damosel will come to you anion, and then speak ye fair to her that she will give you that sword. Anon withal came the damosel unto Arthur, and saluted him, and he her again. Damosel, said Arthur, what sword is that, that yonder the arm holdest above the water? I would it were mine, for I have no sword. Sir Arthur, king, said the damosel, that sword is mine, and if ye will give me a gift when I ask it of you, ye shall have it. By my faith, said Arthur, I will give what gift ye will ask. Well, said the damosel, go ye into yonder barge, and row yourself to the sword and take it and the scabbard with you, and I will ask my gift when I see my time. So Sir Arthur and Merlin alighted and tied their horses to two trees, and so they went into the ship and when they came to the sword that the hand held, Sir Arthur took it up by the handles, and took it with him, and the arm and the hand went under the water.[14]

As in so many instances within epic and mythic story, this magical gift comes with a condition which will cause Arthur trouble later on when the Lady demands the head of a rival damsel, but from this time on Arthur holds the most powerful weapon on Earth, which while he carries it makes him undefeatable. However, as Merlin explain shortly after, the scabbard is every bit as important.

Then Sir Arthur looked on the sword, and liked it passing well. Whether liketh you better, said Merlin, the sword or the scabbard? Me liketh better the sword, said Arthur. Ye are more unwise, said Merlin, for the scabbard is worth ten of the swords, for while ye have the scabbard upon you, ye shall never lose no blood, be ye never so sore wounded; therefore, keep well the scabbard always with you.[15]

Later the scabbard is stolen by Morgan le Fay, and lost, but Excalibur remains with Arthur until the end, when, mortally wounded, he orders his faithful knight Sir Bedivere to return it to the lake, at which the hand once more appears and takes the sword and brandishes it three times before withdrawing it beneath the water. The same story, alone within epic literature, is told of a Sarmatian hero named Batradz, whose deeds closely parallel those of Arthur.

Merlin's part in these events is more than a simple go-between. He clearly knows the Lady of the Lake and is aware of the sword's unique power. For this is no ordinary weapon, but one of the ancient sacred treasures of Britain, virtually an embodiment of the land itself. By accepting it Arthur enters into a contract as ruler over the sacred earth; Merlin and the Lady together stand as witnesses to this agreement, and both will guard and protect the young king throughout his life.

As we shall see in the next chapter, Merlin's relationship with women, especially faery women, is deep and powerful, but is also seen as the cause for his removal from an active role in the Arthurian court. At this moment, however, he is at the height of his powers. Arthur has been chosen king, a group of rival lords has been successfully defeated (not without a little help from Merlin himself, who causes the rebel army to see terrifying visions) and now the king has his magical sword. Only one further act remains for the great enchanter to bring about: the creation of the Round Table and the establishment of a fellowship of knights who will sit around it, and whose names and deeds will continue to live in memory long after Merlin himself has departed.

The Round Table
The first mention of the Round Table comes in the work of the Anglo-Norman poet Wace, who we have already encountered as the author of an adaptation of Geoffrey of Monmouth's *Historia*.

Wace evidently had access to other sources in addition to those used by Geoffrey, and one of these may have contained a reference to the creation of the table. Wace tells us that it was created at the request of Arthur himself, in order to prevent his followers from quarrelling over who should sit closest to him.[16] Again it is Robert de Borron who seems to have been the first writer to elaborate the story and to describe Merlin as the table's actual creator. In this instance the table is not made for Arthur, but for Uther, his father, to whom he tells the story of the Last Supper, which took place at the first table, and of a second, built at the command of Joseph of Arimathea in memory of the first Eucharist. Here the members of the Grail family, a select group of guardians whose task is to protect the sacred vessel, sit to eat and are fed by the Grail. Now Merlin proposes a third table, at which will one day sit a great company whose chivalrous deeds will be honoured around the world.

In the later versions of the story, Merlin has the table made 'round, in the likeness of the world' and presents it to Arthur when he marries Guinevere. Even the suggestion to send out a call for all knights of worship and strength to come and sit at the Table originates with the king's great councillor, who also warns Arthur that a seat should be left empty until the one destined to sit there appears. This is said to be in memory of the seat occupied by Judas at the Last Supper, and later we are shown how anyone foolish enough to disobey this instruction is likely to be swallowed up, as the earth cracks open and a warning voice announces that this chair is only for the destined Grail knight. Long before this, when the Table is installed in the great hall of Camelot, Merlin arranges for statues representing twelve kings overcome by Arthur to be installed, each one holding a candle to light the hall. And when the first fifty knights arrive (there will be at least three times this number in the end), Merlin has seen to it that their names are already inscribed in letters of gold on the backs of each chair. The 'fairest fellowship in all the world' is thus established, with the help of Merlin's magic.[17]

Merlin and Mabon

From here on, Merlin's role as a magician and wonder-worker is well established. We see him appearing to Arthur in various guises – as a fur-clad hunter, as an old man, and as a child, each one blessed with a unique wisdom. On one occasion, when Arthur catches sight of the mysterious Questing Beast, a creature made up of several animals, Merlin appears first as a youth who offers to explain to Arthur the meaning of the creature. When Arthur rejects this information on the grounds that the boy is too young to know of such matters, Merlin walks away then reappears as an old man, to whose words Arthur is far more willing to listen. From this point on, we are given to understand, Merlin will take this form at all times – for in this way he is more certain of being listened to. It may well be due to this moment that we owe the characteristic image of Merlin as a white-bearded elder, though he remained a young man beneath his disguise. His initial appearance as a youth, however, reveals Merlin's essentially otherworldly form as a wondrous child who can accomplish the most remarkable deeds (see plate section, page 3).

We have already examined something of this enduring myth and seen how well the story of Merlin fits within its overall structure. The full story of the Child of Wonder in other cultures is too complex to deal with in detail here, but a brief appraisal of one story which could have affected Merlin's own developing myth, may offer us another clue to the deepest aspect of his nature.

Throughout Celtic myth there are references to Mabon, Son of Modron, a title which simply means 'Son of the Mother' and shows that we are almost certainly dealing with a deity. According to the

Triads of Britain, a vast body of lore assembled in the thirteenth century, this mysterious youth is one of the 'Three Exalted Prisoners of the Island of Britain'. In the *Mabinogion* story of 'Culhwch and Olwen', we learn that the mysterious child was stolen from his mother's side when only two nights old and imprisoned in a stone fastness from which he is later rescued by Arthur and his heroes. Scattered literary references and the evidence of archaeology have identified this elusive child with the Gaulish God of Youth, Maponus, who was worshipped under a variety of names throughout the Celtic world. As an archetype of the Wondrous Child this suggests that Merlin may once have been seen in a similar light, as a being with god-like powers who often appeared as a youth. As Merlin's role became more and more identified with that of the magician, this earlier status was forgotten or deliberately suppressed, leaving behind only an astonishing power which was swiftly subsumed within the new story of his demonic birth. Significantly, in the *Lancelot-Grail Cycle*, we learn that Merlin was so honoured that the Britons called him their holy prophet and the common people regarded him as a god.[18]

Merlin and Virgil

The characterisation of the medieval figure of Merlin – especially those stories which describe him as a magician – may, as mentioned above, owe much to a most unlikely figure: the Roman poet Virgil (70–19 BC) who, though in his lifetime had no actual association with magic, was consistently represented as a magician by the medieval romance writers. This transformation came about through a series of misunderstandings of his poems, as well as reports of miracles that took place in and around Virgil's tomb within a hundred years of his death. The effect was to turn Virgil into a virtual god in the eyes of the medieval thinkers and writers. First, he was given a miraculous birth story, according to the medieval writer Alexander of Neckam (1157–1217) who wrote a *Secret History of Virgil*[19] in which he described how the poet's mother, Magia Pollia, was impregnated by the god Jupiter (Zeus) who took the form of a shower of gold flakes which blew in through the window and landed in her wine glass. The city of Rome was also said to have shaken on the day of his nascence, thus establishing him as yet another type of the Miraculous Youth. Then, while still a young man, he was said to have encountered a powerful spirit trapped in a hole in the ground, who offered him a copy of the magical *Book of Solomon* in return for releasing him. Virgil accepted this and used it to trick the evil spirit back into its hole. Now possessed of great magical powers he entered into a magical battle against the Roman Emperor's sorcerer, not unlike Merlin's encounter with Vortigern's wizards.

We next hear of the wizardly Virgil engaged in a love affair with the daughter of the Sultan of Babylon, whom he visited by creating a bridge of air from his home in Naples to the Far East. Later he builds her a magic castle in which to live, echoing Merlin's creation of such a palace for his mistress Nimue which we shall examine later.

Within a few years of his death, copies of Virgil's writings were being used to make divination – opened at random and a finger placed on a line which was then taken as an answer to a prefigured question. But perhaps the main reason for the association of Merlin and Virgil is a relationship between the Roman poet and the Welsh bard Taliesin who, as we have seen, is represented in the *Vita Merlini* as Merlin's friend and successor.

* * *

Both Merlin and Taliesin began their careers as historical poets and became widely celebrated as magicians in later stories. In part this stems from an acknowledgement of the sacredness and power of the word, especially the written word. Those who had the power of writing or composing words and music were especially gifted. Thus, poets like Myrddin, Taliesin and Virgil were attributed initially with prophetic and later with magical powers. In Celtic tradition it was said that a poet could raise boils on a person's face by writing a scurrilous satire about them.

A curious reference in the fourteenth-century text known as *Hanes Taliesin* (The Life of Taliesin) refers to the origin of his powers as 'the Books of Fferyllt', which though it is sometimes translated as 'philosophers' or 'scientists', is really a Welsh attempt to form the name Virgil. Elsewhere, in a poem attributed to Taliesin are these mysterious lines:

> Golden, gold skinned, I shall deck myself in riches,
> And I shall be in luxury because of the prophecy of Virgil.[20]

This has been seen as referring to a statement in Virgil's Fourth *Eclogue*.

> Now has the last great age begun,
> by Cumae's seer foretold;
> newborn the mighty cycles run
> their course and quit the old.
> Now too, the Virgin reappears,
> and Saturn re-controls the spheres.
> Now a new race is on the way
> from heaven; do thou befriend
> the Infant, all but born, whose day
> the iron brood shall end
> and with the golden fill the earth.
> Chaste Lucina, speed his birth.
> Thy own Apollo now is king.[21]

The prophesied child of this poem is described in terms of the Greek god Apollo, but many early Christian commentators read it as a reference to the coming of Christ. This poem gives Virgil the status of a wise pagan in Christian eyes, while in the medieval world he received acclaim as a magician. The myth of the Golden Age, hinted at in the first line, exercised the Classical imagination a good deal: it signalled the manifestation of an otherworld reality, analogous to the Celtic vision of Avalon, complete with Arthur and his court, which would one day return to Earth. This theme, re-interpreted by Christian teachers as the Kingdom of Heaven, became a potent hope for successive ages in the West.

Taliesin's prophetic utterances, like those of Merlin, placed him at many of the great events of history, including the birth and crucifixion of Christ, while Virgil was widely believed to possess magical, as well as prophetic, powers. All three had miraculous births, were renowned for their wonderworking abilities and possessed immense degrees of wisdom and knowledge.

Such stray pieces of information demonstrate how easily these figures, widely separated in time, could became associated, and how easy it would have been for one to lend aspects of his story to the other. Virgil was certainly known about at the time when the stories of Merlin and Taliesin were being written down, and it is entirely possible that aspects of his story became attached to that of the two great Welsh poets and wonderworkers, each of whom was also a wondrous child.

Shaping the Future

Once the Round Table had been established, Merlin's role began to diminish. He was seen to be aware of the future appearance of the Grail, destined to be the new fellowship's greatest adventure, and to prepare the way for this in various ways. Almost his last act before apparently falling into a trap set for him by the otherworldly Nimue, is the part he plays in the story of two knights, the brothers Balin and Balan.

The story begins in the version composed by Malory, with the arrival of the Lady of the Lake, demanding the gift she had been promised by Arthur, which turns out to be the head of another lady who had only recently asked for help from the fellowship. Caught in a dilemma Arthur refuses and in the ensuing melee, the hot-tempered Balin snatches up a sword and cuts off the Lady of the Lake's head. From this moment he is under a curse and sets out on a series of adventures, shadowed by Merlin at every point. The final act in this tragic series of events occurs when Balin, pursuing an evil knight who attacks people under a cloak of invisibility, accidentally wounds Pelles, the Grail king. This event, known as the Dolorous Stroke, is one of several events which, in the story, take place at this time, and which foretell the coming of the Grail. Shortly after this Balin meets up with his brother Balan, though neither recognises the other since they are disguised in unfamiliar armour. The brothers fight and mortally wound each other. Merlin, who has watched all this, now appears, and taking the sword from Balin embeds it in a stone which he then sets adrift on a river. In an echo of Arthur's drawing of the sword from the stone, Galahad, the Grail final winner (who is also, incidentally, a Wonder Child), will later take this weapon for himself. Merlin meanwhile buries the two dead knights in a single tomb over which he erects a stone. He prophesies that many famous combats between rival knights will take place there.[22]

This story illustrates the nature of Merlin's involvement in the affairs of the Round Table and of King Arthur's realm. Constantly watching, sometimes intervening directly, he is always shaping the future, as though following some secret dream of his own. It is here that we see him in his most typical guise, as a mover behind the scenes, as someone who knows what is to come and sets out to ensure that the destiny of Arthur and his knights is fulfilled.

One cannot help wondering how differently the story might have gone had Merlin remained on the scene. He had already warned Arthur against marrying Guinevere and foretold how she would betray her lord with his best knight. Perhaps he would have arranged for the Grail knights to find their goal more easily than they did, and thus saved many deaths that helped bring about the fall of the Round Table – but the story takes other roads and Merlin's influence begins to dwindle. At this point he is ever-present, subtly effecting events, advising and guiding the young king in his first steps toward the creation of a great earthly kingdom; but the dream was not to be fulfilled, and Merlin himself was to be taken out of the picture in a dramatic fashion, portrayed according to the medieval mindset as an old man doting on a young woman. But there was far more to the picture than this, as we shall see in the next chapter.

4

MERLIN THE LOVER

Dark is the loom tide of the lake.
I have flickered through blind fathoms
To the clear still shallows
Of the water-fasten that holds
My country apart from yours.

Steven O'Brien:
'Nimue of the Pallid Countenance'

To think of Merlin as a lover may seem at variance with the character described in the stories we have been exploring; but while references to his relationships with women are limited, they do exist, and offer both a new insight into his character as well as that of the woman usually described as his nemesis. That he was, by some at least, seen as one who could enchant women is indicated by the words of the twelfth-century Welsh poet Hywel ab Owain Gwynedd, who asks God to award him the power to sing praises to women 'as did Merddin' (*sic*).[1]

* * *

Merlin has had more than one companion during his long lifetime, though it is the latest of these, Nimue, usually portrayed as a scheming betrayer, who is most familiar to us today. Yet there are older, far more interesting figures behind the story than this. One of these, Merlin's sister, Gwenddydd/Ganeida, we have already met. Others, more shadowy still, but no less intriguing, can be glimpsed within older texts and traditions.

The truth is made difficult to see because the nature of the relationship between Merlin and his mistresses has long been misunderstood – as has the nature of these women themselves. Essentially, they were otherworldly women, described as *fées* or faeries by medieval writers. Their role was to act as initiators into the mysteries of the Otherworld, to offer challenges to the heroes who wandered the pathless forests of the Arthurian world. Again and again we read of mysterious women who appear at Arthur's court to ask for help; but when a knight is dispatched to answer such requests it often turns out that far more is involved than was at first supposed.

Some knights ended up marrying the magical women they helped. Thus, the knight Sir Launfal goes off with his faery mistress to live in her enchanted realm; while Sir Gawain had at least two otherworldly wives at various times in his career, as well as numerous faery mistresses.[2]

Merlin, of course, had his own links with the Otherworld, and with its female representatives, as we saw in the previous chapter, where he sought Excalibur for the young King Arthur from the Lady of the Lake. Older stories suggest that there was once a far deeper and more overt relationship between the great enchanter and the otherworldly women who feature so largely in the tales.

Later writers, such as Sir Thomas Malory in the fifteenth century, took a more pragmatic and humanistic view than the tale spinners of earlier times, and so moved away from the otherworldly nature of the stories, or sought to Christianise them. By ignoring the otherworldly aspects of the women in Merlin's story, they appear as scheming rather than wise, necromantic rather than as guardians of the gates to the inner realms. This is very clearly what happened to the story of Merlin's relationship with Gwenddydd. In virtually all the later versions of the story their connection has been so eroded that it no longer bears any resemblance – at least on the surface – to the original version. Merlin's relationship with his sister, who we must assume shared his own non-human blood – has been changed out of all recognition.

Perhaps the medieval scribes who compiled the later Merlin texts were unable to accept the idea of brother and sister living together in the woods, as Geoffrey of Monmouth had described them in the *Vita Merlini*. Such things suggested the possibility of incest, and given Merlin's diabolic parentage, who knew what unspeakable acts might not be perpetrated in the house in the forest! So, they transformed the figure of Gwenddydd from sister to temptress and gave her a new name. However, in so doing, they actually looked back to older sources and thus, almost by accident, preserved something of Merlin's true relationship with the Otherworld.

With these changes it became necessary to portray Merlin's companion as acquiring his wisdom through the use of her wiles, and from here it was only a small step to the unflattering portrayal of Merlin as an old man desperately seeking the love of a young woman, followed by her eventual betrayal of him. What began as a portrayal of a deep spiritual bond of magical and prophetic awareness became skewed into a very human and generally fatal love story, in which Merlin falls for a treacherous fay, who steals his power and uses it to bind him forever. The story of how this happened, and what lies behind it, is one of the most fascinating aspects of Merlin's history.

Nimue's Odyssey

Let us begin with Nimue – or as she is called in the earliest stories in which she appears – Niniane. We first encounter her in the Merlin section of the vast compilation of Arthurian texts known as *The Lancelot-Grail Cycle*.[3] This massive collection of story and polemic was assembled during the first-half of the thirteenth century, by clerks from the Cistercian order, founded by the great medieval theologian Bernard of Clairvaux. Drawing upon a range of older works, many of which were subsequently lost, they preserved some intriguing details of Merlin's life, as well as expanding on themes and ideas first expressed in Robert de Boron's *Merlin* and the *Vita Merlini*.

The *Estoire de Merlin (History of Merlin)*, one of the first books in the sequence, was composed *c.*1280–90 and later translated into English by an anonymous author. It is in this version that we read the story of a forester named Dionas – so called because of his devotion to the goddess Diana – and to whom the goddess herself appeared and made the following prophecy.

> I grant thee, and so doth the god of the sea and the stars ... that the first female child that thou shalt have shall be much coveted by the wisest man that ever was on earth ... and he shall teach her the most part of his wit and cunning by way of necromancy, in such manner that he shall be so desirous after he hath seen her, that he shall have no power against her wish, and all things that she enquires after he shall teach.[4]

The same text continues by relating how Dionas, who had long served the Duke of Burgoyne (Burgundy) is given the latter's daughter for a wife, as well as half the forest of Brooke (Broceliande). When, in due course, the couple have a daughter, she is named Niniane, which, according to the author of the text, is of

Hebrew origin (*sic*), and means, in French, 'I shall not lie'. The child is regarded as being under the protection of the goddess from the moment of her birth, in much the same way as her father is termed her 'god-son' – a euphemistic way of describing him as her devotee.

The interpretation of Niniane's name is not without interest. That it is said to derive from the Hebrew we may set aside as an instance of the common desire of medieval authors to provide authentication for their characters – anything with the rumour of the Biblical, despite in this case its inappropriateness, being acceptable. The deciphering of her name as meaning 'I will not lie' is more interesting. It scarcely bears scrutiny as a piece of orthography, but if we accept it for the moment, we may glimpse another reading of her character: not simply as the 'evil temptress' the later authors endeavoured to make her, but as a prophetess incapable of falsehood. The overall character of Niniane, as she appears here, shows the anonymous author struggling to balance the pagan aspects of her character with her evident humanity. He shows her to have been much put upon by Merlin, and eventually to have hated him enough to justify her entrapment of him as a way of escaping his unwelcome advances.

The Prophecy

The prophecy made about Niniane by the goddess – that she will be loved by the wisest of men – is proved to be accurate. We hear next of the meeting of Merlin and Niniane, whom the former seeks out, disguised as a young squire, at a fountain where she used to often go. There, he demonstrates his miraculous powers by calling up an enchanted garden and summoning knights and ladies to dance and sing for her.

Anon the maiden ... saw come out of the forest of Briogne ladies and knights and maidens and squires, each holding other by the hand, [that] came singing and making the greatest joy that ever was seen in any land; and before the maiden came jongleurs with tymbrels and tabors [medieval musical instruments]and entered the scene that Merlin had made, and when they were within, they began [to sing] carols and [play] dances so great and so marvellous, that one might not say the fourth part of joy that was made there; and because the land was so great Merlin made there a garden, wherein was all manner of fruit and all manner of flowers, that gave so great sweetness of flavour, that marvel it were to tell.[5]

Merlin is certainly in love with Niniane, and in this version demands assurance of her own feelings. Niniane promises to return his love on condition that he teaches her all his wisdom. He agrees to do this, but not immediately, as he must leave her then for other work. Before he goes, however, he teaches her a spell which enables her to conjure up a great river, and beyond it a magical place into which she may go at will and where she will be attended to by magical servants.

There are a number of interesting details here. It is possible to see that the goddess, who spends many days with Dionas, may at one time have been the actual mother of Niniane. This may be the reason why, in a thirteenth-century text known as *The Huth Merlin*,[6] she is repeatedly referred to as 'the Huntress'. This title prompts Merlin to relate a strange tale about the goddess, which may throw further light on the true identity of Niniane.

The story concerns the Lake of Diana in the *Foret en Val* (Forest in the Vale), so called because it was here that Diana lived in a wondrous palace with the hunter Faunus. But in time she fell in love with another man, named Felix, and so wished to dispose of her former love. When Faunus returned one day, wounded from hunting, he sought to take a bath in some healing water. But Diana drained these away and, in a scene reminiscent of Merlin's demise, persuaded Faunus to get into a tomb on which she places a heavy lid with a hole in it. She then pours boiling lead through the hole. Although he had previously abjured her to get rid of her lover, when Felix hears the manner of his rival's death, he is horrified and cuts off Diana's head.

In the light of this story, it has been suggested that the association of Niniane with Diana could be carried a step further – that in fact the writer of *The Huth Merlin* may have known an ancient Celtic story from the *Mabinogion*, a thirteenth- to fourteenth-century collection of Welsh myths drawn from ancient sources.[7] In this the maiden Blodeuwedd is made from flowers by the wizard Math to be a wife for the hero Lleu Llaw Gyffes. However, she falls in love with a hunter named Gronw Pebr and arranges the death of Lleu by having him stand with one foot on a bath, the other on the back of a goat, at which point Gronw casts a spear at him. This curious death is the only way that the hero could be killed and there are certainly some parallels here with the story of Diana and Faunus, especially in the manner of the deaths of the two characters. But the most interesting fact is the suggestion that otherworldly blood flowed in Niniane's veins and that there might be a connection between her and Blodeuwedd.

The Flower Bride

Blodeuwedd belongs to a group of otherworldly women known as Flower Brides or Flower Maidens, who represents the Spring Maiden in Celtic tradition. Every year she is fought over by the champions of summer and winter, their struggle forming a kind of primitive eternal triangle of a woman caught between two men.

This story echoes and re-echoes throughout the Arthurian sagas. In the *Morte D'Arthur* we find it embedded in several episodes in which Nimue plays a part. The first tells how the knight Sir Pelleas loved a maiden named Ettard so deeply that he allowed himself to be taken prisoner so that he would be taken to her castle, where he has at least a chance of seeing her. Ettard, however, hates Pelleas, and sends him away every time. The great Arthurian hero Gawain, coming on a scene in which Pelleas as usual allows himself to be defeated, learns of the story and promises to do all in his power to persuade the Ettard to look with favour on the knight. In fact, he is himself so attracted to Ettard – and the attraction proves mutual – that he ends up in bed with her, having told her that he has slain Pelleas. By chance the lovelorn knight finds them and, though heart-smitten, refrains from killing them, instead laying the blade of his sword across their necks as they sleep in token of their betrayal. When the pair wake Ettard is dismayed at Gawain's duplicity and sends him away. It is at this point that Nimue enters the story. Hearing of Pelleas' intention to starve himself to death, she intervenes, casting a powerful spell which causes Ettard to love Pelleas, and the knight to fall in love with Nimue herself. Thus, the roles are reversed and Ettard, who now loves Pelleas so much that she is likely to die of it, is left to suffer as much as he formerly did. Nimue, meanwhile, becoming his lover from that moment on, carries him away. Later, Pelleas is referred to as being 'wedded' to Nimue, who saved him from meeting death at the hands of any knight he fought with thereafter.[8]

This is a very Merlin-like intervention and also, in its triangular relationships reminiscent of the Flower Bride story. Nimue here shows herself to be not only a powerful sorceress, but also clear-sighted and decisive in her resolution of the tangle of relationships. Her subsequent appearances confirm this. The next episode in which she takes part is that in which Accolon of Gaul, the lover of Morgan le Fay, attempts to kill Arthur with his own sword, which Morgan has stolen, having first told Accolon that Arthur is a rival for her favours. Nimue appears because that Morgan le Fay 'had ordained that King Arthur should be slain that day, and therefore she came to save his life'. By enchantment she causes Excalibur to fall from Accolon's hand, and Arthur retrieves it and wins the battle forthwith. Merlin had earlier warned Arthur of this very event, and it seems very much in keeping with the portrayal of Nimue as the mage's successor that she should participate in this episode. It also further echoes the Flower Bride story in the contrived struggle between Arthur and Accolon for the possession of Morgan.

Nimue's First Test

But if we are to prove that Nimue is a type of Flower Bride, with all its attendant mythical undertones, we should seek for an episode in which she is herself carried off or fought over by opposing champions. In fact, we do not have to look very far. The very first episode in which Arthur and his knights encounter Nimue includes this very theme.

As the knights of the Round Table – then only lately formed – gather to celebrate Arthur's wedding to Guinevere, a white hart bounds into the hall pursued by a bratchet (a small hunting dog). This is followed in turn by Nimue herself, who at this point is unnamed. An unknown knight now jumps up, seizes the dog, and departs quickly from the hall. As Nimue protests loudly, another knight appears and abducts her in turn. At first the fellowship is inclined to dismiss all of this as unimportant, but Merlin himself reproves them, and at his bidding Arthur dispatches King Pellinore, one of his strongest knights, to rescue the abducted lady and either bring back or kill the knight who stole her away.

Pellinore's journey is marked by ominous events from the start. First he encounters a maiden cradling the wounded body of her knight, but when she begs help he refuses to turn aside from his appointed task and after he has ridden away – with the woman's curse ringing in his ears – the wounded knight dies and the maiden kills herself with his sword. Pellinore continues on his way and overtakes Nimue, who is being fought over by two knights, the one who carried her off and another, her cousin, who seems to think he should have the ruling of her. Pellinore defeats the knight who had abducted her from Arthur's hall and makes friends with the other, who is more than glad to give over the protection of his errant cousin into the hands of the older man. It is only then that we learn her name for the first time – Nimue.[9]

Here she is presented as a purely human character, who behaves in a somewhat noisy and helpless way, allowing herself to be pushed from knight to knight without much protest. But what is important is that here Nimue appears as a woman fought over by two knights – just like the Spring Maiden in the Flower Bride myth.

On the return journey with Pellinore they come to the place where the distressed maiden had asked for help, finding only the pitiful remains for her body, consumed save for the head by wild animals. Pellinore now shows shame and regret at his hasty behaviour, and at Nimue's suggestion carries the head, hung about his neck, back to Camelot.

There is no suggestion of otherworldliness here; nor is Nimue yet referred to as one of the Ladies of the Lake. Yet the very next episode in *Le Morte D'Arthur* begins with the account of how Merlin 'fell in a dotage on the damosel that King Pellinore brought [back] to court, and she was one of the damosels of the lake...' This confusion is probably due to Malory's use of various sources, but does suggest that there were two separate traditions, in one of which Nimue was of mortal stock, and in the other of otherworldly origin.

While it is true that Merlin himself does not engage in combat for Nimue, he does engineer her rescue, and the implication is that he then seeks her out because she is an otherworldly woman, a type of Flower Bride who, like himself, may be only half human, perhaps indeed with the blood of the goddess Diana in her veins.

It is in these stories that we begin to catch a first glimpse of Nimue's true nature. The Flower Bride is only one aspect of this, but the archetype appears in so many early Celtic and later Arthurian stories that it is more than likely that the role influenced the shaping of Niniane's character in the later romances.

Merlin's Successor

In each of the incidents described here Nimue also begins to adopt the role of Merlin's successor. How then, does this effect the way we see her imprisonment of the great enchanter?

We have seen the episode variously interpreted as tragedy or comedy, or as an inevitable consequence of Merlin's infatuation, or as the fate he has predicted for himself; while Nimue's role ranges from that of abused woman to scheming fay.

Malory's characterisation of Nimue is certainly far from consistent – though she is unfailingly represented as helpful to Arthur. Indeed, once Merlin has been taken out of the picture, she virtually takes his place, saving Arthur from various attacks by his half-sister Morgan le Fay. In fact, Malory's blunt retelling of the whole episode puts Nimue in a far more favourable light than the earlier French or English texts.

> Merlin fell in a dotage on … one of the damosels of the lake, [named] Nimue. But Merlin would let her have no rest, but always he would be with her. And ever she made Merlin good cheer till she had learned of him all manner of thing that she desired; and he was besotted upon her … and always … lay about the lady to have her maidenhood, and she was ever passing weary of him, and fain would have been delivered of him because he was a devil's son … And so on a time it happed that Merlin showed her a rock where was a great wonder … So, by her subtle working she made Merlin to go under that stone … but she wrought … for him that he came never out for all the craft that he could do. And so she departed and left Merlin.[10]

Map of Merlin's Britain, by John Matthews.

Merlin on the cover of a programme for a production of King Arthur *at the Lyceum Theatre, London, in 1895. (Author's collection)*

Merlin is depicted as a wild man in this illustration from Malory's Le Morte D'Arthur *by the nineteenth-century illustrator Aubrey Beardsley. (Author's collection)*

Merlin as a powerful man in the prime of life, as depicted in this contemporary painting by Nicole Ryan. (Used by permission of the artist)

Above: Lailoken the Madman *portrayed by modern artist Will Worthington. (Used by permission of the artist)*

Left: *Merlin as a Druid by Louis Rhead, from a series of illustrations for Tennyson's* Idylls of the King. *(Author's collection)*

Merlin's Cave. *Engraving by T. Bonles from* Merlin, or the British Enchanter *(1736). (Author's collection)*

Merlin is tricked into entering a cave by Nimue in this 1529 woodcut illustration from Sir Thomas Malory's Le Morte D'Arthur. *(Author's collection)*

The Imprisonment of Merlin *by contemporary artist Joe Machine. (Used by permission of the artist)*

Merlin well verſt-in many an hidden *ſpell*,
His Countries *omen* did long ſince foretell.
Grac'd in his *Time* by ſundry *King* he was,
And all that *he* predicted came to paſſe.

Merlin the Monk. *Illustration from the seventeenth-century publication,* Life of Merlin, *by Thomas Heywood. (Author's collection)*

Above: *Merlin and Vivien,
from a nineteenth-century tile.
Painting by J. Moyr Smith.
(Author's collection)*

Left: *Merlin by Alan Lee.
(Used by permission of the
artist)*

This unflattering portrayal of the aged Merlin, besotted on the beautiful faery damsel, now named as one of the Ladies of the Lake, who cozens him out of his secrets and then uses them to imprison him, seems to be part of the general tendency on the part of medieval writers to reinterpret the more primitive pagan material as they understood it. As Merlin himself became represented as the son of a devil rather than the child of an otherworldly being, so now Nimue, whose father served the goddess Diana, is portrayed as a temptress whose power derives solely from that of Merlin.

Merlin is depicted as following her everywhere, constantly trying to get her alone in some secluded spot where he may 'have her maidenhead'. She, in turn, is afraid of him, referring to him as a 'devil's son', and finally doing all she can to learn his secrets so that she may use them against him.

Malory, as is usual with him, tones down the supernatural element throughout all of this. His vision of Nimue is of a mortal woman beset by an older, more skilful man who just happens to possess magical powers. In the end, she turns those powers against him, imprisoning him for all time. The last we hear of the old wizard is his voice issuing from beneath the rock under which Nimue has penned him. The inference is that the only one who can let him out, is she who put him there. Her tacit refusal to do so speaks for itself.

The Glass Cage

In order to understand the real nature of Nimue's role in Merlin's withdrawal we have to look at a later text: the fourteenth century *Didot Perceval*.[11] Here, Merlin's end is described in very different terms to that of the foolish old man overcome by the wiles of a girl. Here there is no mention of Nimue at all; rather Merlin withdraws from the world by choice.

And then Merlin came to Perceval and to Blayse his master, and he took leave of them and told them that Our Lord did not wish that he should show himself to people, yet that he would not be able to die before the end of the world; '... and I wish to make a lodging outside your palace and to dwell there and I will prophesy whatever Our Lord commands me. And all those who will see my lodging will name it the *esplumoir* (or moulting cage) of Merlin.'[12]

There has been much speculation about the meaning of this word *esplumoir*. [13] No exact equivalent has been found, and the interpretation 'moulting cage' has led to a number of speculations. It may be that the author of the *Didot Perceval* intended nothing more than an elaborate pun on the derivation of Merlin's name from that of a hawk, and that the *esplumoir* is really nothing more than a cage in which hunting birds were kept during moult.

However, several commentators have pointed out that the moulting cage can itself be seen as an image of the otherworld, into which mortals often went but from where they seldom returned. If this is the case, and if Merlin either retires voluntarily or is shut up in the cage, or otherworldly place, by Nimue, then she must, by inference, be seen as an otherworldly figure herself, as, indeed, one of the faery women whose role is often to test – and sometimes to entrap – mortals.

In the *Didot* there is an episode in which a number of otherworldly women, living in an in invisible castle, turn themselves into birds at attack the hero. As he approaches the castle Perceval hears the voice of Merlin warning him not to go there. The voices issue from a shadow (*ombre*) or cloud, which passes overhead four times. This would seem to imply that Merlin is himself in bird form at this point, flying overhead. Birds have long been associated with the faery realm and are among the most common shapes taken by otherworldly women when they transform themselves.

We learn more of such mysterious imprisonments from the Irish myth of Étaín, who is turned into a fly and kept in a kind of glass cage by her lover, the god Aengus mac ind Óic, who keeps her safe in this way while she is in such a vulnerable form. Interestingly, another name for Étaín was Befinn (White One), a variant of which, Bébinn, sometimes written as it was pronounced: *Bhebhionn*. This could easily have developed, in the hands of the French romancers, into Vivianne, another variant of Niniane's name. Befinn means 'White Lady', and Gwenddydd means 'White Day' – surely too similar to be mere coincidence.[14]

The god Aengus, who kept Étaín in a glass cage known as a *grianán*, has himself been compared to Merlin – so that it may be possible to suggest that, at one point in the development of the story, Merlin's house of glass was perceived as not unlike the home of the god – an otherworldly dwelling over which he ruled, accompanied by faery women. There are indeed several instances of such places in both Welsh and Irish tradition. For example, the Glass Tower found in the ninth-century poem '*Prieddeu Annwn*', which is incidentally the first account of Arthur and his men going in search of a magical vessel which predates the Christian Grail story. Lastly, we hear that Nimuë (the new name for Merlin's companion) conjures a tower of glass in which to imprison her 'ancient' lover.

Another possible interpretation of the word *esplumoir* is the Latin *ex-plumare*, which refers to the putting off of the feathers of a bird – in otherwise the semblance or shape of the bird. In Irish the words *énchendraich*, 'bird-garb', is used when describing Étaín's bird-lover, who flies into her window each day and leaves his bird-form on the floor. Could this be the origin of the story of Merlin's conception? That an otherworldly (probably faery) man flies into the chamber of the Princess of Dyfed and having taken off his bird shape, begets upon her the Wonder Child? The overlapping words and situations imply this.

From this a wholly different picture of Merlin's companion begins to emerge, in which Ganeida/Gwenddydd, Merlin's sister, dwells with him in an otherworldly house of glass from which they observe the outside world, prophesying events to come. Ganeida is referred to in the *Vita Merlini* as returning frequently to Merlin's house – a detail which suggests that Merlin could not himself leave there even if he wished.

Here we can see how Merlin, perhaps tired of the world and of the need constantly to intervene in matters pertaining to the kingdom he has helped create, could be seen as retiring to his *esplumoir*, accompanied by his faery lover or sister (who is perhaps one and the same), where he remains, while Gwenddydd, now called Nimue, and prepared by him for the role, takes Merlin's place as helper and advisor to Arthur, whom she continues to protect until his passing to Avalon.

We shall return to a fuller account of the origins and function of Merlin's *esplumoir* in the next chapter; for the moment it is enough to say that its ultimate source is almost certainly to be found in Celtic myth. It is clear enough that *esplumoir* refers to the otherworld, which in many stories is represented as a *grianán*, a building or cage made of glass, or as a house with many windows such as the observatory constructed for Merlin by Gwenddydd/Ganeida.

The Seeress of the Woods

Merlin's otherworldly nature requires a consort who displays similar qualities. We have already seen how Gwenddydd/Ganeida matches him at many levels in the *Vita* and in the Myrddyn poems. Certainly, the parallels between Gwenddydd/Ganida and Nimue are plain enough:

Ganida:	Nimue:
encourages Merlin	is Merlin's helper
tests Merlin	persuades him to perform magic

meets Merlin in the forest	meets Merlin in the forest
makes a secluded observatory	conjures a glass tower
continues Merlin's prophetic task	continues Merlin's work

Now, just as Ganeida's prophetic abilities are seen to grow as Merlin withdraws into his observatory, so once Merlin is entombed, Nimue begins to develop until she is virtually his successor.

Another factor which illustrates this transformation is the reference in one of the Myrddin Poems to a *chwyfleian* who 'foretells a tale that will come to pass'. There has been some debate over the exact meaning of this word and its variant form *hwimleian*. This can be translated as 'a wanderer of pallid countenance' or as 'a seer/ess'. The word *lleian*, from which *hwimleian* comes, is variously said to mean either a nun, a vestal virgin or a priestess. The word is still in use today to refer to a nun, which suggests that it almost certainly carried the connotation of priestess over a long period of time.

But the most interesting point, for our current argument, is the obvious similarity between *chwibleian* and *hwimleian*, and the name of Merlin's mistress Niniane or Vivienne. Either could have derived from the old Welsh word and carried with it the idea of a prophetess or woman of power associated with Merlin.[15]

It seems clear that this is the underlying sense of an episode from the *Vita Merlini* which describes Merlin, together with some companions arriving at a spring. There they find some fragrant apples which, when eaten, cause the mage's companions to go temporarily mad. When they are recovered Merlin explains that the poisoned fruit was in all probability meant for him. It seems that there was, in that district,

... a woman who had formally been infatuated with me and had satisfied her love for me during many years. After I had spurned her and had refused to cohabit with her she was suddenly seized with an evil desire to do me harm, and when with all her plotting she could not find any other means of approach, she placed the gifts smeared with poison by the fountain to which I was going to return, planning by this device to injure me if I could chance to find the apples on the grass and eat them.[16]

Is this the origin of Nimue? A woman who loved Merlin and, on being spurned by him, turned against him and attempted to destroy him by poisoned apples? Interestingly there is an episode towards the end of the *Morte D'Arthur* in which Nimue comes to the court to save Queen Guinevere, who has been accused of murdering a knight named Sir Pinel – with poisoned apples! Nimue is able to reveal that this was all a plot to kill Sir Gawain, but it is interesting that this episode features her in connection with poisoned fruit.

The answer to all of this may lie in the nature of the fruit itself. Apples were considered among the Celts to be of otherworldly origin, and there are numerous stories in which heroes are found sleeping beneath apple trees and carried off by otherworldly women, or are offered apples which have the effect of bespelling them so that they fall asleep and waken in faeryland. If we see Gwenddydd/Nimue as being a guardian or possessor of such apples, then we have come a step nearer to the idea of her as a faery woman who has the power, in her own right, to convey people into the otherworld.

The Goddess of the Door

Virtually all of texts that include her story emphasise Nimue's careful preservation of her virginity, and this suggests a lingering memory of an earlier status – as a priestess. Her age, given sometimes as twelve, but more often as fifteen, supports this, since we know that Vestal Virgins entered the temple in Rome at this age.

Robert Graves, in his seminal study of poetic myth, *The White Goddess,* classes Nimue with Cardea-Cerridwen, a muse goddess who inspires *cerddeu* 'poems' (in Greek *cerdia*). He also quotes the 'The Dialogue of Gwenddydd and Merddin' from *The Black Book of Carmarthen* in which, as we may remember, Gwenddydd instructs her brother to 'rise from his prison and open the Books of Inspiration without fear'. In the same poem she is described as *Gwenddydd wen adlam Cerddeu* which Graves translates as 'White Lady of Day, refuge of Poems'. All of which seems to confirm her status as an inspirer.[17]

If we add to this the evidence presented above, which identifies Gwenddydd as the *Chwifleian* or priestess-sibyl, this makes a very strong case for seeing Nimue as both a priestess and an inspirer. It also gives us a giant key with which to unlock the last mystery of her role in Merlin's history.

When he invokes the name of Cardea, Graves points out that she is the Roman goddess of door hinges and is in nature very similar to both Artemis and Diana with whom she shares the attributes of virgin goddess of the hunt. She obtained her post as guardian of doorways from the double-faced god Janus, in return for her favours. This fact alone affirms Nimue as the successor of Gwenddydd/Ganeida, since Nimue encloses Merlin behind a door which will not open to anyone save she and is only given this power in return for her embraces.

In the *History of the Kings of Britain* Geoffrey of Monmouth speaks of how the princess Cordelia buried her father King Leir in a vault under the River Soar at Leicester, ground which had been sacred to Janus. The tomb was already the meeting place for workmen who would convene here on the first day of the year to begin their work. Again, we note the connection of Cardea/Cordelia with Janus and with sacred work. This image of Cordelia sealing Leir into a vault strangely echoes both the story of Diana and Faunus and of Merlin and Nimue.[18]

The Goddess of the Door also makes an appearance in the extraordinary apocalyptic prophecies of Merlin included in the *Historia*. There she is referred to as the goddess Ariadne, who literally closes the door on the age.

> The twelve mansions of the stars will weep ... the Gemini will cease their wonted embraces and will dispatch Aquarius to the fountain. The scales of Lyra will hang awry ... the tail of Scorpio shall generate lightning and Cancer will fight with the Sun ... the Moon's chariot shall run amok in the Zodiac and the Pliades will burst into tears ... Ariadne will shut [the]door and be hidden within the enclosing cloudbanks.[19]

The Roman historian Varro confirms that Cardea ruled over the Celestial Hinge at the back of the North wind, around which the millstone of the world revolves.[20] Gwenddydd/Ganeida is the creator of Merlin's otherworldly observatory of seventy doors and windows which becomes the centre of his world from that moment onward and offers glimpses into a sometimes-terrifying future.

Within these varied references we catch a glimpse of Nimue as the representative of a native British Goddess of the Door, one who guards the borderlands between this world and the other. Her sacred task is to accompany Merlin, becoming his lineal successor in the Arthurian world. She does not entrap or imprison him, but rather opens a door between the worlds, allowing him to enter there and shed his old form to become renewed in the mysterious *esplumoir* of his glass observatory.

The Myth Reforged

The view of Nimue as a temptress bent upon the destruction of Merlin is thus shown to be not only untrue but also a huge oversimplification. As we have seen, Nimue is a far more complex figure when all the versions are examined; she functions not only as an essential helper to Arthur, but as a prophetess and priestess of considerable abilities. Her unfortunate metamorphosis is largely due to a fundamental misunderstanding of both her own and Merlin's natures. Merlin's withdrawal from the world is just that – the idea that he was entrapped by a faery woman reads like a piece of medieval rationalisation of a much older theme – one that is still clearly preserved in the *Vita Merlini*.

Even in Malory this is still sustained. There, far from being the evil enchantress or femme fatale that most people see, Nimue is described as someone who 'did great good to King Arthur and all his knights.' Her role is one of continuing Merlin's work. She helps Arthur against the plots of Morgan le Fay. Later, she appears in the story of the poisoning of Sir Pinel. Her final appearance in the *Mort D'Arthur* is as one of the queenly women in the barge which ambiguously carries Arthur either to his death or to be healed in Avalon. Other commentators have suggested that Nimue is there specifically to counterbalance Morgan. The two women, Arthur's helper and his chief opponent, are brought together at the end to balance each other out, as well as adding to the ambiguity of Arthur's fate. In fact, the apparent turn in Morgan's character is not what it seems, but the way in which Malory understood it upholds the theory of the two women as magical opponents, balanced in polarity at the end of the Arthurian dream.

Merlin's companion is thus seen clearly at last – in the shape of an empowering priestess and prophet every bit as important and powerful as he, and very possibly with the blood of a goddess in her veins. How the story changed so that, from her original relationship, she became Merlin's nemesis, is not so very hard to see. Gwenddydd/Ganeida had distinct otherworldly traits, as did Niniane/Nimue, and to the medieval romancers that made her a fay. And fays were all assumed to be beautiful, lustful and dangerous. Therefore, when Merlin, the great enchanter, encounters one such – he could not, by the later development of the legend, be seen as having an actual sister – sparks were bound to fly. Instead of a sister and helper, Gwenddydd/Nimue becomes a temptress and betrayer, whose only defence against Merlin's wiles is to flatter him and smile at him until she has gained enough of his knowledge to turn it against him. Thus, the empowerer becomes the betrayer, and as so often in the world of Arthurian romance, the role of the woman is subverted and changed from positive to negative. But enough of the original archetype was preserved in the figure of Nimue to ensure that in texts such as the *Mort D'Arthur* she continued to fulfil her role as an otherworldly lady of the lake, while in the *Vita Merlini* her true function as the holder of the ways between this world and the otherworld could still be seen.

Nor should we forget that in the *Vita,* Merlin *wants* to be enclosed, that he requests of Ganeida that she build him a shelter; while in the later romances he is entombed against his will. This is a significant change, since it alters the role of Merlin's companion from that of empowerer to imprisoner. Once again, the clerical minds of the medieval writers could not grasp the true significance of Merlin's withdrawal into the otherworld, as represented by the observatory in the woods, any more than they were willing to entertain the priestessly aspects of the woman he chose for his companion.

Merlin's relationships with women are, as one might expect, not at all straightforward. There are other aspects of his story embedded within the accounts of his perilous love for Nimue that lead us to a consideration of his last, and perhaps most important incarnation – as an all-wise sage and keeper of ancient wisdom. It is to this aspect of his character that we turn next.

5

MERLIN THE SAGE

There the wise Merlin .... went (they say)
To make his wonne [home] low underneath the ground,
In a deep delve, far from the view of day,
That of no living wight he might be found,
When so he counselled with his spirits encompassed round.

Edmund Spenser:
'The Faerie Queene'

The mystery of the *esplumoir*, the Moulting Cage into which Merlin retires, as we have seen, is a great deal older than at first appears. It is also an important key to the unlocking of the final stage of Merlin's changing role and status through the ages. He was always seen as exceptionally wise, beyond the wisdom of ordinary men, as his skill as a prophet and later as one blessed with magic demonstrates. We have also seen how at least some part of his wisdom derives from his relationships with women, one of whom, variously called Nimue, Vivienne, Gwenddydd or Ganeida, provided him with a permanent base from which to operate. It is this base, and its more ancient aspects, which we will be examining in this chapter, as well as the treasures guarded within it. Not only does the history of the *esplumoir* cast light on Merlin's history, it also shows us just how far back in time, and how deep, his connection with the Island of Britain actually goes.

Merlin's Enclosure

Preserved with the collection of *The Triads of Britain* which, as we saw in Chapter 1, hold valuable references to Merlin's early history, is a manuscript which, in its present form, dates from the fifteenth century but yet again contains material of a far older provenance. In it is a list of The Names of the Island of Britain (*Enweu Ynys Prydein*). The first entry is of immediate interest:

> The First Name that this island bore, before it was taken or settled: Myrddin's Precinct [*Clas Myrddyn*]. And after it was taken and settled, the Island of Honey. And after it was conquered by Prydein son of Aedd the Great it was called Prydein (Britain).[1]

This is an important statement, suggesting as it does that Merlin's connection with the island is a lot older than we may suppose. While it is clearly unlikely that prehistoric Britain was named after a sixth-century character, a suggestion put forward by the writer Geoffrey Ashe is that Myrddin might have been the name of a local god associated with a particular site where he had once been worshipped, and that this was transferred to a wider context. Carmarthen (Moridunum) obviously leaps to mind as a possible candidate for this site since, as we saw earlier, it appears to have possessed a long-standing association with Merlin.

The idea that Britain was surrounded by an enclosure built by the great sage is one that resurfaces elsewhere. As late as the seventeenth century, the poet Edmund Spenser, in his epic poem 'The Faerie Queene', which is known to have preserved folklore and traditions since lost, refers to Merlin encompassing the town of Carmarthen with a wall of brass. Having painted a dramatic picture of Merlin's underground workshop, filled with loud groans and sounds like brazen cauldrons being struck with hammers, the poet remarks:

> The cause some say is this: A little while
> Before that Merlin died, he did intend,
> A brazen wall in compass to compile
> About Cairmardin, and did it commend
> Unto these sprights, to bring to perfect end.
> During which work the Lady of the Lake,
> Whom long he loved, for him in haste did send,
> Who thereby forced his workmen to forsake,
> Them bound till his return, their labours not to slake.[2]

This is almost certainly a reflection of a long-held belief that an actual enclosure once encircled the entire island – though what the nature of that enclosure was is nowhere described. It may well have originated with Plato's account in *Timaeus* of a similar wall surrounding the fabled city of Atlantis. Or perhaps it may also be considered as a kind of psychic barrier, a magical ring of protection designed to keep the island and its people safe from harm. As we shall see, much of this is a direct link with the true nature of the *esplumoir*. It is also very much a part of what may be termed the mythical history of Britain, in which the country is founded by a runaway princess (Albina), a hero from Troy (Brutus) in a land populated by giants.

Geoffrey of Monmouth, the indefatigable mythographer who gave us so much of Merlin's history, also included in the *Historia* the story of Brutus, the grandson of the more famous Aeneas, who arrived in Britain and established a kingdom here, naming the island after himself.[3] A second myth, written down in the thirteenth century in an anonymous Anglo-Norman poem,

Dez Grantz Geanz ('The Origins of the Giants'),[4] takes us even further back with the arrival of Albina and her twenty-nine sisters who set up home on the island, named Albion after their leader, who in time cohabit with demons and give birth to the same giants whom Brutus must later defeat in order to found his kingdom.

These stories are of a kind known as foundation myths, establishing an ancient lineage from which all future descendants can claim their heritage. Thus Brutus builds the city of Troy-Novant (New Troy) which is later to be renamed London after another mythical king: Lud. It seems reasonable to suggest that the idea behind Britain being originally known as Clas Myrddin, may well refer to another such story, now lost, in which Merlin was recognised as a significant founder of the ancient land. It would also certainly resonate with the idea, admittedly late, that Merlin was seen as a god.

Just when this idea surfaced, we cannot say with any certainty, since nothing exists in written form before the twelfth century, but it encourages the notion that Merlin's appearance could be very much earlier than his medieval history would suggest.

The Moulting Cage

As we saw in the previous chapter, it has become customary to view the end of Merlin's career in a certain light: as an ageing wizard captivated by a young woman. In this scenario Merlin is beguiled into giving away his secrets in return for sexual favours and, once the temptress has succeeded in extracting this knowledge, she then uses it to imprison her aged lover, sometimes under a great rock, sometimes in a glass tower. From there he is said to utter elusive prophecies or gnomic sayings. In some versions, the *Perron de Merlin*, Merlin's Stone, which marks his last resting place, becomes a starting point for adventure, to which those in search of the strange or mysterious resort to await events or instructions.

But there is another interpretation, which we can trace through Geoffrey of Monmouth's *Vita Merlini* to the *Didot Perceval* and the Myrddyn poems. Beyond these we enter the mists of Celtic mythology, where the same idea is found. In this scenario Merlin has reached a great age, or a particular stage of spiritual development, or simply tires of the world, and decides to retire from it of his own accord. He is, sometimes, still accompanied by a female companion, and lives in a tower, or on a mysterious island. In each case these are places of Merlin's own choosing.

We have heard also how Merlin himself lets it be known that he will no longer remain active in the world, but that he will build a place close to the walls of Camelot, which will be known as Merlin's *esplumoir*, or 'moulting cage'. For a long time, it was thought that this term really applied to a falcon's cage, and that because Merlin happened to share his name with an actual bird of prey, an elaborate pun was intended. In one sense this was right, for just as birds moult in order to change, to grow fresh plumage, so Merlin himself wants to change himself in some profound manner. However, the bird imagery is itself interesting.

We have also seen in Chapter 1 how Merlin displays shamanistic abilities; in particular the accounts of him in the *Historia* and the *Vita Merlini* have a strong flavour of this ancient path. Both these texts have been shown to embody material from a much earlier time, and from the evidence they present it is possible to see how the figure of Merlin matches precisely with a kind of inspired, half-mad poet and prophet known to the Celts as a *gelt*, and who also just happens to fly.

The word *gelt*, which is usually translated as 'inspired madman' is probably the nearest we have to a native word for shaman. The best-known figure to whom it is applied comes from ancient Ireland; he is known as Suibhne Gelt, to whom Merlin has been compared before. Like the sage, Suibhne also had a passion for trees, and spends a great deal of time in their branches, dressed in a cloak of feathers which enabled him to fly. It is possible that Merlin once possessed this ability also, and that when we read of him entering his 'moulting cage' he is simply taking off the feathered cloak of the shaman – a costume widely attributed to shamans of many lands.[5] In the *Didot Perceval*, Merlin is heard speaking from within a cloud, whose shadow crosses the ground beneath him, while in the French romance of *Meraugis de la Portlesguez*, which is the only other text to mention the *esplumoir* by this name, the term is applied to the Roche aux Pucelles (Rock of Ladies), a place with no path to the summit – implying that the only way to get there was by flying.[6] Yet again this offers evidence for the *esplumoir* as a magical place which only someone with bird wings can reach – such a place, indeed, as Merlin's 'moulting cage', where the hawk retires to renew itself. It is perhaps also worth noting that in the writings of the monk Nennius, which as we saw earlier, is one of the primary sources for the story of Merlin and the dragons, we find mention of a glass tower, lying close to the sea, on top of which are found *quasi homines* (half-men)[7] who either cannot speak or choose not to, we can see how this idea may have been passed on, along with the story of Emrys, to later writers.

The Dream Ended

We do not have to seek very far for another, more pragmatic reason for Merlin's withdrawal. At the beginning of the Arthurian era he is active, arranging for the birth of the future king, finding him his magical weapon, helping to establish the Round Table and guiding the knights through their first adventures. But as the king grows more independent Merlin's role diminishes, and it is at this moment that an event occurs that sows the seeds for the future destruction of the kingdom. On the eve of a great battle Arthur unknowingly sleeps with his half-sister and begets a child who will grow up to be his nemesis. When Merlin learns of this – having been distracted by other events – he tells the king roundly that:

> ... ye have done a thing of late that God is displeased with you, for ye have lain with your sister and on her ye have gotten a child that shall destroy you and all the knights of your realm.[8]

Soon after this Arthur meets and falls in love with Guinevere, the woman who will be his future queen. This time Merlin is on hand and warns Arthur that one day the queen will betray him with his best knight, Sir Lancelot. Arthur chooses to ignore the advice of his councillor and marries Guinevere anyway. But with this act the seeds are sown that will indeed bring about the end of the Round Table – for Lancelot and Guinevere do fall in love, and their illicit passion splits the fellowship into embittered factions. In the wars that follow, the dream of Arthur and Merlin will fail.

It is perhaps no accident that when Malory's Merlin warns Arthur against Mordred (the fruit of his incestuous union) he chooses this moment to foretell his own end – which he himself describes as 'shameful'. But even if it were not for this, or for Arthur's increasing independence of spirit, we can see why Merlin might choose to turn his back on a world where the darker aspects of human nature disturb the perfect earthly kingdom which his wisdom was intended to shape.

Hidden Kings

But there are deeper reasons still for Merlin's decision to withdraw into the seclusion of the *esplumoir*. For clues to this we have to look outside native British tradition, where we find that there are other figures who share Merlin's attributes as prophet, magician, and seer, and who withdraw into dimensions which are not of this world.

These figures are known by the term 'hidden' or 'inner' kings – beings who, though still living, have chosen to withdraw into another dimension. From there they continue to have responsibility for a particular tradition or teaching and to influence events in the world outside. Among the most notable of these are three figures most familiar to us from Biblical and Jewish sources – Melchizedek, Enoch, and Elijah, each one notable for the extended span of life they are given and the great wisdom they possess.[9] Despite their many differences, these figures share certain important aspects. They are all mysterious, shadowy beings, who appear at a time of crucial import to a particular group of people, and who have neither an orthodox beginning nor end to their lives. Finally, each withdraws or disappears, leaving conflicting accounts of their actual existence, function or allegiance.

The mysterious Biblical priest-king, Melchizedek, who is described as being 'without beginning or end', was seen as a precursor of Christ. He is said to have brought bread and wine to the patriarch Abraham after a great battle, and to have offered these in a way that foreshadowed the Eucharist. He became, like Merlin, synonymous with wisdom, while some sources portray him as reborn in the likeness of the prophets Enoch and Elijah. If we examine the history of these two figures, we will see some interesting parallels with Merlin.

Enoch, who according to the Bible 'walked with God and was not', seems never to have been born at all. He is first mentioned, in Jewish traditional sources, as living in a hidden enclave, not of heaven or Earth, from which he watches and records the deeds of mankind and holds occasional converse with God. Later he is represented as a king who ruled over mankind for more than 200 years before being summoned by God to rule over angelic hosts as a replacement for the fallen angel Lucifer. To this rather sparse account we can add, from various other sources, that Enoch visited heaven often while still in the flesh, and that he received instruction from the archangel Michael, after which he wrote some 366 books of wisdom – echoing the prophetic books supposedly written by Merlin. When he is finally translated to heaven, Enoch has bestowed upon him a vast catalogue of qualities:

extraordinary wisdom, sagacity, judgement, knowledge, learning, compassion, love, kindness, grace, humility, strength, power, might, splendour, beauty, shapeliness and all other excellent qualities', and received besides: 'many thousand blessings from God, and his height and breadth became equal to the height and breadth of the world, and thirty-six wings were attached to his body to the right and to the left, each as large as the world, and three hundred and sixty-five thousand eyes were bestowed upon him, each as brilliant as the sun.[10]

This description continues for several more paragraphs, outlining a truly cosmic figure. At the end it is revealed that Enoch – whose name, not surprisingly, means 'the enlightened one', received a new title. As the text puts it: 'A magnificent throne was erected for him beside the gates of the seventh celestial palace, and a herald proclaimed throughout heaven concerning him, who was henceforth to be called Metatron.'[11]

God then declares:

I have appointed my servant Metatron as prince and chief over all other princes in my realm … whatever angel has a request to refer to me, shall appear before Metatron, and what he will command at my bidding, ye must observe and do, for the Prince of Wisdom and the Prince of Understanding are at his service, and they will reveal unto him the science of the celestials and the terrestrials, and knowledge of the present order of the world, and the knowledge of the future order of the world. Furthermore, have I made him guardian of the treasures of the palace of heaven, Arabot, and of the treasures of life that are in the highest heavens.[12]

Enoch has thus become a Lord of Hosts and a guardian of the Treasures of Life in heaven. More interestingly perhaps he is also said to have assumed the position left vacant by the fall of Lucifer. It may not be stretching the facts too far to see here a precursor of the seat left empty at the Round Table, destined one day be filled by the most successful Grail knight. The revelation of sciences celestial and terrestrial, the knowledge of present and future, offer another analogy to the knowledge and wisdom of Merlin, derived from within his *esplumoir*, built outside the walls of a palace in the *Didot Perceval*, a detail which strikingly recalls the throne created for Enoch outside the gates of the seventh celestial palace.

Many ages after the withdrawal of Enoch another figure appears to represent the mysterious hierarchy of withdrawn kings. This is Elijah, who was carried up to heaven in a chariot of fire at the end of a greatly extended life, and who even in Biblical sources comes across as a cantankerous, argumentative character, not at all above telling God how things ought to be done. A traditional Jewish story relates that when the time came for him to ascend to heaven, the Angel of Death was reluctant to admit him. In fact, Elijah argued so vehemently before the gates of heaven that God himself was forced to intervene and gave permission for a wrestling match between Elijah and the Angel. Elijah was victorious and now sits with Enoch and Melchizedek, like them recording the deeds of mankind. He is also seen as a guide, who stands at the crossroads of Paradise to guide the righteous dead to their appointed place. He is thus, like both Enoch and Merlin, a way-shower and, like Enoch, he rules over a part of Paradise. He is still remembered in Judaic spirituality at the celebration of the Passover, when a place is set for him at every table in Orthodox Jewish homes.[13]

Many stories are told of Elijah's travels through the world, and of his many disguises, through which he becomes something of a trickster, though always remaining a stern judge of human frailty. He is often to be found traveling the roads with some unsuspecting companion, behaving in an extraordinary manner or laughing unaccountably as one who knows the inner truth of the situation from an unknown source. In this he closely resembles Merlin, especially when we recall the instances of Merlin's laughter, when he perceives things unseen by others and finds the foolishness of men too comical to restrain his mirth.

The Bird's Nest

But there is more yet to the mystery of the *esplumoir*, and it takes us into some very strange seas. Celtic literature has a whole genre of stories called *immrama,* meaning literally 'rowings about' but generally translated as 'voyages'. One of the most famous of these is *The Voyage of Maelduin*, dating from around the beginning of the eleventh century in its present form but believed to have originated in the eighth.[14] In this we find an episode where the voyagers arrive at an island where they see an ancient eagle fall and renew itself in the waters of a red lake. When one of the crew drinks some of this water he is said never again to be troubled with bad eyesight or toothache, so strong are its properties. We may remember that Merlin was already connected with healing waters. In the *Vita Merlini* he is healed by the waters of a fountain, newly sprung from the earth; in the *Historia* he is responsible for the erection of the great stones of the Giant's Dance, which bestowed healing properties to water poured over them. An obscure poem from a sixteenth-century manuscript which bears the title 'Arthur and the Eagle', contains a dialogue between the king and the eponymous bird, said to be a reincarnation of Eliwlod, Arthur's own nephew and grandson of Uther.

Arthur

A wonder I see

On the top of the oak

A vision of an eagle.

Eagle

Arthur, of great fame,

Joy to your host,

This eagle you have seen before [...]

Arthur

Eagle of blameless aspect

Whose discourse is true,

Are you Eliwlod my nephew?

Eagle

Arthur the audacious,

If I am Eliwlod

Am I worthy of your sight?[15]

The detail of the poem is more Christian than pagan, but there are shadows of an older tale lurking within, and it again recalls the imagery of Merlin and Elijah.

The *Voyage of Maelduin* adds its own Biblical reference to lend validity to the episode. The quotation is from *Isiah* 40:31 which says: 'You shall renew yourselves as eagles'. This suggests another possible source for the *esplumoir* in the traditions of the Bible and Judaism. If we turn to the *Zohar*, one of the most important mystical texts from the Judaic religion, we do indeed find a description of paradise which not only recalls the stories of Enoch and Elijah but takes us a step further towards an understanding of Merlin's *esplumoir*.

In the passage in question we learn of a part of heaven in which is 'a certain hidden place, which no eye has seen but those to whom God shows it,' and which is called the Bird's Nest. Within this the Messiah, who according to Jewish tradition could be one among many, lies sick, 'in the fifth hall of Paradise, in the Castle of Souls, the Bird's Nest, visited only by Elijah, who comforts him.'[16]

Interestingly, the texts comprising the *Zohar* were compiled at the same time that the medieval Grail romances were being written down, and the image of the ailing Messiah conjures up a scene familiar from this source. In the many different texts that describe the castle of the Grail, we find an old, sick king lying in a hall, who is also visited by Merlin. When we discover that, in one of these romances, this same wounded king is called 'Messias' – a name which could only have come from the Hebrew – the parallel becomes even more significant. What, then, is this 'Bird's Nest'? The *Zohar* describes it as a place of prophetic vision:

> The Messiah enters that abode, lifts up his eyes, and beholds the Fathers [or Patriarchs] visiting the ruins of God's sanctuary. He perceives mother Rachel with tears upon her face; the Holy One, blessed be He, tries to comfort her, but she refuses to be comforted.
>
> Then the Messiah lifts up his voice and weeps and the whole Garden of Eden quakes, and all the righteous saints who are there break out in crying and lamentation with him. When the crying and weeping resound for the second time, the whole firmament above the Garden begins to shake, and the cry echoes from five hundred myriads of supernal hosts, until it reaches the highest throne.[17]

Merlin also, when he enters his *esplumoir*, is able to see things that others cannot – glimpses of British history just as the Messiah sees glimpses of Jewish history. There is also a marked similarity between the apocalyptic descriptions in the *Zohar* and the extraordinary visions of Merlin in both the *Vita Merlini* and the earlier *Prophecies* set forth by Geoffrey of Monmouth in the middle of the twelfth century. Merlin too is said to cry out from his withdrawn place.

Nor should we be surprised by these points of similarity between Christian and Judaic authorities; the barriers between the two cultures in the Middle Ages were far less severe than is often supposed. It is more than likely that any one of the widely read, much-travelled mediaeval romance writers, responsible for the Arthurian legends, could have encountered the tradition of the Bird's Nest within the *Zohar* or elsewhere, and that this became a seed planted in the soil of their own vision.

In Celtic literature also, long recognised as a primary source for the Arthurian myths, are descriptions of the Otherworld in which both Enoch and Elijah are described as living on a mysterious island until the Day of Judgment; and in an early poem attributed to the bard Taliesin, who as we have seen is closely identified with Merlin, we find the line: 'I was an instructor to Elijah and Enoch.'[18]

The Thirteen Treasures

Just as Enoch became a guardian of the treasures of life, so Merlin is likewise said to retire to a glass house in which are the Thirteen Treasures of Britain. Part of Merlin's withdrawal into a place between the worlds is intimately connected with his role as the guardian of these mysterious treasures. A fifteenth-century manuscript describes him retiring to a place called Enlli, identified by some authorities as Bardsey Island, off the coast of Wales.[19] The same source lists the Thirteen Treasures – though like the *Triads,* it refers to them in connection with stories we know little or nothing about.

1. Dyrnwyn (White Hilt), the Sword of Rhydderch the Generous: If a nobleman drew it, the blade burst into flames. It would come into the hand of anyone who asked for it, but everyone rejected it because of this ability.

2. The Hamper of Gwyddno Garanhir: if food for one was put into it, food for a hundred would be taken from it.

3. The Horn of Bran the Niggard, from the North: it contained whatever drink one desired.

4. The Chariot of Morgan the Wealthy: it took a man quickly to the place of his desire.

5. The Halter of Clydno Eiddyn, which was fastened by a staple to his bed-foot; the horse of one's desire could be found in the halter.

6. The Knife of Llawfodedd the Horseman: it would serve twenty-four men.

7. The Cauldron of Dyrnwch the Giant: it would not boil the meat of a coward, only that of a hero.

8. The Whetstone of Tudwal Tydglyd: if a hero sharpened his sword on it his opponents would bleed to death; if a coward did so, his opponent was no worse.

9. The Coat of Padarn Red-Coat: it was the right size for any nobleman but would fit a peasant.

10. and 11. The Crock and Dish of Rhygenydd the Cleric: which provided the food of one's desire.

12. The Chessboard of Gwenddolau ap Ceidio: the men were of silver, the board of gold; the pieces would play by themselves.

13. The Mantle of Arthur in Cornwall: it made the wearer invisible though he could see everyone.

This is not the place to explore these treasures in detail, however, we can see that items 2, 3, 10 and 11 serve much the same purpose, offering the food most desired by those who own them – a feature shared by the Grail in later romances. The Sword of Rhydderch is also a Sword of Light, a weapon wielded with great effect in the quest for the Cauldron of the Otherworld and referred to in the Myrddyn poems. The Horn of Bran the Niggard, the importance of which is discussed below, is probably a corrupted reference to the cauldron of the Celtic hero-god Bran the Blessed. The Chessboard of Gwenddolau is mentioned in several places, including stories from the *Mabinogion* and in the Myrddyn poems. The magical chessboard is a paradigm of the land of Britain itself, over which contending sides battle. The Mantle of Arthur is worn long after Arthur's passing by the hero Caswallawn when he kills seven guardians of Britain.

These items are interesting enough in themselves, and though ultimately mysterious, they reflect the status of the person chosen to guard them. A note scribbled in a sixteenth-century manuscript develops the idea further:

> Myrddyn came there to ask for those treasures of everyone who had them; and everyone agreed that if he should obtain the Horn of Bran the Niggard he should obtain theirs from them, supposing that he should ever get the Horn. And nevertheless, Myrddyn obtained the Horn, and after that he obtained them all, and went with them to the Glass House, and they (the Thirteen Treasures) remain there forever.[20]

Here Merlin, in a story no longer extant, is seen to actively seek out the Treasures and then when he has collected them all, he takes them to a place of safety – a Glass House, which almost certainly derives from the observatory built for him by Ganeida. The early nineteenth-century scholar, Lewis Morris, interpreting this in his own particular way, suggested that there must have been

> ... a museum of rarities in King Arthur's time ... which Myrddin ... carried with him to the house of glass in the isle of Enlli

or Bardsey ... This house of glass, it seems, was the museum where they kept their curiosities to be seen by everybody, but not handled; and it is probable that Myrddin ... was the keeper of their museum in that time ...[21]

The choice of the word 'museum' may read strangely to our ears, but it makes the point that Merlin's *esplumoir* was both a treasure house and a place of prophecy, as is the Bird's Nest to which both Enoch and Elijah withdrew. Within it, Merlin guards the sacred treasures of Britain, and notes down the history of mankind. In the *Didot Perceval*, where this is reported, the name of the clerk who copies out his words is given as Helyas, a corruption of the name Elijah!

The Faery Paradise

In the Jewish texts quoted above, we have seen that the Bird's Nest, with all its analogies to Merlin's *esplumoir*, is a meeting place between the worlds, or within the higher levels of Paradise, where the Messiah sits viewing the ongoing history of Creation and where both Enoch and Elijah also dwell. Among the scattered references to Merlin's Enclosure, Britain itself is described as either a magical realm or at very least a kind of antechamber to the faery realm. For example, in a text relating to the adventures of Ogier the Dane, a hero once as famous as Arthur, we find him carried off to Avalon by Morgan le Fay. The description is interesting:

> The barge on which Ogier was, floated across the sea until it came near the Castle of Loadstone, which is called the Castle of Avalon, which is not far this side of the Terrestrial Paradise, whither were wrapt in a flame of fire Enoch and Elijah, and where was also Morgan le Fay...
>
> *Le Roman D'Ogier le Danois*[22]

Here we have an amalgam of the otherworldly island of Avalon and the terrestrial Paradise, and among its inhabitants are the two Biblical prophets and the greatest enchantress of the Arthurian myths. It also combines a number of themes and ideas which reoccur throughout the Arthurian corpus, especially the Grail myth, which speaks of a sacred island (sometimes known by the Hebrew sounding name of Sarras) as the final resting place of the sacred vessel. Another text, the thirteenth-century poem called 'Sone de Nansay', includes a detailed account of this which could easily be a description of Merlin's isle and the treasure house of ancient sacred objects.

It stood in the open sea at a distance where no machine could hurl anything to harm its crenelated walls that rose up out of the living rock. On its outer wall were four towers that looked the finest in the world, and in the centre, midway between them, a greater one surpassing the others. This contained the palace; and surely nothing more sumptuous had ever been built.

In every direction it was a hundred feet wide because it was perfectly circular. At the centre of the central tower was a fireplace that rested on four gilded pillars that supported a pure copper pipe, four feet high, decorated with gold coloured mosaics that crossed the reception hall. I am sure no more wondrous place had ever been built.[23]

This in turn leads us very swiftly to the *Vita Merlini*, where we find a description of Britain which leaves us in no doubt that this island was long held to be an earthly paradise.

... foremost and best, producing in its fruitfulness every single thing. For it bears crops which throughout the year give the noble gifts of fragrance to man, and it has woods and glades with honey dripping in them, and lofty mountains and broad green fields, fountains and rivers, fishes and cattle and wild beasts, fruit trees, gems, precious metals, and whatever creative nature is in the habit of furnishing.[24]

This is Avalon as much as it is Britain, and it is also Merlin's Isle, where adventures begin at the stone that bears his name, and where his voice may be heard upraised in prophetic utterance. Together with Enoch, Elijah, Melchizedek and many more, Merlin has become a withdrawn or inner king, one who has chosen to enter a place from where he will continue to mediate events in the world – but at a deeper level.

The Real Esplumoir

This is the true nature of the *esplumoir*, the moulting cage where ties with the world are unmade and those who enter it journey towards another state of being. There are parallels for this in other traditions, including Sufism and the Jewish Kabbalah. The shifting jigsaw of people and places takes place outside time, where different names are given to the same people, manifesting throughout time and at each junction taking on a new aspect with an ongoing purpose. Thus, a late medieval manuscript source, pondering how so wise a man as Merlin could have allowed himself to be entrapped by a girl, tells us that

... there are a variety of opinions and talk among the people, [who] hold that ... Merlin was a spirit in human form, who was in that shape from the time of Vortigern until the beginning of King Arthur, when he disappeared. After that, his spirit appeared again in the time of Maelgwn Gwynedd, at which time he was called Taliesin, who is said to be alive yet in a place called Caer Sidia. Then, he appeared a third time in the days of Morfran Frych son of Esyllt ... and in this period, he was called Merlin the Mad. From that day to this, he is said to be resting in Caer Sidia, whence certain people believe firmly that he will rise up once again before Doomsday.[25]

Here Merlin is seen as still active from within the sphere of Caer Sidia, which is yet another name for the Celtic Otherworld. In the other, Biblical, version we have discussed, Enoch/Metatron begins as a replacement for Lucifer, righting the balance of power in Heaven; he reappears as Melchizedek, initiating a line of priestly kings who lead to Christ. He reappears next as Enoch, who becomes Sandalphon, the way-shower. Perhaps we are not stretching this idea too far if we suggest that the next reappearance of this mighty being is as Merlin himself, who takes the sacred treasures of Britain into his own Bird's Nest, the *esplumoir*.

This is all a far cry from the view of a lovesick old fool who allows himself to be tricked into an imprisonment from which he cannot escape. We have seen instead that Merlin's withdrawal is a willing one, made from choice, to allow him the freedom to grow and change and to protect the treasures of life. It is also where he can relate to the feminine wisdom offered by Nimue or her kin. This can best be brought about within the place of the withdrawn kings, which lies somewhere between Earth and heaven. In the light of these materials Merlin appears as one who travels through the world for a while, only to withdraw again into an inner place from which he may one day come again.

The Alchemical Tradition

The next development in the story was not so much a transformation of Merlin himself, but of what he represented. The transformation was in the way that magic, and those who practised it, were perceived. As the Middle Ages drew to a close and the

Renaissance began, a wind of change blew throughout Europe, and in its wake came shifts in perception that would affect the way Merlin was understood forever.

After the fall of Constantinople in 1453, the Classical remnants of the great libraries found their way west to the ready soil of medieval Europe. Thus began a rekindling of arts, philosophy and hermeneutics, where the narrow scope of medieval Christianity was expanded by contact with neo-Platonic and Classical world views. During this time, several physical embodiments of Merlin's wisdom appeared throughout Europe. Figures such as Marcilio Ficino (1453–99), Athanasius Kircher (1602–80) and Dr John Dee (1527–1608) revealed themselves as polymaths of comprehensive Druidic stature, prime movers in political strategy and in esoteric philosophy alike.

Dee made much of his Welsh descent and possible kinship with King Arthur. As Merlin to Queen Elizabeth's Arthur, Dee served as her esoteric adviser, masterminding the discovery and colonisation of the New World, as well as maintaining a closet coterie of esoteric practice. The account of his discourse with spirits is well documented, revealing that his concern with mapping inner worlds matched his desire to chart the unexplored regions of the New World.

For Merlin these historical changes brought about a different kind of metamorphosis. We have seen him as a seer, as a manipulator of the elements, as a creator of wonders, and as a sage possessed of almost limitless wisdom. In the next strand in his development many of these aspects were combined – he became an alchemist.

Alchemy has a long and complex history of its own. Its origins were seen as dating back to Ancient Egypt or even Atlantis, but its real flowering was not until the sixteenth century. After this it was the primary expression of magic until the dawn of the so-called Age of Enlightenment in the eighteenth century, when it gradually transformed into the new discipline of science. But alchemy was always more concerned with what might be called the science of magic, and it promoted an investigation into the very structure of the cosmos which was both mystical and pragmatic.[26]

One of the strangest texts relating to Merlin shows him in this light and demonstrates that when it came to discussions of alchemical mysteries, his name and presence was as potent as ever. The text was edited by the great seventeenth-century antiquary Elias Ashmole, who published it in his *Theatrum Chemicum Britannicum*[27] in 1652. The work's only modern editor suggests that the original was written towards the end of the fifteenth century. The text takes the form of an 'Argument Between Morien and Merlin', here described as father and son. Most of it is taken up with a discussion of the alchemical process involved in the production of the Philosopher's Stone, a magical object that could prolong the life of the one able to create it.

> The Father of that City shall die
> But the Mother shall live always.
> And when the Child is borne of the Mother free,
> He shall be washed with water warm.
> So that the Child shall take no harm,
> Look that thou wash him in waters twelve,
> And keep each water by itself.
> And the last water will be then clear
> Without any foul matter.
> And then hast thou a Child fair and bright,
> But then it is young and hath no might.
> And then to make the Child hardy and strong.
> I shall thee teach 'ere it be long.
> First thou must put him to nourishing:
> Yet know her well that shall have him in keeping,
> That she be of meane [medium] stature,

And also bright of colour.
And look that she be of body clean and pure,
And also perfect, good and sure [...]
And then take unto her Mercury the Child,
And she shall him tame if he be wild.
And with her milk shall make him white
And then is the Child of great might.

The choice of imagery is interesting. Here the Child Mercury is the product of chemical compounds brewed in the alchemists vat; but the metaphors are all ones that could just as easily apply to the mysterious Child of Wonder – to Merlin himself.

But there is more than one kind of alchemy. We most often hear about the kind that concentrated on turning lead into gold or discovering the Elixir of Life, but there is another kind – spiritual alchemy, which is in many ways closer to Merlin's magic. This alchemy is more interested in refining the baser qualities of the human soul, and in turning it to the gold of spiritual enlightenment. As one great alchemist, Nicholas Flamel, wrote around the middle of the fifteenth century:

> Our work is the conversion and change of one being into another being, as from one thing into another thing, from debility to strength ... from corporeality to spirituality.[28]

This, surely, is exactly what Merlin does for Arthur, and for the fellowship of the Round Table, each of whom he helps to grow and develop.

Magic itself was being constantly redefined through the ages, either in religious terms, or as philosophy. Each age took up the fragments of a magical past and impressed their own synthesis upon it, so that magic went from a religious discipline to a philosophy and back again. In late-medieval Europe a mixture of shamanic spirituality and neo-classical magic brought about the reformation of the wizard's character and role, and transformed him into a keeper of wisdom and knowledge.

Finally, the magical tradition became secularised and at the same time the image of the magician changed from that of a wise and powerful wonderworker into that of a proto scientist. The great thinkers and natural magicians of the Renaissance were first and foremost Christian; other options were scarcely open to them. Yet there also were older traditions: those of Greece, Egypt, Persia. And so there began slowly to emerge a new system based on the ancient mysteries but seen as taking place within the framework of the Christian world.

Many of these ideas were still perceived as heretical, but the magicians who practised them saw things differently. For them the ancient deities of the pagan world became transformed into spirits of the air, angelic beings created, like humanity, to serve God and creation. A new breed of magician emerged from this – one who was recognised as a keeper of divine knowledge and wisdom, whose worldview included the mysteries of the stars and the very nature of creation itself. Not, of course, that this was in any sense new – magicians and wizards had been working with such matters since the beginning of history. What was different was that they now approached their work with the precision and exactitude of scientists.

The Wisdom of Merlin

Merlin fitted this role perfectly. He was so widely known as an archetypal magician – ironically since, as we saw earlier he was never actually given this title until the sixteenth century – that his name was constantly on the lips of the new magicians, who used examples of his works as a springboard for their own experiments. But the nature of the wisdom which Merlin came to represent was, as one might expect, as chameleon-like as his character. In the Myrddin Poems it is seen as a deep relationship with the natural world. In the *Vita Merlini* it is concerned with the heavens and the divine mysteries of creation. In the later medieval texts, his knowledge is already looking forward to the Renaissance and the mysteries of alchemy.

From the moment he stepped upon the stage of the Arthurian sagas he was destined to recognised as a sage, as the living embodiment of wisdom which derived from both human and non-human knowledge. Whether, like Elijah and Enoch, he received this wisdom from God or, as in the medieval variations of his story, from demonic sources, he chose to use this knowledge for the good of humanity. With it he shaped the dream that was the Arthurian kingdom – an Earthly Paradise full of magic and love and the ideals of chivalry.

In each case the moulting cage of the *esplumoir* is seen as a place of study and learning, a place where the prophet and wise man could retire to synthesise his knowledge into a whole. In this way, instead of a half-mortal living in our world, he becomes a deeper inhabitant of the otherworld itself – but one who yet remains interested in worldly affairs. The *esplumoir* is a necessary place of transmutation, a place between the worlds where Merlin can fully enter into his role as a guardian of the treasure house of life itself.

The Cry of Merlin

Merlin's end is as mysterious as his life. As we have seen, the story goes that he was ensnared by an otherworldly woman who imprisoned him, according to which version one follows, in a cave, beneath a stone, in a castle of glass, or in a forest. But the motivations vary according to the writer. In Malory, Merlin is an old fool who in his dotage falls for a beautiful maiden (one of the Ladies of the Lake); in the 'Lancelot-Grail' there is a greater tenderness between the enchanter and his love. The Welsh writer Elis Gruffydd – who, we may remember, wrote of Merlin's reincarnation – writing in the fifteenth century, expressed his astonishment that someone as wise as Merlin 'would allow a maiden to deceive him in his own art'.

Another Welsh text, *Y Seint Greal*, a fifteenth-century version of the *Quest del San Grail* containing many variants from the original, describes how, when Lancelot, Gwalchmai (Gawain) and Arthur are on their way to visit King Peleur (Pelles) they stop at a chapel next to an ancient hall– later identified as Tintagel. There they encounter an old priest, who shows them a sepulchre said to belong to Merlin. But the priest comments:

'Lords', he said, 'The body of Merlin was put into this sepulchre. And know truly that his body is not there at the present time, for the moment his body was placed inside, it was spirited away. I know not whether it was God's work or the Devil's.'[29]

Aside from the striking parallel between this description and accounts of the resurrection of Jesus, it was clearly felt that Merlin was too important, too powerful figure to simply vanish with no chance of returning.

But as we have already seen Merlin's imprisonment is not what it seems to be. In the *English Merlin*, also known as *The Prose Merlin*, composed in the fifteenth century, there is a coda to this, in which Sir Gawain, having suffered an unfortunate encounter with a magician and been turned into a dwarf, seeks the aid of Merlin, only to discover that the enchanter has been himself enchanted. The last words of Arthur's great councillor, issuing from within the rock beneath which he has been imprisoned, are moving and powerful:

'Me shall you never see again … for from hence may I not come out, nor shall I ever come out, for in all the world is not so strong a place as this where I am, and it is not of iron, nor steel, nor timber, nor stone, but it is of the air without any other thing, [made] by enchantments so strong that it may never be undone while the world endures, nor may I come out nor no one enter, save she that me here hath enclosed, that keeps me company when she likes, and goes hence when she likes... Nor never shall no man speak with me after you, [Sir Gawain], therefore for nothing might any man seek for me; and for yourself, as soon as you have turned from hence, you shall never hear me speak; and therefore now return and greet well king Arthur, and my lady the queen, and all the barons, and tell them how it is with me...' 'Now,' said Merlin, 'I beseech you to God that [He] keep the king Arthur and the realm of Logres [Britain], as for the best people of the world.'[30]

Gawain is astonished to hear that Merlin is a prisoner and asks him how this may be since he is 'the wisest man of the world'. Merlin's response follows the story of Nimue's trickery and his enslavement to her, but despite the seeming finality of this, it was certainly not the last of Merlin. People still heard the voice of the prophet issuing from his prison of air, and many spoke of the 'Cry of Merlin' which was capable of invoking wondrous occurrences.

If anything, Merlin's withdrawal made him more accessible than ever. From the depths of the *esplumoir* he was to emerge in countless new forms, re-imagined and restored in the hands of new generations of writers, thinkers and believers. His last metamorphosis turned out to be only the first of many, and today he is as alive as ever in the many contemporary versions of his story. It is to these we turn now for the latest chapter in the history of the wisest man in the world.

6

THE RETURN OF MERLIN

He was my genius, this juggler, always the more impressive part
of me. Or was I merely a facet of him, designed to lead and care
for men?

Parke Godwin:
Firelord

In no two contemporary accounts is Merlin ever the same; even
allowing for the idiosyncrasies of the various authors who have
written about him, the divergence is so great that it would be
difficult to imagine that it was the same figure were it not for the
common factors which reveal the character hidden at the heart
of this constellation of disguises. Merlin has remained 'dark and
mysterious' as he said he would in the *Didot Perceval*. Yet
somehow, none of those who have chosen to write about him have
been able to resist asking the question: who – or what – is he? Their
answers have been as diverse as they possibly could be, picturing
Merlin as god or jester; as prophet, wise man or warrior; as an
old lover caught in the silken wiles of his young pupil; as an alien
being brought to earth on cosmic business; as a Wondrous Child or

an Atlantean priest; as a servant of many gods or of one goddess; as a charlatan or a liar and a madman. But always, between the disguises, we glimpse a pilgrim and wanderer, sent here long ago to guide and guard the destiny of kings and of men – a majestic mage steering the barque of the island that was once named after him: Clas Merlin – Merlin's Enclosure.

In this book we have seen Merlin in his most familiar guises – as a shaman, flying amid the treetops or living wild in the forests of Celtic Britain; as the wise and foresighted prophet who stands behind Arthur in the early days of his reign; as a lover of Otherworld women; or latterly as a repository of wisdom, and a keeper of ancient treasures. But how has Merlin fared in our own age – how has the mirror of contemporary media perceived him and how, if at all, has this changed our perception of the most famous visionary of all time? Modern fictional versions of the older story of Merlin do exist, but it is at the works which have sought to recreate and redefine his character that we need to turn if we are to answer these questions.

Atlantean Origins

The span of Merlin's years seems to be immense; possibly, like the angel Melchizedek, he is 'without beginning or end'. But surprisingly few writers of this or any age have looked for his beginnings or have added to the medieval tale of his conception by a demon and birth to an innocent maiden. It was not in the realm of fiction or poetry that writings that a history which accounted for his extended life and mysterious powers first emerged, but in the writings of an early-twentieth-century mystic named Dion Fortune (1890–1946). Inner spiritual forces shaped her vision of Merlin as a priest of Atlantis, who fled the destruction of the lost continent, bearing with him the princess Igraine, destined to become the mother of Arthur.[1]

Though Dion Fortune wrote no novel of Merlin, her ideas resurfaced in two very different works of fiction: *The Mists of Avalon* (1982) by Marion Zimmer Bradley, and *Merlin and the Dragons of Atlantis* (1983) by Rita and Tim Hildebrand. In the latter, Merlin is a scientist from Lemuria, a land adjacent to Atlantis but far older, which has adopted more peaceful and mystical ways than those of its powerful neighbour. The Lemurians now seek to perfect a race of genetically engineered dragons to protect their vast cities and great domains. Merlin's thirst for scientific knowledge brings him into alliance with those working on the project, but when it is successful and the dragons are set free, they are taken over by evil forces, and Merlin subsequently helps to destroy them – thus also initiating the premature fall of Atlantis and the destruction of all that he loves. But Merlin himself does not die; he places himself in an induced state of hibernation from which he will one day awake to bring about the realisation of a new dream, the creation of a new Atlantean state in the world of Arthurian heroes.

Dragons of Atlantis represents an attempt to see Merlin as a transcendent figure who operates over vast distances of time and space, through the use of knowledge no longer current in our world. Atlantis becomes the latest image of the otherworldly realm from which Merlin has long been recognised as coming, while the image of the sage himself is much as we would expect him to be in our time: as a scientist rather than a wizard; as someone imbued with endless curiosity about the nature of Creation and its foremost offspring: mankind.

In Marion Bradley's book 'The Merlin' is a title borne by many successive men, an idea which has gained favour in recent years, though there is no actual evidence for it. Here, as in numerous recent versions of the story, the setting is post-Roman Britain, in which Merlin aids those seeking to unite the shattered country into an unshakeable power under the banner of Arthur. But already, even before this dream is begun, a division exists between followers on the newly arrived Christians and those who honour the goddess of the Earth. Bradley's interpretation actually says more about the current spiritual divide between orthodox religion and eco-paganism than about anything existing in post-Roman culture. Nevertheless, her personal colouring of events gives the book its vigour and also allows her Merlin to voice a genuine observation:

> There are now two Britains ... their world under their One God and the Christ; and beside it and behind it, the world where the Great Mother still rules, the world in which the Old People have chosen to live and worship.[2]

Ygrane, soon to be the mother of the young king, remembers an older time, an earlier incarnation. In a waking vision, she stands on Salisbury Plain and watches the fiery sun rise over the great stone circle – and beyond:

> To the West, where stood the lost lands of Lyonesse and Ys and the great isle Alamesios, or Atlantis, the forgotten kingdom of the sea. There, indeed, had been the great fire, there the mountain had blown apart, and in a single night, a hundred thousand men and women and little children had perished. 'But the Priests knew' said a voice at her side. 'For the past hundred years, they have been building their star temple here on the plains, so that they might not lose count of the tracking of the seasons... These people here, they know nothing of such things, but they know we are wise, priests and priestesses from over the sea, and they will build for us, as they did before.[3]

The speaker is Uther, who shares Ygrane's reincarnational memories. From their love will issue Arthur who, with Merlin's aid, will attempt to build a new and perfect expression of human endeavour – a new Atlantis. Here, Merlin represents the latest of a line of priests descended from the people of the drowned land, who have carried the memories of the past within them until it can be brought into manifestation again. Bradley's familiarity with Dion Fortune's writings can clearly be seen in this strand of her book, and it adds a significant aspect to the modern understanding of Merlin's role. *Mists of Avalon* was and remains a hugely influential piece of writing, which became the one true account of the Arthurian world for an entire generation. Several sequels, some by Bradley and others by Diana Paxson, along with a TV film of the book have kept it in the forefront of contemporary awareness.

Against the Dark

The theme of Merlin's role as the protector and guide of humanity's evolution is expressed again, though in a somewhat different way, in Andre Norton's *Merlin's Mirror* (1975), where the central premise concerns a race of alien beings known as the Sky Lords who, in the infancy of the human world, leave behind them a hidden computer installation programmed to begin its work many thousands of years later, creating heroes and leaders who will raise the race of men to the level of the Sky Lords themselves. There is an implication that these beings will themselves have perished by the time the computer begins its work, perhaps as a result of a long struggle with an opposing force called simply 'the Dark Ones'. These beings are not described as intrinsically evil, but they are directly opposed to the Sky Lords' declared aim to hasten the development of humanity.

This is very much a science fiction version of the story, and in it we have Merlin created by artificial insemination, his mother seeing only a computer-generated image of a beautiful golden man – an ingenious twist to the story of Merlin's birth in the medieval accounts. Even more ingeniously, just as Merlin represents the Sky Lords, so the Dark Ones are represented by Nimue, and the ancient destiny of the king, his wizard, and the priestess who brings about their downfall, is played out in images drawn from the world of science fiction. In the end, Merlin, who has read the future in his computer-operated 'mirror', sees that his dream of a united land under the figure of Arthur is doomed to fail, and retires, like the Merlin of the Hildebrand novel, into a self-induced sleep to await a more auspicious time when he may try again to create the dream of man.

Merlin's Task

Again and again Merlin is shown as a councillor of kings, sent from a far-off land or planet where civilisation is more advanced than in the world of everyday humans. He is also shown to possess occult knowledge or prophetic gifts – to represent in fact the archetypal figure of the wizard. This aspect of his function has been perfectly described by one of the greatest writers of the twentieth century, who created a Merlin-like figure, who does not bear his name but occupies a position in almost every way the same as that of Merlin.

> Warm and eager was his spirit … opposing the fire that devours and wastes with the fire that kindles and succours in wan hope and distress; but his joy, and his swift wrath, were veiled in garments grey as ash, so that only those who knew him well glimpsed the flame that was within. Merry he could be and kindly to the young and simple, and yet quick at times to sharp speech and the rebuking of folly; but he was not proud, and sought neither power nor praise, and thus far and wide he was beloved among all those that were not themselves proud. Mostly he journeyed unwearyingly on foot, leaning on a staff; and so he was called among men of the North, Gandalf, the 'Elf of the Wand'.[4]

In Tolkien's mythology, Gandalf is one of the Istari, emissaries of the Valar, great angelic forces who watch over the world and mediate between God and creation. In Tolkien's greatest work, *The Lord of the Rings*, he is the guiding force behind the attempts to destroy a ring of power created by the evil lord Sauron. Many have seen this as an allegory for the creation of the nuclear bomb, and though Tolkien denied this in his lifetime, the ring may well be seen as a manifestation of the darker side of human nature. Gandalf's role in all of this is to help a fellowship drawn from the various races of Middle Earth – men, elves, dwarfs and hobbits – to bring about the destruction of the ring and the establishment of the first solely human kingdom on earth. Everything about this is in line with the task allotted to Merlin in many of the original stories written about him – where he is set to guide and shepherd the destinies of men. It is this theme that has attracted the majority of modern authors, who have chosen to represent Merlin in this light in books as varied and far apart in scope as John Cowper Powys's *Porius* (1951), Mary Stewart's *Merlin Trilogy* (1970–79), Peter Vansittart's *Lancelot* (1978) and Linda Haldeman's fantasy *The Lastborn of Elvinwood* (1980).[5]

The Oldest of the Old

The Merlin of *Porius* is half-man and half-god, a huge, slow earthman, smelling of mould and green things and clearly deriving from the oldest version of the character. Like many of the characterisations of Merlin in more recent times, his work is devoted to the return upon Earth of a new Golden Age, the age of Saturn/Cronos, of which god he sees himself as a true avatar. Descriptions of him abound in Powys's extraordinary book.

> Myrddin Wyllt was dressed in his long black mantle; and at the place where his great beard reached the level of his navel, it was

tied with ... gold thread whose tassels hung down to his knees. His head was bare, and his long fingers at the end of his long arms were making slow majestic movements as if writing upon the interior darkness of the tent... But it soon occurred to Porius that what the man was doing lent itself to another and quite different interpretation; namely, that instead of inscribing things on the air he was tracing out things that had already been written upon it![6]

Powys's Myrddin is linked with an ancient race of aboriginal giants, the children of the god Cronos, whose last remnant live out their days in the fastness of the Welsh mountains. Linda Haldeman returns to this idea in *The Lastborn of Elvinwood,* where Merlin is again associated with the destiny of a race of gigantic people, though in this instance they have remained hidden through the ages, but have dwindled in size, becoming known as the denizens of Faery. They have no love for Merlin, whom they call 'the Old One', blaming his actions in a dim and distant time for their own present state. Their traditions tell how once, their giant ancestors

... dwelt in the mountains to the north ... herding and farming and minding their own business. He, the Old One, lived alone in the south. What he is and where he came from, I cannot say. Perhaps your legend of him being the offspring of a demon has some truth in it. I don't pretend to know. We call ourselves the First Folk, because it is our belief that our gigantic ancestors were the first people to live on this island. Yet they called him the Old One [even then].[7]

This looks back very clearly to older tales regarding the first comers to Britain as giants, or as defenders of the land against incomers like Albina and Brutus of Troy. The present-day protagonists of the book, seeking to enlist Merlin's aid, find the

Old One living in semi-retirement in a cottage in the depths of the English countryside. On their way to visit him they discuss his history – the story of him being the son of the devil, and of his entrapment by Nimue:

> Ah yes, Nimue ... A naive ruse, but one that worked. It was the end of what he calls his political phase ... Arthur turned out to be a bitter disappointment, more interested in holding bloody tournaments than in planting gardens ... and unnaturally preoccupied with his wife's activities ... Arthur is one of the main reasons he's down on the Celts ... he decided to retire. Arthur refused to let him go, so he paid Nimue to invent the cave story and slipped off to live in blissful solitude.[8]

Here the vision of Merlin is tinged with irony, yet he can be a difficult and even dangerous character, both chancy and unreliable in his dealings with humanity.

Peter Vansittart, in his novel *Lancelot*, paints a thoroughly ironic portrait. Merlin is generally referred to simply as 'He' – a mark of respect and caution towards one whom one should never address by name unless invited to do so. 'He' seems, at first glance, an unprepossessing character:

> Despite the familiar dirt caking his ears, beard, bare feet, the sack like gown under gaudy robes, he repelled me less, his hierophantic mendacities more lively than the dismal hush that passed for entertainment with Artorius. Last year his hand motions had induced a snowfall when least required, his explanations being acceptable as minor poetry by anyone without scholarship or sensitivity. He had also acquired an adroit method of inclining his head so that a shadow of a bird or animal was reflected on the wall behind him.[9]

This Merlin seems more of a charlatan than a true worker of magic, but behind the irony of Vansittart's unique vision of the Arthurian world lies a very real respect for the power and authority of the sage.

Merlin is brought back to life – literally since he is summoned from his grave – by the current king of the Britons, to assist in a last desperate attempt to stem the tide of the invading Saxons in Nikolai Tolstoy's *The Coming of the King: The First Book of Merlin* (1988). This is the first in a projected trilogy, still incomplete at the time of writing, and follows on from Tolstoy's excellent historical study *The Quest for Merlin*, which appeared in 1985.

The Coming of the King is an immensely long and discursive book, frequently interrupting the flow of the narrative for long digressions on matters of siege warfare or for huge set pieces such as the feast of Maelgwn Gwynedd, in which devils and demons are conjured up to join in the baroque festivities. The setting of the book is northern Britain, two generations after the departure of Arthur, and consists in part of Myrddin's (Tolstoy opts for the more traditional spelling) rambling memoirs, in which he recalls not only the time of Arthur but mythological time as well. He is conflated somewhat with the figure of Taliesin, which gives Tolstoy an excuse to retell the powerful myth of the shapeshifting bard, and to lead the way into the depths of Annwn itself. For this is not just a tale of historical characters and events – it is a vast spiritual tract, an allegory as densely allusive as Spenser or Bunyon.

> It seemed to King Ceneu and his companions that there arose from the centre of the gorsedd a man greater far in stature then the men of their own time. His clothes were but the undressed skins of beasts, his hair thin and grey and flowing, and his aspect paler, emaciated, wild. He lacked his left eye, which was but a puckered, sightless socket. His gaze seemed to portend both pain and anger.[10]

This is a bardic retelling, which draws on both the Mabinogion and the Myrddin poems to fuel a powerful and extraordinary imagination.

Tolstoy is primarily a historian and Celticist, and the immense structure of his learning, which is intended to support the book, at times hampers the story. Yet the figure of Myrddin that emerges is probably the closest anyone has got since Geoffrey of Monmouth to the real figure: immemorially ancient, powerful and almost merging with the land itself. In this Tolstoy is closest to J.C. Powys in his delineation of the character of the old mage.

Atlantis Again

Stephen Lawhead's *Pendragon Cycle* (1987–2001) again harks back to Atlantis but develops the theme further than ever before, describing an Atlantean community ruled over by King Avallach and his son Prince Taliesin within the land of Celtic Britain. The second volume in the series *Merlin* (1988), concentrates on the figure of Avallach's grandson, who is not only named Merlin but is the inheritor of the Atlantean bloodline. The book follows the outlines of the *Vita Merlini* in its general shape and structure, though developing the character and story of Merlin far beyond the scope of the medieval tale. Here Merlin is both King of Dyfed and a reluctant seer, whose pain and passion in the wilderness is starkly set forth. The story is told in the first person, and at the very opening of the book Merlin recalls the various ways in which he has been recognised:

> Emrys is the name I have won among men and it is my own. Emrys, Immortal... Emrys, Divine... Emrys Wledig, king and prophet to his people. Ambrosius it is to the Latin speakers, and Embries to the people of Southern Britain and Lloegres.... But Myrddin Emrys am I to the Cymry of the hill-bound fastness of the west.[11]

His long life, including years of wandering in the wilds of the hills, is chronicled, as is his love for Ganeida, his association with Ambrosius, Uther and finally Arthur himself. Lawhead's long and intricately woven chronicle places Merlin squarely centre stage, and links him both to the dim and distant realm of Atlantis and to the founding of the great Arthurian kingdom which is so much his own work. Of all the recent portrayals of Merlin it is one of the best and certainly the most moving.

The Wider Arc

Most contemporary writers to deal with the character of Merlin have tended to be from within the old Celtic lands of Britain and Ireland or in North America, but the European continent has not wholly neglected him. France especially has produced a number of novels featuring Merlin, including René Berjavel's *The Enchanter* and Jacques Roubaud's *Grail Fiction*. The Spanish writer Álvaro Cunqueiro Mora (1911–1981), in his *Merlin & Company* paints a wittier and more universal portrait. In his book Merlin and Guinevere, following the departure of Arthur, have retied to a house in the province of Galicia. There, in a series of almost picaresque episodes, they are visited by the representatives of the crowned heads of Europe, each of whom has a problem that needs Merlin's particular talents to solve. Thus, the Emperor of Byzantium has been seduced by a faery woman, the Lady of Aquitaine has been turned into a fawn and a French bishop's magical umbrella no longer turns night into day. In each instance Merlin uses cunning, age-old wisdom and native skill to turn these problems around. The book is narrated by Filipe, his aged page, and through his eyes we see a landscape of wit and magic that draws equally on the Celtic tales of Merlin and Don Quixote, whose own chronicle features Merlin as a cave-dwelling mage. Mora's gentle humour presents us a far more urbane Merlin than most we have seen, but one every bit as entertaining and magical as any of those discussed here.

Another visionary and esoteric novel, *The Testament of Merlin* by Théophile Briant (1891–1956), remained unpublished during the author's life and was only translated in 2016, nineteen years after its author's death. Briant shared many of the esoteric ideas set forth in Dion Fortune's books, and he drew heavily on the Breton poet Hersart de le Villemarqué, whose own work on Merlin makes for interesting reading. *The Testament of Merlin* is referred to as a 'pseudo-historical' novel,[12] and on the surface deals with Arthur's battles against the Saxons. He also manages to cover the founding of the Round Table by Merlin, the death of Arthur, the return of Excalibur to the Lake and the conducting of Arthur to Avalon, as well as Merlin's love for Vivienne (here a faery) and his own death at the hands of shepherds near Drumelzier in Scotland. The story is told through the eyes of Merlin's 'apprentice', the knight Adragante – a character invented by Briant based on characters from Malory and Spencer – whose own initiation at the hands of his master is a highlight of the book.

Initially Merlin is portrayed as a master builder, the designer of ship with a lateen sail that seems powered by magic; but beyond this he is known as the White Druid of Broceliande – the magical forest in Brittany where Merlin's Well can still be seen. His inspired chanting before battle leads Arthur's warriors to victory, but he is also a healer and a poet, whose words hold magical power. At the heart of the book is the struggle between the old ways of the pagan world and the nascent Christian religion. Merlin is himself conflicted and declares that '… one can become a son of God without turning away from nature, and both may be resolved in the blood'[13] on p264 of the French edition.

The book is something of a curiosity among modern accounts of Merlin's life, but as a picture of the old and new magics it is of great interest. Its current translator, Gareth Knight, himself an expert on ritual magic, comments that the book is 'of great contemporary relevance in the current confrontations between Christian and Neo-Pagan dynamics – the religion of Divine Love and the religion of Ancestral Wisdom. The question being – are they so irreconcilable as is sometimes thought?'[14]

The Historical Adventure

Fictional retellings of the historical side of Merlin's life are rare. Most contemporary novelists prefer the drama of sorcery and ancient power, but at least one writer, M.K. Hume, in her *Merlin's Prophecy* trilogy, set out to reconstruct the life of an historical Merlin as a prince of the Deceangii. Hume, a retired academic who has studied Arthurian literature and history, is also the author of three other series, ranging from Arthurian to Celtic history and myth. Her writing is uneven, but her grasp of the world in which Arthur and Merlin may have lived is considerable. In first volume of the Merlin sequence, *Clash of Kings,* she tells the story of Myrddion Merlinus (her Romanised version of his name) from birth to boyhood, following the traditional pattern of the story as told by Nennius and Geoffrey of Monmouth, though with her own spin. Beginning in the time of Vortigern, High Chief of the North, at a time of comparative peace – soon to be broken by his marriage to a Saxon queen – Myrddion, here the product of a brutal rape, is spurned by his mother as the offspring of a demon, thus neatly avoiding the more otherworldly story of Merlin's birth. Myrddion is apprenticed to a skilful healer but his destiny soon catches up with him as the story of the crumbling castle of Dinas Emrys unfolds. The boy begins to be aware of his own nascent skills and his prophetic outpouring before Vortigern earns him a place at court. But the young man's life is changed forever when the king hints at the identity of Myrddin's real father, and in the second volume, *Death of an Empire*, Hume takes us far from Britain, following her hero's search for his origins across France and Italy to Constantinople, the heart of the Byzantine Empire.

Serving as a healer under General Flavius Aetius, Myrddion takes part in the Battle of the Catalaunian Plains, saving thousands of lives. From there he journeys to Rome and the world of Emperor Theodosius, where, recommended by his former master, Myrddion becomes a physician to the imperial court. He saves the life of Cleoxenes, who is soon to embark on a mission to meet with Attila the Hun in an attempt to negotiate peace. But while this encounter is taking place a far deadlier conflict begins between the two opposing emperors: Theodosius and Valentinian, stage managed by the scheming Senator Petronius Maximus. Caught up in this conflict, that will spell the fall of the Empire, Myrddion is forced to choose sides and face some hard decisions.

The third volume, *Web of Deceit*, takes us back from Constantinople to Britain, where Myrddion finds the land in the grip of a savage war against the Saxons. Coerced into obedience by the violent warrior Uther Pendragon, Myrddion finds himself serving Uther's brother Ambrosius, a wise and honest ruler. Myrddion's skills are now put to good use as he sets up a network of spies whom he trains as healers. But when Ambrosius is poisoned, his untimely death propels Myrddion back into the callous hands of Uther, who now seeks to become High King and to destroy the fragile foundations of the kingdom, now abandoned by Rome as the Empire begins to fade. Myrddion uses his skills as a seer and prophet to fight against the seemingly inevitable destruction of his homeland.

The books are tumultuous and at times astoundingly brutal, but the overall impression is of a world riven by doubt and destruction, in which this version of Merlin represents all that is good. As one of the few fictional accounts of an historical Merlin it sets the scene for the later sequence dealing with Arthur and in the process it shows Merlin as an intelligent, haunted man whose bitter life gives him the power to hold his own in the context of a fractured Dark Age world.

The Prophet & the Lover

Two aspects of Merlin's character which we have explored in this book – those of prophet and lover, have been somewhat neglected by contemporary storytellers. Merlin's prophetic gifts are so much a part of his character that they almost seem to pass unnoticed at times, though it is by this means that he is enabled, primarily, to bring about the shaping of the destiny of others. Mary Stewart, in her trilogy of books (*The Crystal Cave, The Hollow Hills* and *The Last Enchantment*) makes these powers central to her characterisation of the mage.

In the first volume, Merlin discovers his ability to 'see' future events; but his vision are the product of fits brought on by staring into a pattern of crystals, rather than by inner or magical contact, and throughout the remainder of the book and those which follow it, ingenious solutions are found for many of the more mysterious aspects of Merlin's life. Thus we read nothing of his magic, only his technical skills, which enable him to position the 'Hele Stone' of Stonehenge at its present site, rather than (as in the medieval stories) raising the whole monument or causing it to fly through the air or float across the Irish Sea.

This portrait of Merlin succeeds in flattening out the character in an effort to explain it – psychological motivation accounting for most of his life – though he remains a prime mover in the setting up of a stable kingdom under the enlightened rule of Arthur.

The first and second volumes draw primarily on Geoffrey of Monmouth, augmented by a solid background borrowed from the medieval accounts. The third recounts the relationship with Nimue in great detail. In Mary Stewart's version, with Arthur established as king over all of Britain, Merlin retires to the wilderness. There, weakened by a subtle poison administered to him by Arthur's half-sister Morgause, he is nursed back to health by a youth named Ninnian, who of course turns out to be a girl, Niniane, or Nimue:

> The dim-seen figure in the mist [seemed] so like the lost boy, that I had greeted her and put the words 'boy' and 'Ninnian' into her head before she could even speak. Told her I was Merlin: offered her the gift of my power and magic, gifts that another girl, the witch Morgause – had tried in vain to prise from me, but which I had hastened eagerly to lay at this stranger's feet.[15]

Thereafter, the story follows the familiar track, though always subtly reshaping it for modern perceptions. Here Nimue becomes Merlin's pupil until, in the end, his powers begin to fade, and she takes over the role of guardian of Arthur's realm as she does in the medieval romances. Finally, Merlin withdraws, promising to return. His end is left uncertain.

The only significant treatment of Merlin as a lover, is in a book by the American author, James Branch Cabell (1879–1958). Cabell is something of an oddity among those who have dealt with Arthurian themes in fiction in that he sets his book, *Something About Eve* (1935), within the framework of an invented universe of chivalry and eroticism, spanning vast areas of time and space. In a chapter entitled 'The Chivalry of Merlin', the old wizard is summoned, with King Solomon and Odysseus, to give an account of himself before he passes 'into the realms of Antan' (Cabell's name for the otherworld), to discover the true meaning of his life:

> 'I was Merlin Ambrosius. This wisdom that I had was more than human ... but I served heaven with it...' Then [he] told about the

child Nimue who was the daughter of the goddess Diana, and of how old, wearied, overlearned Merlin had come ... [to love her]. Then Merlin told to Nimue, because she pouted so adoringly, the secret of building a tower which is not made of stone, or timber, or iron, and is so strong that it may never be felled while this world endures. And Nimue, the moment he had fallen asleep with his head in her lap, spoke very softly the old rune ...[16]

Merlin confesses that he was happy for a long time while in his tower, until he saw his 'toys', the men and women of the Arthurian age, begin to destroy each other and to become filled with hate and lust and barbarity. Yet, despite this he has lingered on, happy with his child love and the peace of his tower – only now seeking enlightenment in the Otherworld, where perhaps he may find reasons for the failure of his dream. Much of this is drawn directly from the *English Merlin*, where Nimue is a priestess of Diana, but Cabell gives it his own spin by setting it within the compass of the universe in which many of his books are set.

Apocalypse Now

Merlin's role as a saviour of humanity is one that runs through every version of his story from the ancient Myrddin poems to the latest novels and movies. The most apocalyptic account of this theme is A. A. Attanasio's extraordinary Arthor series (1986–2000) In the first of these, *The Dragon and the Unicorn*, the author plays all kinds of tricks with the original material, making Merlin an ancient demon in his own right, and borrowing the name Lailoken from the mad wild man who appears in the oldest accounts of Merlin's life. Tricked into assuming human form, he becomes Merlinus, a wandering wise man versed in magic, destined to work for the good of humanity. Against him is ranged the Furor, an ancient Norse god who does everything to frustrate the mage's plans for the Arthurian kingdom. In the beginning of the book he encounters a unicorn, a spirit also trapped in earthly form, which leads him to find Ygrane, the future mother of Arthor, who is described as a queen of the Celts. She it is who sets him the task of finding a man she has only ever seen in seen in a vision but fated to be her king and lover.

Combining the world of Arthur with black holes, gods and alternate timelines, Attanasio produces a world full of mythology and history. Perhaps the most striking aspect of the books is the mixture of love and hatred, horror and joy that Merlin experiences in his relationship with the ancient goddess of time and the earthly women who represent her – including Nimue. A memorable passage sums this up in Merlinus' own words:

> Woman. Everything I am I owe to Her. All the good and the bad in my life. All the sorcery and mystery. All the wisdom and madness. Even in the very beginning, before there could be space, or time either, when every point of each of us touched every point of each of the others, She was there. She was Herself the one point out of which everything has come. And She was the coming, too. Why do you think we left but to follow Her?[17]

This is the most intricate modern portrait of Merlin yet attempted. In the end it captures every aspect of the mage, from shaman to wizard, and shows them to us though a fragmented mirror.

The Teacher

Whatever Merlin's destiny, whatever his origins, he never ceases to be concerned with this world and the people who live in it. His function within the secret history of Britain varies hardly at all from Geoffrey of Monmouth to Mary Stewart. As the prime mover in the setting up of Arthur's kingdom, and the founding of the

Round Table; as prophet, guardian and sometime tutelary spirit of Britain, he remains true.

In Parke Godwin's *Firelord* (1980), Merlin assumes another of his old guises, that of the Wonder Child, in order to awaken something within the young Arthur:

> The boy was seated on a flat rock... He looked maddeningly familiar with his shock of blond, curly hair and blue eyes glistening with secret excitement: things to do and tomorrows that couldn't be caught up fast enough. He shimmered all over, he made me tingle with the energy that came from him...[18]

Here Merlin is, in some sense, Arthur's own inner self, able to show him a vision of the great king and warrior whose presence draws the very utmost effort from the men who follow him – the man that Arthur is to become, driven by the Merlin within:

> Deep in me, Artos stirs. Stay away, I tell him. Go back to sleep. But Artos wakes ... opens his eyes inside me. 'It's time' he says. Time for what? 'I know what Merlin wanted to teach me,' whispers Artos in my soul. 'To be a king over men. To know what they are and the price of knowledge.'[19]

Merlin's function here is very much that of a teacher – a task which he often performs in his own unique way. In *The Sword in the Stone* (1938), the first and best known of T. H. White's great quartet of novels which make up *The Once & Future King* (1958) he teaches by example, turning Arthur into animal, fish or bird. From his encounter with a great pike that lives beneath the walls of his foster-father's castle, the boy learns that power for its own sake leads nowhere; while from a position high above the earth, Arthur as a bird discovers that boundaries are an illusion fought over without reason. And of course, all that he learns stands him in good stead when he comes to draw the famous sword from the stone – the act that will make him King:

> All round the churchyard there were hundreds of old friends. They rose over the church wall all together, like Punch and Judy ghosts of remembered days, and there were otters and nightingales and vulgar crows and hares and serpents and falcons and fishes and goats and dogs and dainty unicorns and newts and solitary wasps and goatmoth caterpillars and cockindrills and volcanoes and mighty trees and patient stones. They loomed round the church walls, the lovers and helpers of the Wart [Arthur] and they all spoke solemnly in turn…[20]

Nor is it surprising that Merlin should choose to teach using parallels drawn from nature. In his oldest incarnation he is a creature of the woods, whose closeness to the natural world is so compete that he is able to converse with animals and trees.

In America the ideas set forth by White – who was himself a teacher at the prestigious Stowe school in Buckinghamshire – were proposed as a perfect model for the education of young people by the educator Barbara Lerner.

> That was Merlyn's magic, the old magic of teaching and learning. Not the in-passing, by-the-way, among-other things, peripheral-vision kind of learning that became the norm in so many post-modern classrooms, but the sort of focused, concentrated, full-attention learning that absorbs you so completely that it lifts you right up out of yourself and your own situation, taking you to another place entirely, plunking you down in whole new worlds beyond our own.[21]

It is as the tutor and guide to the young king that we really know Merlin best, and as such he appears again and again in modern retellings. Catherine Christian in *The Sword and the Flame* (1982) has Merlin arranging for Arthur to acquire his second, more famous, sword – just as he does in the mediaeval tales. But in a variation from the more traditional episode, in which he receives it from the Lady of the Lake, here Merlin assists in its forging by an ancient smith-god, from a lump of meteorite:

> It is now. Listen ... the stream sings for it. The fire-spirits call for it. Fetch the King-sword here, to the anvil, and finish its forging, while the power of the Dragon and the power of the Merlin are together in this place to give you strength.[22]

A more recent series of books, *The Camulod Chronicles* (1998–2003) by Canadian author Jack Whyte, takes this idea even further, describing the forging of Excalibur by a Roman-born smith who is revealed as the grandfather of Arthur. The series, numbering nine volumes, features the figure of Caius Merlyn Britannicus, soldier and leader who offers a Romanised version of the mage, every bit as memorable as any other portrait written to date.

Nor should we ignore the presence of a very Merlin-like teacher in the *Harry Potter* books by J.K. Rowling. Albus Dumbledore, the venerable headmaster of the Hogwarts School of Witchcraft and Wizardry, bears a striking resemblance to the popular conception of Merlin. Since the appearance of *Harry Potter and the Philosopher's Stone* (renamed *Harry Potter and the Sorcerer's Stone* in the USA) the series has attained cult status around the world, triggering a huge amount of interest in magic and magicians. Harry is only a nine-year-old boy when the series opens, but he finds himself inheriting the skills and abilities of his parents much as Merlin ingests those of his demonic father and human mother. Harry Potter is gradually introduced into a kind of parallel world where magic is the accepted norm. Reading the accounts of Harry's adventures, we get a glimpse of what the Merlin's own youthful exploits might have been like if we knew more of them.

For an actual account of Merlin's young days, we have to turn to another very successful series, *The Lost Years of Merlin* by T.A. Barron (2000–2012). This twelve-volume saga (actually two linked series) follows the sometimes-painful development of a boy born with unique powers. Blinded by an accident and with no memory of his birth or parents, he discovers that his inner vision is far clearer than his ordinary sight had been. Throughout the early part of the series we watch him gain the awareness and skill which will stand him in good stead in his years as Arthur's guide and councillor; the second sequence traces his growing strength and first adventures in the world of Arthur. The books are qualified by a good deal of wisdom aimed at their young readers, with Merlin's struggles offering examples of how a boy with a disability can triumph over adversity.

Rest and Rebirth

Arthur's life is often portrayed as extending beyond a single lifetime, as we see in those versions of the story where both he and Merlin return after a long sleep, whether in Avalon or the *esplumoir*, to continue the work left unfinished at the end of the Arthurian Age. In the final part of C.S. Lewis' *Peralandra* trilogy (*That Hideous Strength*, 1945), Merlin is awakened by the striving of the forces of good and evil – here represented by Ransom, Lewis' space voyager, and a totalitarian group seeking control over the Earth. As in J.C. Powys's *Porius*, Merlin is seen as almost a god – a force as old as time itself; a massive, primitive power virtually without limit. When he and Ransom first meet there follows a marvellous riddling exchange reminiscent of those indulged in by Celtic bards, in which they test each other's knowledge. When Ransom has successfully answered a whole string of questions, Merlin asks another which he deems even harder: where is Arthur's Ring?

'The Ring of the King,' said Ransom, 'is on Arthur's finger where he sits in the House of Kings in the cup-shaped land of Abhalljin, beyond the seas of Lur in Peralandra. [Lewis' name for Venus.] For Arthur did not die; but Our Lord took him to be in the body until the end of time ... with Enoch and Elias and Moses and Melchisedec the King. Melchisedec is he in whose hall the steep-stoned ring sparkles on the finger of the Pendragon.'[23]

Here Lewis draws upon his considerable knowledge of the Arthurian literature to unite aspects of Merlin's life which, as we saw in Chapter 5, are seldom revealed. Ransom is later shown to be Arthur's successor, the new Pendragon, to whom Merlin once again pledges his service, and whom he aids in the final overthrow of the modern-day forces of evil. References to Numinor and the 'Far West' in the book show that Lewis, who knew J.R.R. Tolkien well, recognised the identification of Merlin with Gandalf.

The theme of the recurring lives of Merlin and Arthur is taken up again by the science fiction writer Tim Powers in *The Drawing of the Dark* (1977). Here, Merlin is the guardian of the wounded Grail King, who is kept alive, by a curious twist of the old story, not through the daily descent of a dove bearing a wafer in its beak, but by a yearly draught of a unique elixir – Hertzwestern beer! Merlin, the owner of the inn where this mysterious drink is brewed, summons the latest incarnation of Arthur, a seventeenth-century Irish mercenary named Brian Duffy, to help him protect the elixir against an ancient and implacable enemy. The substance of the book is concerned with Duffy's adventures and with his unwillingness to allow memories of himself as Arthur to come to the surface. But throughout the story the figure of Merlin moves subtly. He is very old, an undying figure eternally destined to pit himself against the enemies of light.

Merlin's Laughter

Merlin the trickster, whose laughter echoes the wild visionary gifts of the shaman, has his own champions. Apart from Linda Halderman's book, which touched upon this aspect of Merlin's character, there are two others: Robert Nye's *Merlin* (1978), and Thomas Berger's *Arthur Rex* (1979), which both deal with this side of his nature.

Berger is closest in many respects to Malory's version, though his book is a comic masterpiece shot through with gleams of high fantasy. In a scene near the beginning of the book, two knights seek out Merlin at an enchanted fountain in the forest:

> And both the knight and the horses, being sore thirsty, drank from the crystal water of the spring (into which one could see forever because there was no bottom) and by the time they had soaked their parched throats the men had been transformed into green frogs and the horses into spotted hounds... 'None may drink of my water without my leave,' said a voice, and looking aloft the frogs saw it was the raven that spake. Then the glossy black bird flapped his wings twice and before their bulging eyes he was transformed into a man with a long white beard and wearing the raiment of a wizard... And the next instant Merlin (for it was he) caused both knights and horses to return to their proper forms and only then did he laugh most merrily.[24]

Nye, on the other hand, aims for a comedy of Eros, and in the process plumbs the depths of Merlin's character as very few writers have managed to do. At once outrageous, irreverent and profound, beneath its scatological humour and endless wordplay, lies a deeply researched picture which draws upon nearly all the many disguises of Merlin to reveal him, at last, as a strangely sorrowful creature, mourning for the even more sorrowful creatures in his care. From within the crystal cave of his retirement, Merlin views past, present and future with a jaundiced eye. He describes himself dryly as:

> Merlin Ambrosius. Merlin Sylvester. Merlin the magician. Merlin the witch. The wisest man at the court of King Arthur, and the greatest fool. Well, shall we say the only adult. My mother was a virgin. My father was the devil.[25]

For Nye, as for the medieval authors he has studied, this is the crux of the matter – Merlin partakes of both natures – human and non-human, good and evil, god and devil. Within him are the legions of hell and the armies of heaven. He is the battleground, and the object of conquest and defence is humanity. It is part of the subtle alchemy of Nye's book that he is able to show up the dark side of human nature – as well as its silly side: all libido and bluster – and yet give a sense of the triumph of man over his own shortcomings. Merlin is a *deus-ex-machina* who stands ready to intervene, who laughs and plays the fool but who, underneath, cares for his children.

Deeper Portraits

Other than Robert Nye's account, no single work of fiction has yet appeared which attempts to deal with all the aspects of Merlin's character, and perhaps there could be no such book. Nye comes closest, while a recent collection of stories by Jane Yolen, published under the title *Merlin's Booke* (1986), has great diversity but lacks the coherence of a novel; nevertheless, Merlin's story is brought up to date in a most intriguing way. The story is set in the near future, when a group of reporters have been summoned to a news conference at which it is revealed that Merlin's tomb has been discovered beneath Glastonbury Tor, and that along with the ancient wizard's mummified body is a strange box, which is to be opened by the Prince of Wales under the eyes of the world's press. Each of them sees something different, but one, who is of Celtic origin, sees more than any – though what, he dares not say:

> Could he tell them that at the moment the box had opened, the ceiling and walls of the meeting room had dropped away? That they were all suddenly standing within a circle of Corinthian pillars under a clear night sky. That as he watched, behind the pillars one by one the stars had begun to fall. Could he tell them? Or more to the point – would they believe?
>
> 'Light,' I said. 'I saw light. And darkness coming on.'. . .
>
> Merlin had been known as a prophet, a soothsayer, equal to or better than Nostradamus. But the words of seers have always admitted to a certain ambiguity... 'My darlings,' I said, 'I have a sudden and overwhelming thirst. I want to make a toast to the earth under me and the sky above me. A toast to the arch-mage and what he has left us. A salute to Merlin: ave magister. Will you come?'[26]

Among the new generation of writers who have added significantly to the Arthurian mythos is the Canadian writer Charles de Lint. His understanding of the darkly wooded world of the Celts runs as deep as any previous writer. In *Spiritwalk* (1992), a section appears called 'Merlin Dreams in the Mondream Wood'. This is almost a separate piece of writing from the rest, though it opens up themes which are further explored throughout the remainder of the book. In it one of the characters comes to live in the Tamson House, a gateway between the worlds where figures from the Otherworld enter and depart at will. Here, in the garden of the house, she encounters a mysterious being:

> In the heart of the garden stood a tree. In the heart of the tree lived an old man who wore the shape of a red-haired boy with crackernut eyes that seemed as bright as salmon tails glinting up the water. His was a riddling wisdom, older by far than the ancient oak that housed his body. The green sap was his blood and leaves grew in his hair. In the winter he slept. In the spring, the moon harped a windsong against his antler tines as the oak's boughs stretched its green buds to wake. In the summer, the air was thick with the droning of bees and the scent of wildflowers that grew in stormy profusion where the fat brown bole became root. And in the autumn, when the tree loosed its bounty to the ground below, there were hazlenuts lying in among the acorns.
>
> *The Secrets of a Green Man*[27]

This Merlin is old, older perhaps than any of the others we have considered. He is both Arthur's Merlin and Geoffrey's Merlin and something else as well – the Old Earth Man, the Green One, the Walker in the Woods who had been on this Earth from the beginning. De Lint's contribution, though slight in volume, is as significant of the way we regard Merlin as any other writer in this age or the past.

Since this time, only one new portrait of Merlin has significantly added to our understanding of the charter. This is in the late Robert Holdstock's powerful series, *The Merlin Codex*. Book I, *Celtika*, appeared in 2001, followed by *The Iron Grail* in 2003 and *The Broken Kings* in 2007. Holdstock had approached the figure of Merlin before, in his ground-breaking *Mythago Wood* sequence, but in these books, he chose to go back to the beginning, to a time centuries before Arthur, when the young but eternally ageless Merlin wanders the Earth. Here we have the most shamanic portrait of Merlin to date, and Holdstock extends the picture by setting the books outside the usual Arthurian world. Thus, in Book 1, Merlin joins the resurrected crew of Jason's *Argo* (which has a personality of its own) to sail on a fantastic voyage in search of the hero's long-lost sons, stolen from him by the enchantress Medea.

In Book 2, *The Iron Grail*, many hundreds of years have passed. Merlin, still wandering across the world in search of his own destiny, hears stories of a screaming ship, and realises that it is the *Argo* and that the screams are those of Jason, still searching for his long-lost children. Joining them again, Merlin accompanies them on a fresh journey, deepening the magic and revealing more of Merlin's power, which, in an unusual touch, he must harbour, since every time he used it lessens his abilities. From the frozen seas of the far north to the desolate isle of Alba, that will one day become Arthur's kingdom, to the shores of ancient Greece, Merlin's quest continues, weaving Celtic and Classical myth into a remarkable tale of courage, death, and magic.

In Book 3, *The Broken Kings*, the *Argo* sales once more to Alba and lies hidden in a cavern beneath the fortress of Urtha (Holdstock's name for Uther). Aboard it is Jason and his crew, locked in an enchanted sleep, as well as Niiv, Merlin's sometime lover and potential nemesis. Above them, the dead are awakening, and otherworldly beings spill out into the world of men. An immerse struggle now begins between the heroes of the past, and those of the *Argo* and the natives of Alba. Merlin himself moves in and out of time, desperately trying to manipulate the tides of magic to bring about the birth of the Arthurian world.

Robert Holdstock was a maker of myths, and for this complex and compelling series he ransacked both the mythology of the *Mabinogion*, the writings of Geoffrey of Monmouth and the mysterious world evoked in the ninth-century poem *'Prieddeu Annwn'*, as well as Greek myths of the quest for the Golden Fleece. Characters from both worlds meet and mingle and exchange roles with each other. These books are not really comparable to any of the ones discussed above; together they make one of the most profound and penetrating accounts of Merlin in contemporary literature. Holdstock was later to return to some of the themes of his earlier books in *Merlin's Wood*, completed shortly before his untimely death in 2009. Here he linked the *Mythago* sequence with the *Merlin Codex*, but this book has nothing of the triumphant mythic purity of the earlier work.

Merlin in Film and TV

Inevitably the figure of Merlin has loomed large in recent years in the most magical of all modern media: motion pictures. Merlin on the silver screen has shone forth in a variety of guises which reflect his various incarnations.

One of the finest portraits of the mage to date in this or any other medium is in *Excalibur* (1983), directed by John Boorman and co-written by Boorman and Rospo Pallenberg. At one time the intention was to call this film 'Merlin' and it is the figure of the mage which dominates the action. Here we encounter him in each of his major aspects. As the controller of destinies, he engineers the birth of Arthur, the giving of the magical sword, the shaping of the Round Table, and the quest for the Grail. But he is not of human blood and follows the old ways, which, as he tells his pupil Morgana, 'are numberéd'; and as he tells Arthur later, he is already fading: 'My time is almost over. The days of men are here to stay.' Like Gandalf, when his work is done, he must depart into the West to become 'a dream to some, a nightmare to others.' Throughout the shifting patterns of the film, Merlin emerges in Nicol Williamson's astonishing portrayal, as tetchy, loving, ingenious, amused, surprised. Possessed of god-like powers, vision and cunning, he is all of the Merlins in one. Finally, he is as baffling as ever, escaping before us like smoke blown across the blood-soaked field of Camlann.

It was perhaps inevitable that Merlin would feature in more than one film by the Walt Disney Company. In fact (not including brief appearances) he features in three. The animated version of T.H. White's *Sword in the Stone* in 1963 (currently being remade as a live-action production) followed in 1995 by *A Kid in King Arthur's Court,* and in the same year by *Kids of the Round Table*. In the first of these Merlyn (*sic*) is treated in humorous fashion, as he is in the original book. Living 'backwards' he has access to modern ideas and knowledge of Arthur as the subject of books histories and films – as he tells the young Arthur. The point of the film is to show that while Arthur begins as a simple boy taught by a venerable wizard, in the end (following a dispute with Merlyn) he must make his own way – helped by the various creatures encountered during his teachings – to reach the point where he can become king. The film is bright and witty and features songs by Richard M. and Robert B. Sherman, and with a strange version of Morgan le Fay, renamed Madam Mim, who is reduced to a pantomime villainess akin to those that feature in so many of Disney's earlier animated features.

Kids of the Round Table, featuring Roddy McDowell as Merlin, is played out against the background of an American high school. The characters of Arthur, Lancelot, and Guinevere are played by teenagers Alex, Luke, and Jenny, with Alex claiming Excalibur (here, as so often, confused with the Sword from the Stone), and meeting Merlin, who teaches him how to wield its power. Alex is told that no one else can be allowed to see the sword, because 'its power comes from faith'. Enter then Luke, who behaves in a Lancelot-like fashion, with Jenny as the object of both boys' affections. The boys come to blows and Alex invokes the invisible power of Excalibur to win – which he does, but this misuse of power loses him Jenny's affection for a time. The remainder of the film is taken up by showing Alex discovering his natural strength, catching bank robbers though his own abilities while thinking he is drawing upon the power of the sword. Encountering Merlin again, Alex asks if he will ever get Excalibur back. Merlin implies that the sword's qualities are not magical but '… only what you make of it… Excalibur is not a thing… Excalibur is the good in you.' With its rather heavy-handed lesson delivered, the film ends with a vision of another time, when a girl pulls the sword from stone.

The second film *A Kid in King Arthur's Court* (1995) is set in the time of Arthur, who is portrayed as a type of *roi feanéant*, a weak king who has given up on life and can no longer wield Excalibur. It brings Ron Moody to the role of Merlin, who is here represented as a spirit living on in the Well of Destiny. Arthur (Joss Ackland) is played as a man destroyed by the loss of Guinevere and Merlin, both of whom have died. No longer able to wield Excalibur, his kingdom is placed in the hands of the villainous seneschal Belasco (Art Malik). Merlin in desperation sends out a spell across time to bring a worthy champion to save the kingdom. The spell transports a hapless young American baseball player named Calvin Fuller (Thomas Ian Nichols) who becomes a reluctant hero – taught by a master swordsman played by a young Daniel Craig. In time he realises his potential and saves the day, bringing Arthur back to his old self and giving Excalibur into his hands. With all set to rights in Camelot, Calvin is returned to his own time, to take part in a triumphant baseball match, watched by various reincarnations of characters from the past, including Arthur and Merlin.

Here, yet again, we see Merlin playing the part of an all-powerful wizard determined to save the broken king and the broken kingdom. The film is very loosely based on Mark Twain's *A Connecticut Yankee at King Arthur's Court*, and there are some witty moments – but by and large the film is a poor sample of ill-judged characterisation and torpid dialogue that fails to bring the story to life.

A greatly wasted opportunity is the 1985 *Arthur the King* (also known as *Merlin and the Sword*) directed by Clive Donner and starring a range of excellent actors including Edward Woodward as Merlin, Malcolm McDowell changing his wizard's hat for a crown to play Arthur. Candice Bergen is Morgan le Fay, with Rupert Everett as Lancelot, and Patrick Ryecart as Gawain.

Originally shot as a 3-hour TV special, then cut to 2 hours and finally released on DVD as a 90-minute shambles, it has rightly earned its place as one of the worst Arthurian movies to date. The story revolves around Merlin and Niniane, who are discovered in an ice cave below Stonehenge, where they have dwelt for a thousand years. Merlin, however, has left an opening through which he can observe the starry skies (an echo of the observatory built for him Ganeida in the *Vita Merlini*). Through this hole falls a modern-day woman called Katherine (Diane Carroll) and it is to her that Merlin and Niniane recount their story in a series of flashbacks to the time of Arthur. Central to the film, and possibly the only time it has been adapted for the screen, is the story of Gawain and Ragnell, in which the great knight is trapped into marrying a hideously ugly woman, who turns out to be under a spell cast by Morgan le Fay. Only when Gawain gives her the right to choose whether she will be ugly by night or day is the spell broken, and Ragnell permanently regains her beauty.

All the stories are about love conquering all, and we gradually learn that Niniane had betrayed Merlin because Morgan had her father in her power. She had been told to get a spell to entrap Merlin, but the spell backfires and both Merlin and Niniane are trapped in the cave of ice. Finally, the spell is broken when Merlin and Niniane are reconciled, with a little modern psychology from Katherine. Merlin then returns to Camelot where he will help Arthur in his fight against Morgan and her allies.

The stories intercut into this somewhat muddled tale are actually quite well executed, and one wishes one could see the full-length version to judge it better. The drastic cuts turned it into a mishmash, and a poor script and some indifferent acting add to the general mess. The scenes in the ice cave remind one somewhat of the entrapment of Merlin in *Excalibur*, but everything about the film is far beneath Boorman's epic.

Merlin is presented as a good man of great power – though apparently not enough to release himself from his own spell – whose attempts to win Niniane bring about his downfall. Woodward is excellent, given the terrible script and Liam Neeson appears in the role of the villain, returning to the Arthurian universe having played Gawain in Boorman's film.

One of the few attempts to place Arthur in a more rationalised world is the 1997 film *Guinevere*. This is a TV adaptation of a trilogy of novels by Persia Wooley (*Guinevere, Child of the Northern Spring,* and *Queen of the Summer Stars*). The story focusses on the struggles leading to the ushering in of a golden age in Britain under the rulership of Arthur (Sean Patrick Flannery) and Guinevere (Sheryl Lee). Merlin (Donald Pleasance) is seen as something of an anachronism, and his plans to raise Arthur to the kingship and marry him to Guinevere are constantly frustrated by Morgana Le Fay (Brid Brennan) who hates Merlin and sees Arthur as the product of the rape of her mother by Uther. The film is very much a feminist take on the legend, with Guinevere in the forefront, becoming a leader when Arthur is captured by Morgana and her ally Malgrim.

The portrayal of Merlin is more realistic than in many of the films and books considered here. He has no magic and seems human (he dies towards the end of the film) using his wisdom to bring about Camelot's golden age. But it is Guinevere who is really the driving force, coming up with a whole new idea of kingship as a service to the people. She is even responsible for the creation of the Round Table and becomes the caretaker of Merlin's dream. Despite some flaws and an occasionally indifferent script, the film manages to offer a new take on the stories that is true to its own vision.

The Teacher and the Mage

Several of the films discussed above cast Merlin in the guise of teacher or mage, offering worldly wisdom from a magical point of view. In the latest manifestation of his character, the 2018 film *The Kid Who Would be King*, which harks back to *Kids at the Round Table,* an old Merlin is played by the redoubtable Patrick Stewart, and his younger self by Angus Imrie. The film is a curiosity, especially considering the date of its release – 2017 – a time when most films are dark and negative in tone, this offers a simpler, cleaner and more optimistic world, where Arthur and Merlin and their friends can reincarnate in the form of modern school children. The story begins with an ordinary boy – once again named Alex (short for Alexander) – played by Louis Ashbourne Serkis, is typically bullied by two older kids until he discovers the Sword in the Stone in the middle of desolate building site – a veritable wasteland – and is plunged into a whirlwind adventure in which he is, again, pitted against Morgana (Rebecca Fergusson) in full sorceress array.

We learn at the beginning how the original Arthur and Merlin defeat Morgana and imprisoned her beneath the ground, bound in place by tree roots. In our own time, as Merlin notes on his first appearance (disguised as an owl – an idea borrowed from T.H. White) Britain is a divided land, the hearts of its people grown hollow, focussed only on trinkets, games and fleeting pleasures. Joe Cornish, who wrote and directed the film, had a vision of it when he was thirteen and never gave upon the idea of making it. In fact, the story turned out to be extremely prescient, given that it appeared at the time of actual division concerning the proposed departure of the UK from the European Union.

Chased onto a building site young Alexander Eliot (named after the hero of the classic Spielberg film *E.T.*) finds the sword in the stone (here, as so often, confused with Excalibur) and pulls it out in time to defend himself against the school bullies Lance (Tom Taylor) and Kay (Rhianna Dorris). No one, least of all his mother, struggling to raise him alone following the departure of her husband, believes him – with the exception of his best friend Bedivere (Dean Chaumoo). But the taking of the Sword disturbs the imprisoned Morgana who begins to break free and sends a dead warrior to kill Alex and bring her the sword. Enter Merlin, jumping though a portal at Stonehenge and taking the shape of a teenage boy to take Alex under his wing. Presented as both a mage in his older form, a boy with magical knowledge, and something of a trickster, he acknowledges Alex as the new Once and Future King and explains that Morgana, unless stopped before the eclipse of the sun in four days, will take over the kingdom – and in time the world – bringing death and gloom in her wake.

Alex gathers some modern knights – his friend Bedders, and surprisingly, his adversaries Lance and Kay, whom he 'knights' with the sword, winning them over by sheer eloquence. Discovering a book of *King Arthur and his Knights* in the loft at home, which had been inscribed to 'My Once and Future King' by his absent father, Alex decides to go in search of him, believing he must have known what was to happen. The boys, accompanied by Merlin, set off for Tintagel, the place in Cornwall most famously associated with Arthur. There, they encounter his sister who tells Alex that their father has moved on, and that he is struggling with his own 'demons'. At this point of defeat, Merlin, appearing as his ancient self, tells them:

Legends are mere rumours whispered down the centuries, written and rewritten, told and retold – sometimes by the rich and powerful.

Meanwhile Morgana is waking up and she looses her army of long-dead warriors armed with flaming swords against the kids. Alex works out that the sorceress is hidden beneath Glastonbury Tor and the boys proceed there and break through into the underworld. While Merlin and the rest hold the phantom knights at bay Alex tackles Morgana, who appears as a monstrous dragon-like creature, naming herself 'the last of the living Pendragons'. Alex stabs her to the heart with Excalibur and the underworld caves in.

Believing his work completed, Alex returns the sword to the Lady of the Lake – seen as an arm rising from water – and the kids head home. But Morgana is not dead and emerges now even stronger with her army of undead knights. Alex retrieves Excalibur by filling a bath with water and calling upon the sword's guardian – who is said to live in every bit of water whether large or small. Alex and his friends – aided somewhat by Merlin – persuade their entire school to join them in defending the land against the sorceress. A huge pitched battle now ensues with Morgana appearing as an even larger dragon. Alex cuts off her head and she is sucked back into the underworld forever. All her followers vanish as the sun comes out. In the closing scenes Merlin gives Alex his own book of King Arthur, which has been rewritten to be about him and his friends. Alex throws Excalibur back into a local pond.

This unusual and charming film shows Merlin in his most fascinating guise, as the young/old mage and trickster, guiding the footsteps of the young Arthur. An excellent script and some fine acting by the whole cast, make this one of the more memorable reappearances of Merlin in recent years.

In another of the more recent chapters of Merlin's filmic history, *King Arthur* (2004) written by David Franzoni and directed by Antoine Fuqua, Merlin is portrayed as a freedom fighter, struggling to preserve his people (the Picts, who may be the oldest inhabitants of Britain) against both the Romans and Saxons. Here Merlin is stripped of most of his magic – though there are elements of the shaman still embedded in the character. Stephen Dillane's portrayal makes us aware of a raw power, scarcely held in check, which might at any moment break free. This promises to be one of the most interesting accounts of Merlin in recent years, and in its stark realism may come as close as possible to the human being behind the mage.

In the most recent Hollywood epic to deal with Arthur, British director Guy Ritchie sacrificed much of the original story to bring in elements designed to appeal to contemporary games enthusiasts. His film *King Arthur: The Legend of the Sword* (2017), borrows tropes from *Lord of the Rings*, the writings of H. P. Lovecraft and contemporary gangster flicks in a bizarre amalgam in which Arthur becomes a street kid leading a band of unlikely heroes. Vortigern (Jude Law) is transposed from his early role in Merlin's story to that of primary villain, backed up by a monstrous creature who lives in a cave beneath his castle and consumes members of Vortigern's family. Merlin does not appear under his own name, but his role and several of his aspects are taken on by The Mage (Àstrid Bergès-Frisby) a strange combination of Merlin and Nimue, whose magic is the most believable thing in the film, and whose role remains mysterious enough to add to an otherwise unsatisfactory blend of old and new.

Other Arthurian films, including a possible full-length version of T. H. White's *The Once and Future King*, and at least two TV series, are under way at the time of writing. They are bound to assure the continued presence of Merlin in cinema history.

Merlin does not always appear on the small screen in immediately recognisable form. In the hugely successful TV franchise *Star Trek*, it takes little effort to see the age-old gallery of characters arranged at a new Round Table, the deck of the USS *Enterprise*. Captain James T. Kirk (William Shatner) fills the role of Arthur, with the alien Mr Spock (Leonard Nimoy) as his sardonic, but always wise, Merlin.

Nowhere within a contemporary framework is the character of Merlin more clearly represented than in George Lucas' *Star Wars*. In the character of Obi Wan Kenobi, as played first by Alec Guinness, we see Merlin at his most wise and powerful. In the more recent movies, where a younger version of the character is played by Ewan McGregor, Merlin as warrior and maybe even as trickster enters the story. Nor should we overlook Jedi master Yoda, a diminutive portrait of a Merlin-like, mystical wizard, who shares many of the traits of the ancient sage.

Throughout the whole series runs the idea of the mystical Force. This represents one of the clearest restatements of an ancient idea that is part of Merlin's life as it is of virtually every wizard who has ever lived. The Force is part of the natural order of things and manifests in those who learn how to sense it and allow it to flow through them. They, in turn, learn to master their own inner forces and to manipulate the world around them. In the movie *The Empire Strikes Back* (1980) Yoda says to his apprentice, Luke Skywalker: 'You must feel the Force around you. Here, between you ... me ... the tree ... the rock ... everywhere!' This could easily stand as a description of Merlin's power, which comes not from himself but from a harmonious relationship with nature.

The cinematic treatment of Merlin as a central character has been sparse and uneven. *Merlin, the Return* (2001), wasted the talents of its excellent cast in a pointless story of Merlin's continuing battles with Mordred and Morgan le Fay in the twentieth century. Much better are two striking modern portraits of Merlin, both made for TV. In the miniseries *Merlin* (1998) the sage is excellently played by Sam Neil. Here the whole myth is reworked and places Merlin at centre stage. Unusually, we see a boy gifted with magic who is so hurt by the loss of his family and friends that, as in the *Vita*

Merlini, he goes mad and rejects everything he has believed or stood for. But his powers are such that he can never truly leave them behind, and in his love for Nimue – portrayed sympathetically by Helena Bonham Carter – he finds rest at last. Despite elements of fantasy, this version of the story reflects the increasingly pragmatic direction in which the character of Merlin has been taken of late. There is a deeper concentration on the humanity of the figure than before; he is less of a wizard, less of a seer and prophet and more of a man, suffering all the pains and doubts of humanity in general.

A TV show which certainly put the character back into general consciousness, initially between 2008 and 2012 with a run of sixty-five episodes, and continuing to gather fans on Netflix today, is the fantasy adventure series *Merlin,* created by Julian Jones, Jake Michie, Julian Murphy, and Johnny Capps. It is very loosely based on the Arthurian legends, though taking a very different tack by making both Arthur (Bradley James) and Merlin (Colin Morgan) boys growing up together at the court of Uther Pendragon (Anthony Head). Merlin is here described as a warlock, who has his powers but is generally reluctant to use them – especially since King Uther has banned all magic in his kingdom. Guided by a mysterious voice in his head Merlin finds his way to a cavern beneath the palace and these discovers the Last Dragon in the West, imprisoned there by Uther for reasons that are never really made clear – though there are hints that the banning of magic may be intended as an echo of the Christian belief that all such things are evil. From the dragon (voiced by John Hurt) Merlin leans that it is his destiny to become the guardian of the young Arthur, who will one day rise to be king and unite the land of Albion. There is a good deal of boyish humour in the show, preventing it from carrying much weight, and familiar characters drift in and out without much focus. Morgana (aka Morgan le Fay, played by Katie McGrath) is Uther's daughter and from a slow beginning comes to the fore as the main villainess, hating her own father and determined to destroy Arthur to gain the throne. Arthur meets and falls for Guinevere (Angel Coulby), here a servant at the castle, played – with aplomb – as the first Guinevere of colour.

Merlin grows slowly from a clumsy youth to a powerful young man, but never quite attains the degree of characterisation the character demands. The anachronistic settings and low budget sets bring the story down still further, though the dragon was a spirited effort on behalf of the studios' CGI experts to render a very believable creature. Despite this, the show gained a strong fan following with many young writers trying out their skills as story tellers using the characters from the show. Though ultimately disappointing, *Merlin* reminded everyone of the continuing fascination with the characters.

A less familiar show, written by Tom Richards and directed by David Winning, appeared in 1998 under the title *Merlin: The Magic Begins* (or *Merlin: The Quest Begins*) with Jason Connery in the name part. It ran for twenty-two episodes, beginning with the youth of Merlin, learning to use his raw talent. Thereafter it is a fairly straightforward account of the rise of Arthur, in this version opposed by a very sword-and-sorcery style villain named King Vidus. Connery is excellent at the youthful Merlin. The existence of the parallel UK series seems to have prevented it from being shown here or indeed to get much coverage.

The Return

Returning for the moment to fictional retellings of Merlin's life we find him portrayed as an eternal being. In *Firelord* Parke Godwin says something immensely important about Merlin's inherent mystery. As Arthur is dying – or fading, however one wishes to see it – Merlin appears, a boy again, juggling with brightly coloured balls:

The coloured balls soared higher, four of them now, five, six. The shimmering boy balanced and timed their flight so skilfully that they moved in a smooth circle like the sun. 'Don't they shine, Arthur? Shaped from the finest tomorrows. Not an easy job, you know. Another dreamer to be born in the same old place: where's he's needed.' He was my genius, this juggler, always the more impressive part of me. Or was I merely a facet of him, designed to lead and care for men?[28]

Merlin is ever eternal. The further we get from his original time, so we seem to curve back to an even earlier age, when Merlin is virtually a god, when the elements which went into the creation of his character were stirring in the hearts and minds of the first storytellers.

This is why Merlin will never be forgotten, why he keeps returning, under the guise of such diverse characters as Mr Spock, or Obi Wan Kenobi or as Gandalf. Even in mainstream novels like Lawrence Durrell's *The Revolt of Aphrodite* (1974) or Walker Percy's *Lancelot* (1979) we may detect him, looming up against the backdrop of contemporary dreams or boardroom politics.

Merlin cannot fade. He is too much a part of us all, too deeply rooted in our hearts and minds and souls. He is as much the Spirit of Britain as is Arthur, and it would be hard to imagine one without the other. In this book we have traced his career from its beginnings as a shaman and man of the woods, though various incarnations as wizard, prophet and sage. In our own time all of these images have coalesced into something new, a magic mirror held up to our desires, hopes and fears. As elusive as a stag in a forest, Merlin continues to fascinate, enchant, and lead the way into a place where we may catch a glimpse of him passing by. A wink of sunlight, an echo of laughter, and he is gone. But never far, and never for long.

7

ENVOI

We may think that we have learned all there is to learn about Merlin – but a recent discovery made in Bristol Central Library in January of 2019 suggests otherwise. The press release trumpeted the 'chance discovery, hidden away in a series of sixteenth-century books deep in the archive' of the library.[1] Seven fragments of parchment were found, bound into a four-volume collection belonging to a French scholar named Jean Gerson (1363–1492). They were all from a version of the thirteenth-century *Lancelot-Grail* cycle published in Strasbourg between 1492 and 1502 and were written in French. They were from a part of the sequence known as the *Estoire de Merlin* (History of Merlin). On examination they were found not to contain any strikingly different details from other editions of the manuscript, despite some minor variants, but are of interest to scholars for the fact that they were created for a specific family and contained other romance manuscripts. A small group of Arthurian and medieval scholars are examining the pages, which will be published, with a full commentary, in the near future. Meanwhile, the pages are assumed to have been scraps from the printer's workshop, possibly disposed of following the publication of Malory's English version, *Le Morte D'Arthur*, which made extensive use of the original *Lancelot-Grail*.

This may not add anything significant to our knowledge of Merlin, but it opens the door to the possibility of further such discoveries in the future, while the level of interest generated among the general public once again shows how important the character of Merlin remains.

Appendix 1

THE POEMS OF MYRDDIN WYLLT, NEWLY TRANSLATED BY JOHN MATTHEWS, WITH A TRANSLATION OF '*PEIRYAN VABAN*' BY CAITLÍN MATTHEWS

1 '*Afallenau*' (Apple Trees)
2 '*Oianau*' (Greetings)
3 '*Y Bedwenni*' (Birches)
4 'The Dialogue of Myrddin and Taliesin'
5 'A Fugitive Poem of Myrddin in his Grave'
6 'A Dialogue Between Myrddin and his Sister Gwenddydd'
7 '*Peiryan Vaban*' (Commanding Youth)

Apart from the books of prophetic writings included by Geoffrey of Monmouth in the *Historia Regum Brittaniae*, the essential prophecies of Merlin are contained chiefly in poetic dialogues either between himself and the bard Taliesin, or his sister – Ganeida or Gwenddydd – who was herself recognised as a prophet. All are set during a period when Merlin lived in the wilderness and was visited by various people in search of wisdom. Though most were not copied out until the fourteenth or fifteenth centuries, they clearly include materials from older times. They are the nearest we can get to the authentic voice of Merlin.

The prophecies are for the most part of a general kind, referring to political events, battles and so on – and to known events and people. These are identifiable as separate from the underlying matter of the poems, remembering the terrible battle in which he lost his reason. He thinks often of his sister Gwenddydd, who has deserted him because he (apparently) killed her son, and of his enemies, who seek his destruction. Interspersed are prophecies of events which took place long after – anywhere from the eighth to the eleventh century, when heroes such as Cynan and Cadwaladyr had replaced Arthur as the expected deliverer of the Welsh.

At one time these poems may have formed verse interludes of a longer prose account of Myrddin's life – such as evidently formed the basis of Geoffrey of Monmouth's *Vita Merlini*, which tells the story at greater length, making evident use of the poems attributed to Myrddin.

In the '*Oianau*' ('Greetings') several verses are omitted here, as being later additions made after the coming of the Normans. As it is, verses 5 to 7 almost certainly belong in this category, with references to the Franks (Normans) which were probably inserted within the individual verses to replace references to the Saesons, Picts, or Scoti – the Dark Age enemies of Arthur and his men. Much of the poem still clearly refers to the story of Myrddin as it appears in the *Vita Merlini* – and to his long sojourn in the wilderness, 'snow to my knees, ice in my beard'. The rest is a pitiless catalogue of battle and death. The final image, of two bridges, suggests bridges of human bodies, which can almost never be sufficient until the end of time – a bleak prospect, as one might expect from the isolated spirit of Myrddin.

'*Afallenau*' ('Apple Trees') and '*Y Bedwenni*' ('Birches') consist of a series of prophecies, again mostly added long after Myrddin's time, which refer to events current at the time they were written down, probably in the fourteenth or fifteenth centuries. However, interspersed with these is a powerful account of Myrddin's madness, his escape from the Battle of Arderydd and the visions which followed.

The next poem takes the form of a dialogue between Taliesin and Merlin, in which both the similarities and differences between the two major bardic figures becomes clear. The poet who wrote this piece, whoever he may have been, clearly recognised the individuality of his characters. The prophecies are again of a general kind, with several interpolated references to medieval events. The reiterated sevens, the stark images of war and battle, bear the weight of truth. The two great bards strike sparks from each other as their *awen* lifts them into the realm where they can see what has been and what will be.

In 'A Fugitive Poem of Merlin in His Grave' and 'A Dialogue between Myrddin and his Sister Gwenddydd', which again follow the theme of the poet's life, underpin the prophetic content. In the latter poem, the initial two lines of Gwenddydd's questioning make reference to her brother's time in the forest. It is possible that the end of the poem, which shows some evidence of Christian doctoring, may once have formed part of a separate elegy on the death of Merlin written in the voice of his sister. Much of the imagery is unforgettable in its stark simplicity.

Finally, a poem called *Peiryan Vaban* ('Commanding Youth' or perhaps 'Cauldron Boy') gives us further clues to Myrddin's story. This is such a difficult poem that it has hardly ever been attempted in English. Caitlín Matthews' new version, included here, opens the door onto a scene in which Myrddin addresses either a younger version of himself, or possibly Taliesin, who was born from the inspirational Cauldron of Ceridwen. This difficult poem is found in a fifteenth-century source (Pen. 50, tt.36–8), between two poems that Merlin made in his madness, and, in stanza 3, refers to Merlin as a warrior.

The poems have been translated before, notably by W. F. Skene in the nineteenth century, and more recently by John K. Bollard, and Gwyneth Lewis & Rowan Williams. The former is far from satisfactory both in language or understanding of the meaning expressed by the poems; the latter are far better, though Dr Bollard sacrifices some of the poetic quality for the sake of accuracy. The new versions by Williams and Lewis are striking in their poetic content and form. In the translations which follow here, an attempt has been made to provide diplomatic accounts in which the obvious interpolations have been for the most part edited out, giving an idea of the quality and content of the original poems.

I

'Afallenau' ('Apple Trees')

Sweet appletree, your branches delight me,
Luxuriantly budding, my pride and joy!
I prophesy before the lord of Macreu,
That on Wednesday, in the valley of Machawy
Blood will flow.
Lloegyr's blades will shine.
But hear, O small pig!
On Thursday the Cymry will rejoice
In their defence of Cyminawd,
Furiously cutting and thrusting.
The Saesons will be slaughtered by our ashen spears,
And their heads used as footballs.
I prophesy the unvarnished truth –
The rising of a child in the secluded South.

II

Sweet and luxuriant appletree,
Great are its branches, beautiful its form!

I predict a battle, filling me with fear.

At Pengwern, men drink mead,

But around Cyminawd is a deadly hewing

By a chieftain from Eryri – till only hatred remains.

III

Sweet, yellow, appletree,

Growing in Tal Ardd,

I predict a battle at Prydyn,

In defence of frontiers.

Seven ships will come

Across a wide lake,

Seven hundred men come to conquer.

Of those that come, only seven will return

According to my prophecy.

IV

Sweet appletree of luxuriant growth!

I used to find food at its foot,

When, because of a maid,

I slept alone in the woods of Celyddon,

Shield on shoulder, sword on thigh.

Hear, small pig! listen to my words,

As sweet as birds that sing on Monday –

When sovereigns come across the sea,

The strength of the Cymry is blessed.

V

Sweet appletree in the glade,

Trodden is the earth at its base.

The men of Rhydderch see me not.

Gwenddydd no longer loves nor greets me,

I am hated by Rhydderch's strongest scion.
I have destroyed both his son and daughter:
Death visits them all – why not me?
After Gwenddolau no one will honour me,
No diversions attend me,
Nor fair women visit me.
Though at Arderydd I wore a golden torque
The swan-white woman despises me now.

VI

Sweet appletree, growing by the river,
Who will thrive on your wondrous fruit?
When my reason was intact
I used to lie at its foot
With a fair, eager girl, of slender form.
Now, fifty years the plaything of lawless men,
I have wandered in gloom among spirits.
After great wealth, with vociferous minstrels,
I have been here so long, not even sprites
Can lead me astray.
I never sleep, but tremble at the thought
Of my Lord Gwenddolau, and my own native people.
Long have I suffered unease and longing –
May I receive freedom in the end.

VII

Sweet appletree, with delicate blossom,
Growing, hidden, in the wood!
At daybreak the tale was told to me
That my words had offended a powerful man,
Not once, not twice, but three times in a day.
Ah! that my end had come

Before the death of Gwenddydd's son
Was upon my hands!

VIII

Sweet appletree with your delicate blossom,
Growing amid the thickets of trees!
The *Chwyfleian* foretells,
A tale that will come to pass:
A staff of gold, signifying bravery
Will be given by the glorious Dragon Kings.
The graceful one will vanquish the profane,
And before a child, bright and bold,
The Saesons shall fall, and bards flourish.

IX

Sweet appletree of crimson colour,
Hidden in the wood of Celyddon –
Though men seek your fruit, their search is vain,
Until Cadwaladyr comes from Cadfaon's meeting
To Teiwi river and Tywi's lands,
Till anger and anguish come from Aranwynion,
And the Long-Hairs are tamed.

X

Sweet appletree of crimson colour,
Growing, concealed, in the wood of Celyddon:
Though men seek your fruit, their search is vain,
Till Cadwaladyr comes from Rhyd Rheon's meeting,
And with Cynon advances against the Saesons.
The victorious Cymry, glorious their leaders,
Shall have their rights again,

All Britons rejoice, sounding their horns,
Chanting songs of joy and peace!

2

'*Oianau*' ('Greetings')

Listen, small pig,
Happy small pig!
Don't go rooting
On the mountain top.
Stay here, instead,
Secluded in the wood –
Hidden from the dogs
Of Rhydderch the Faithful.

I will prophecy –
It will be the truth! –
From Aber Taradyr
The Cyrmy will be bound
Under one warlike leader
Of the line of Gwynedd.
Usurpers of the Prydein
He will overcome them all.

Listen, small pig,
We should hide
From the huntsmen of Mordei
Lest we be discovered.
If we escape –
I'll not complain of fatigue! –
I'll predict,
From the back of the ninth wave,

The truth of the White One
Who rode Dyfed to exhaustion,
Who built a church
For those who only half believed.
Until Cynan comes
Nothing will be restored.

Listen, small pig!
I lack sleep,
Such a tumult of grief is within me.
Fifty years of pain I have endured.
Once I saw Gwenddolau,
With the gift of Princes,
Slaughtering prey on every side;
Now he's beneath the sod –
But restless still.
He was the Lord of the North,
And the gentlest man.

Listen, small pig,
Don't sleep yet!
Rumours reach me
Of perjured chieftains,
Of tight-fisted farmers.
Soon, over the sea,
Shall come men in armour –
Two-faced men
On armoured horses,
With destroying spears.
When that happens,
War will come,
Fields be ploughed

But never reaped.
Women will be cuckolds
To the corpses of their men.
Mourning will come to Caer Sallawg.

Listen, small pig,
Pig of truth!
The Sybil has told me
A wondrous tale.
I predict a Summer full of fury,
Treachery between brothers.
A pledge of peace will be required
From Gwynedd,
Seven hundred ships from Gynt
Blown in by the North wind.
In Aber Dyn they will confer.

Listen, small pig,
Blessed pig!
The Sybil has told me
A frightful thing:
When Llogria encamps
In the lands of Eddlyn,
Making Deganwy a strong fort
Between Llogrian and Cymru,
A leaping child will appear,
And the Franks will flee.
At Aber Dulas they will fall,
Sweating in bloody garments.

Listen, small pig,
Go to Gwynedd,

Seek a mate when you rest.
While Rhydderch feasts in his hall
He does not know
What sleeplessness I bear
Every night –
Snow to my knees,
Ice in my hair –
Sad my fate!

Listen, small pig!
Blessed pig!
If you had seen
All I have seen
You would not sleep,
Nor root on the hill.

Listen, small pig,
Is not the mountain green?
In my thin cloak
I get no repose!
I grow pale because
Gwenddydd does not come.

Listen, small pig,
O bit of brawn!
Don't bury your snout.
Love is neither pledge nor play.
This advice I give to Gwernabwy:
Don't be a wanton.
I'll predict now the battle of Machawy,
Where ruddy spears will shine in Rhiw Dymdwy,
– the work of contentious chiefs.

Men will sit, breasts heaving, on their saddles,
And there will be mourning, and woeful looks.
A bear will arise in Deheubarth,
Whose men will infest Mynwy.
A blessed fate awaits Gwenddydd
When Dyfed's prince comes to rule.

Listen, small pig!
Are not the thorn buds green
Is not the mountain fair,
The earth beautiful?
I will predict the battle of Argoed Llewifain,
Bloody biers after Owein's assault.
When stewards dispute,
When children are perjured,
When Cadwaladyr conquers Mona –
The Saeson will be driven out!

Listen, small pig!
Wonders there will be
In Prydein –
But I shall not care.
When the people of Môn
Ask questions of the Britons,
There will come a troublesome time!
A superior lord will appear:
Cynan, from the banks of the Teiwi.
Confusion will follow –
But he shall have the music of Bards to hear!

Listen, small pig –
Do you hear the birds at Caerleon?

I wish I stood on Mynydd Maon
Watching the Bright Ones dance.
Instead I'll prophesy
Battle after battle:
At Machawy, on a river,
At Cors Fochno, at Minron,
At Cyminawd, at Caerleon,
And the battle of Abergwaith,
And the battle of Ieithion ...
And when this music shall end,
A child will come,
And the Britons will know better days.

Listen, small pig,
O little, spotted friend!
Can you hear the seabirds crying?
A day will come when even minstrels
Will be sent away without their portion.
Though they stand at the door,
No gift will come.
A far-flying seagull told me
That strangers will come:
Gwyddyl, Brython, Romans.
There will be confusion then!
And the names of the Gods
Will be taken in vain!
Fighting on both banks of the Tywi.

Listen, small pig,
O stout-legged, little one!
Listen to the voices of the sea-birds –
Great their clamour.

Minstrels will get no honour,
No fair portion theirs;
In a time when hospitality is rejected,
A youth with strong feelings will come.
Then two Idrises will contend for the land,
And their contention will be long.

Listen, small pig!
It's no use my hearing,
The scream of the gulls.
My hair is thin,
My covering likewise.
The vales are my barn –
But short on corn.
My summer harvest
Brings small relief.
Once, my passion was boundless;
Now I predict,
Before the world ends,
Shameless women,
Passionless men!

Listen small pig –
Little trembling one!
Under this thin blanket,
I find no repose.
Since the battle of Arderydd
I no longer care,
If the sky falls
Or the seas overflow.
But I predict that after many kings
With one bridge on the Taw

And another on the Tywi,
There will be an end to war.

3
'Y Bedwenni' ('Birches')

Blessed is the birch in the Valley of Wye,
Whose branches fall one by one, two by two.
Still it will stand when battle comes to Ardudwy,
When cattle moan round the ford of Mochnwy,
And Spears and war-cries are heard in Degannwy;
When Edwin holds sway on Môn,
And pale, untried youths
In bloody clothes command.

Blessed the birch on Plynlimon!
It will see the stag exalted,
It will see mail-clad Franks,
Hearths bearing food, only for wild beasts,
Monks fighting every day on steeds!

Blessed the birch on Dinwythy height,
That will know when battle comes to Ardudwy,
When spears are raised in Edryfwy,
And bridges on the Taf and Tawy,
And a third, unfortunate,
On both banks of the Gwy.
The one who makers them, his name will be Garwy,
May the chieftain of Môn rule well.

Women will lie down for the Danes,
And men feel affliction.
Happier than I the man who lives to see

The time of Cadwaladyr –
May he sing a good song!

4

'The Dialogue of Myrddin and Taliesin'

MYRDDIN

How sad, how sad,
Cedfyl and Cadfan are fallen!
The slaughter was terrible,
Shields shattered and bloody.

TALIESIN

I saw Maelgwn battling –
The host acclaimed him.

MYRDDIN

Before two men in battles they stand,
Before Erith and Gwrith on pale horses.
Slender bay mounts they bring,
Soon after comes the host of Elgan.
Alas for his death, after such a great journey!

TALIESIN

Gap-toothed Rhys, his shield a span –
To him came battle's blessing.
Cyndur has fallen, deplorable beyond measure.
Generous men have been slain –
Three notable men, greatly esteemed by Elgan.

MYRDDIN

Again and again, in great throngs they came.
There came Bran and Melgan to meet me.

At the last, they slew Dyel,
The son of Erbin, with all his men.

TALIESIN
Swiftly came Maelgwn's men,
Warriors ready for battle, for slaughter armed.
For this battle, Arderydd, they have made
A lifetime of preparation.

MYRDDIN
A host of spears flew high, drawing blood
From a host of warriors –
A host, fleeing, a host, wounded –
A host – bloody – retreating.

TALIESIN
The seven sons of Elifer, seven heroes,
Will fail to avoid seven spears in the battle.

MYRDDIN
Seven fires, seven armies,
Cynfelyn in every seventh place.

TALIESIN
Seven spears, seven rivers of blood
From seven chieftains fallen.

MYRDDIN
Seven score heroes, maddened by battle,
To the forest of Celyddon they fled.
Since I, Myrddin, am second only to Taliesin,
Let my words be heard as truth.

5

'A Fugitive Poem of Myrddin in His Grave'

He who speaks from the grave
Knows that before seven years
King March will die.

I have drunk from a bright cup
With fierce and warlike lords;
My name is Myrddin, son of Morvran.

I have drunk from a goblet
With powerful warlords;
Myrddin is my given name.

When the black wheel of oppression
Comes to destroy exhausted Logres
Defence will be bitter and sustained.
The White Mount will see sorrow
A long regret to the people of the Cymry.

Protection won't be found
From the Boar of the Hosts,
Even in the heights of Ardudwy
Or the Cymry's secret ports.

When the redhaired Normans come
And a castle is built at Aber Hodni
Greatly taxed will be the Logrians –
Predictions too will be costly.
When the Freckled One comes
As far as Ryd Bengarn,

Men will face disgrace,
Their sword-hilts will break,
The new King of Prydain
Will be their judge.

When Henri comes to claim
Mur Castell on Eryri's border
Trouble across the sea will call him.

When the Pale One comes to London
Upon an ugly horse –
He will call for the lords of Caergain.

Scarce the acorns, thick the corn
When a young king appears
Causing men to tremble.
A youth of great renown
Conqueror of a hundred cities –
Tender and frail will be his life.
Towards the weak he will be strong;
Towards the people of the upland too –
His coming will bring dark days.

Wantonness will rule,
Women be easy prey –
Even children will need to confess.
But a time of order will follow
When churls will do good deeds;
Maidens will be lovely,
Youths resolute.

A time will follow, near the end of the age,
When the young will fail from adversity
And cuckoos die in May.

There will be a time of hunting dogs,
Of buildings in secret places,

When even a shirt will cost a fortune.
There will be a time of profanity,
When vices are active, and churches empty.
Words and relics will be broken
Truth will vanish, falsehood spread
Faith will grow weak, disputes abound.

There will be a time when clothing seems delightful
When counsellors become vagrants;
Bards will go empty-handed,
Through priests are happy;
Men will be despised, and often refused.

There will be a time of windless days without rain,
With little ploughing and less food,
One acre of land worth nine.

Men will be weak and unmanly
And corn grown under trees –
Though feasts will still take place.

When trees are held in high estate
There will be a new spring
But an evil king –
A cowshed worth more than a cow.

On Wednesday, a time of violence,
Blades will wear out,
Two will be bloodied at Cynghen.

At Aber Sor there will be a council
Of men following on the battle,
A bright ruler ruling the camp.

In Aber Avon the host of Môn congregate
Angles gather at Hinwedon;
Meryon's valour will be long remembered

In Aber Dwyver a leader will fail
From the actions of Gwidig
After the battle of Cyvarllug.
A battle will be on the River Byrri,
Where Britons will have victory.
Gwhyr's men will be heroes.

An Aber Don a battle will happen
And spears be unequal.
Blood on the brows of Saxons.
Servile you are today, Gwenddydd!

The mountain-spirits come to me
Here in Aber Carav.

6

'A Dialogue Between Myrddyn and His Sister Gwenddydd'

GWENDDYDD
I have come here to tell
Of the rule I have in the North;
Every region's beauty is known to me.

MYRDDIN
Since the action at Arderydd and Erydon
Gwenddydd, and all that happened to me,
I am Dull of wits –
Where shall I go for delight?

GWENDDYDD
I speak to my twin brother
Myrddin, wiseman and diviner,
Since he is used to making disclosures
When a woman goes to him.

MYRDDIN

I will sing like a simpleton,

Ominous with fears for the Cymry.

The wind tells me

Rhydderch Hael's standard cannot fall.

GWENDDYDD

Though Rhydderch is pre-eminent

And all the Cymry under him –

Who can possibly follow him?

MYRDDIN

Rhydderch Hael, feller of foes,

Dealt many wounds

On the blissful day at the ford of Tawy.

GWENDDYDD

Rhydderch Hael, while he is the enemy

Of the bardic city in Clyd

Where will he come to the ford?

MYRDDIN

I will tell the fair Gwenddydd

Since she has asked so skilfully –

After tomorrow Rhydderch will cease to be.

GWENDDYD

I ask my far-famed twin,

Intrepid battler,

Who comes after Rhydderch?

MYRDDIN

As Gwenddolau was slain at bloody Arderydd,

And I have come from amid the furz –
Morgant Mawr, son of Sadyrnin.

GWENDDYDD
I ask my far-famed brother,
Who fosters song amid the streams –
Who will rule after Morgant?

MYRDDIN
As Gwenddolau was slain at bloody Arderydd,
And as I wonder why anyone should see me –
The country will call to Urien.

GWENDDYDD
As your hair is white as hoar frost
And God has answered your need –
Who will rule after Urien?

MYRDDIN
Great affliction has fallen upon me,
And I am sick of life –
Maelgwyn Hir will rule over Gwynedd.

GWENDDYDD
I pine every time I leave my brother,
Tears furrow my tired cheek –
After Maelgwyn, who will rule?

MYRDDIN
Rhun is his name, impetuous in battle,
Foremost in the rank of the army –
Woe to Prydain when his day dawns.

GWENDDYDD

As both friend and companion of slaughter
Men will name you leader –
Who will rule Gwynedd after Rhun?

MYRDDIN

Rhun, renowned in battle!
What I say will come to pass!
Gwynedd will fall next to Beli.

GWENDDYDD

I ask my far-famed twin brother
Stalwart in the face of hardship –
Who rules after Beli?

MYRDDIN

Since mountain spirits have taken my reason
And I myself am full of thoughts.
After Beli, his son Iago.

GWENDDYDD

Since mountain spirits have taken your reason,
And you are filled with thoughts.
Who will rule after Iago?

MYRDDIN

He that comes before me with a lofty brow,
Seeking social advancement.
After Iago, his son Cadvan.

GWENDDYDD

Your words have always predicted

That one of universal fame shall appear.
Who will rule after Cadvan?

MYRDDIN
The world shall hear of Brave Cadwallawn.
The heads of his enemies shall fall
And the whole world will admire it.

GWENDDYDD
Though I see tears on your cheeks,
I am bound to ask –
Who will come after Cadwallawn?

MYRDDIN
A tall man conferring with others
All of Prydain under one rule –
The Cymry's best son, Cadwaladyr.
Whoever comes after one so great
Seems worthless.
After Cadwaladyr, Idwal.

GWENDDYDD
I ask you gently,
far-famed, best of men –
Who will rule after Idwal?

MYRDDIN
There will rule after Idwal
As a result of another being summoned
White-shielded Howel, Cadwal's son.

GWENDDYDD
I ask my far-famed twin brother,
Brave in war:
Who will come after Howel?

MYRDDIN

I shall tell of his great fame,
Gwenddydd, before our parting,
After Howel, Rodri.

Cynan will come to Mona
Failing in his authority;
And before the son of Rodri is called
The son of Caeledigan will appear.

GWENDDYDD

On the world's account I ask
And answer me if you will –
Who will rule after Cynan?

MYRDDIN

Since Gwenddolau was slain at Arderydd
You feel only fear –
Mervyn Vrych, from Manaw.

GWENDDYDD

I ask my renowned brother
Lucid in song, best of men
Who will come after Mervyn?

MYRDDIN

I declare without anger,
But from concern – Prydain will be oppressed:
After Mervyn will come Rodri Mawr.

GWENDDYDD

I ask my far-famed twin brother,
Intrepid at the sound of the war-cry
Who will rule after Rodri Mawr?

MYRDDIN

On Conway's banks in the midst of the conflict
Admired will be the eloquent lord –
Anarawd – the aged sovereign.

GWENDDYDD

I address my far-famed twin brother,
Who bravely faced mockery –
Who will rule after Anarawd?

MYRDDIN

He who comes next
Is nearer the time of the unseen visitors –
Sovereignty will be in the hands of Howel.
The Borderers, men who hold back,
Will never reach Paradise –
Church or laity, both are as bad.

GWENDDYDD

I ask my beloved brother
Whom I have heard so often celebrated –
Who will rule after the Borderers?

MYRDDIN

A year and a half of chattering barons
Their rule short-lived –
Any who stumble will be cursed.

GWENDDYDD

As a companion of Cunllaith,
Mercy be to you –
Who will rule after the Barons?

MYRDDIN

One will arise from obscurity
Who nonetheless will fail –
Cynan of the Dogs will hold the Cymry.

GWENDDYDD

On the world's behalf I ask you –
Answer me gently –
Who will rule after Cynan?

MYRDDIN

A man from a far country
Who will batter down our cities –
They say – a king raised from a baron.

GWENDDYDD

On the world's account I ask,
Since you know the truth –
Who will come after the Baron?

MYRDDIN

I foretell the name of Severn Wyn,
A true, white-shielded messenger,
Brave, strong as a prison wall.
He will cross the lands of the traitors
Who will tremble as far as Prydain.

GWENDDYDD

I ask my blessed brother,
Indeed, I require it –
Who will rule after Serven Wyn?

MYRDDIN

Two white shielded Belis

Will appear to cause tumult.

Golden peace there will not be.

GWENDDYDD

I ask my far-famed twin brother

Intrepid among the Cymry –

Who will rule after the Belis?

MYRDDIN

A passionate, beneficent lord

Who councils defence,

Will rule before a great disaster.

GWENDDYDD

I ask my far-famed twin brother,

Brave in battle

Who is this passionate one

Whom you predict –

What name, what man, and when?

MYRDDIN

Gryffyd his name, brave and handsome,

He will throw lustre on all his kin,

And he will rule over Prydain.

GWENDDYDD

I ask my far-famed brother

Intrepid in battle –

Who shall possess the land after Gryffyd?

MYRDDIN

I declare it without rancour,

Oppression will follow –

After Gryffyd, Gwyn Gwarther.

GWENDDYDD

I ask my famous brother

Intrepid in war –

Who will rule after Gwyn Gwarther?

MYRDDIN

Alas fair Gwenddydd! the oracle's words

Are as terrible as those of the Sybil

Of odious stock will be the two Idrises;

For land admired, for judgement vilified.

GWENDDYDD

I ask my far-famed brother,

Intrepid in battles –

Who will come after them?

MYRDDIN

I predict what no youth will venture –

A king, a lion with a steady hand,

Gylvin Gevel with a wolf like grasp.

GWENDDYDD

I ask my profound brother

Whom I have tenderly nourished –

After that who will reign?

MYRDDIN

To the very number of the stars

His followers are compared –
Mackwy Dau Hanner.

GWENDDYDD
I ask my naked brother
The difficult question, the lord's beneficence –
Who will rule after Dau Hanner?

MYRDDIN
Tongues will cry out in battle,
At the fierce conflict among the Cymry –
He is a lord of eight Caers.

GWENDDYDD
I ask my pensive brother,
Who has read Cado's book –
Who will ruler after this lord?

MYRDDIN
From Rheged he comes –
Since I am seriously questioned –
The whelp of illustrious Henri
Never in his time will deliverance come.

GWENDDYDD
I ask my brother, renowned, famous,
Undaunted among the Cymry –
Who will rule after the son of Henri?

MYRDDIN
Two bridges there will be –
One on the Tav, one on the Tywi.
Confusion upon Llogres.

After Henri's son
Many kings will bring trouble.

GWENDDYDD
I ask my blessed brother,
And it is I who ask it –
Who will rule after these kings?

MYRDDIN
A foolish king will come
And the men of Llogres will confuse him;
The land will case to prosper under him.

GWENDDYDD
Fair Myrddin, of fame-conferring song,
Wrathful you are concerning the world –
What will be in the time of the foolish one?

MYRDDIN
With Llogres groaning,
And Cymyr full of woe,
An army will traverse the land.

GWENDDYDD
Fair Myrddin, gifted in speech,
Tell me no falsehood –
Who will follow this army?

MYRDDIN
There will come one of six
Long hidden in concealment;
He will have mastery over Llogres.

GWENDDYDD

Fair Myrddin, of famous stock,
Let the wind revolve within the house –
Who will rule after that?

MYRDDIN

Owein will come,
Right to the gates of London,
Bringing good tidings.

GWENDDYDD

Fair Myrddin, most gifted and famed,
I believe your words –
How long will Owein rule?

MYRDDIN

Gwenddydd, listen to rumours.
Let the wind moan in the valley,
Seven years, as was long since known.

GWENDDYDD

I ask my profound brother,
Whom I have tenderly nourished,
Who will then be sovereign?

MYRDDIN

When Owein comes to Manaw,
The battle for Prydain will be close at hand,
There will be one commanding others.

GWENDDYDD

I ask my profound brother,

Whom I have tenderly nourished,
After that who will be sovereign?

MYRDDIN
A good and noble ruler will he be,
Who will conquer the land,
And bring joy to all.

GWENDDYDD
I ask my profound brother,
Whom I have tenderly nourished –
Who will be sovereign then?

MYRDDIN
Let there be a cry in the valley!
Beli Hir and his whirlwind warriors –
Blessed by the Cymry, woe to Gynt.

GWENDDYDD
I ask my far-famed twin brother,
Brave in battle –
After Beli who will possess the land?

MYRDDIN
Let there be a cry in Aber!
Beli Hir and his numerous troops –
Blessed by the Cymry, woe to the Gwyddyl.

GWENDDYDD
I address my far-famed brother,
Mighty in war –
Why woe to the Gwyddyl?

MYRDDIN

I predict that one prince above others
Will rule Gwynedd, and after affliction
Will have victory over all.

GWENDDYDD

The lord of Marvryn, how strong for us
Is Myrddin Vrych with his mighty host –
What comes before this joy?

MYRDDIN

When Cadwaladyr descends
With a great host,
He will defeat the men of Gwynedd –
But then will the men of Caer Gamwedd come!

GWENDDYDD

Don't depart from converse,
From a dislike of questioning –
In what place will Cadwaladyr descend?

MYRDDIN

When Cadwaladyr descends
To the valley of the Tywi,
Hard pressed will the Abers be –
Britons shall depose Brithwyr.

GWENDDYDD

I ask my profound brother,
Whom I have tenderly nourished –
Who will rule after that?

MYRDDIN

When a fool knows three languages
In Môn, and his son be honoured –
Gwynedd will be rich.

GWENDDYDD

Who will drive the Llogrians back?
Who will move upon Dyfed?
Who will succour the Cymry?

MYRDDIN

The great rout and tumult of Rhydderch,
The armies of Cadwaladyr.
Above the river Tardennin
The key will be broken.

GWENDDYDD

Don't leave me here
Because you hate converse –
What death will carry off Cadwaladyr?

MYRDDIN

A spear will pierce him
Made of wood from a ship.
That day will disgrace the Cymry.

GWENDDYDD

Do not depart from me
Because you hate converse –
How long will Cadwaladyr rule?

MYRDDIN

Three months of a long year,

A full three hundred days,
With many battles he will rule.

GWENDDYDD
Do not depart
For fear of questioning –
Who will ruler after Cadwaladyr?

MYRDDIN
I declare to you Gwenddydd,
From age to age I predict:
After Cadwaladyr, Cynda.

A hand on the cross of every sword,
Let all take care of their lives –
With Cynda there is no reconciliation.

I foretell that one prince will come,
A prince of Gwynedd, after much affliction,
Who will overcome all opposition …

From that time the Cymry suffer
Without help, and failing in their hope –
It is impossible to say who will rule.

Gwenddydd, delicate and fair,
First will be the greatest in Prydain –
Lament, wretched Cymry!

When killing becomes the first duty
From sea to sea, across all the land –
Is the world at an end, lady…?

GWENDDYDD

My twin-brother, well you have answered me,
Myrddin, son of Morvran the skilful –
Yet your tale is sad.

MYRDDIN

I declare to you, Gwenddydd,
Since you have asked me seriously,
Warfare, lady, will have an end.

All that I have predicted
To you Gwenddydd, this glory of princes,
Will come to pass – to the smallest detail.

GWENDDYDD

Twin-brother, since these things will happen'
Even to the souls of our brethren –
What sovereign will come after?

MYRDDIN

Fairest Gwenddydd, courteous one –
I declare it powerfully –
There will be no more kings!

GWENDDYDD

Alas, dear one, for the separation to come.
After this tumult
You may well be placed in the earth
By a king who is brave and fearless.

I am left cheerless by the thought
Of your passing –

A delay will be the best respite
For he who has spoken truth.

Arise from your rest,
Open the book of *Awen* without fear.
Hear the discourse of a girl,
Give repose to your dreams.

Dead is Morgenau, dead Cyvrennin Moryal.
Dead is Moryen, bulwark of battle –
The heaviest grief is for you, Myrddin.

MYRDDIN
I feel heavy affliction.
Dead is Morgenau, dead Mordav,
Dead is Moryen ... I wish to die!

GWENDDYDD
My only brother, chide me not.
Since the battle of Arderydd I have suffered.
It is instruction I seek.

MYRDDIN
I also, I commend thee
To the Chieftain of Chieftains –
Fair Gwenddydd, refuge of songs.

GWENDDYDD
Too long have my songs continued,
Concerning things to be.
Would that they should come to pass!

MYRDDIN

Gwenddydd, be not dissatisfied.

Have not all burdens been consigned to earth?

Everyone must give up what he loves.

While I live, I will not forsake you,

And until death will keep you in mind –

Your fear is the greatest weight.

GWENDDYDD

Swift the steed, free the winds –

I commend my blameless brother

to the supreme Caer.

MYRDDIN

I too commend my sister

To the supreme Caer.

7

'*Peiryan Vaban*' ('**Commanding Youth**')

Translated by Caitlín Matthews

[I]

Commanding Youth, cease your sadness!

God protect you from the Irish tribes,

On the road to the Irish Hill, fiendish encounter,

Thick with Franks and Irish.

Aedan will come across the spreading sea,

And hosts in their hundreds from Manaw will join him,

From the islands on the way to the Irish Hill.

Fiendish battle! Mighty assault!

[II]

Commanding Youth, cease your sighing!

Aedan will come across the spreading sea,

But the Youth shall not be caught by thunder nor by lightning.

Many forays and tramplings, many weapon-holders in Aedan's pay,

Many long-headed lances, many tall spears,

Come to seize the land. Gafran increases.

Many breastplates, many helmets on heads, intent on cattle;

Many red swords, many gruff squires bent on warrior slaughter,

Many lively steeds, many light, broad shields shining.

And he says to Gwenddydd, when daylight dawns, then the
   prophecy will unfold,

And he says to Gwasawg, he respects neither shelter, fold nor
   church.

[III]

Commanding Youth, stem your weeping!

Out of the dark air we usually hear rain.

Aedan will come with host after pelting host.

But Gwenddydd does not know what his hands will do.

Brother joins zealously with brother

Because they will not tolerate invasion here nor oppression.

Except one who has been led into affliction.

Alas, that loss of skill is upon him!

Myrddin son of Morwyn was a white hawk

Whenever there was a fierce resistance to fight,

Whenever there was joyous death, whenever shields waved

Whenever there was heart's blood to avenge.

Out of respect for the memory of Gwenddolau and his
   companions,

Woe is upon me, till death slow that day's approach!

[IV]

Commanding Youth, take your counsel!

It is natural that the generous take precedence.

From Rhydderch Hael's encounter may there be deliverance,

But if it goes ill, no life will be spared.

Mine have been the prophecies among the deeps and shallows,

With the van of the battle because their courage.

Once there was a time when I sat in a court,

Attired in red and purple;

But today, neither my cheek nor body is comely.

It is easy for maidens to overlook me.

[V]

Commanding Youth, end your sadness.

Lamentation is not joyful, nor is it best.

Merlin will come, great his purpose,

Because of the slaughter of my brothers and Gwenddolau;

Llewelyn. Gwgon, best of the generous;

Einion, Rywallon, lord of every battle.

The clash of Rhydderch with Aedan at Alcluid,

Resounds clearly from north to south.

And he says to Gwenddydd, when the bright dawn breaks

The woods will be full of armed men.

[VI]

Commanding Youth, seek your rest.

It is normal to sing sweetly when sleep is desired.

It is natural to give food to suppliants, natural for lovers to love
    each other.

It is usual for there to be rivalry between equally matched men.

But it is unnatural for there to be hatred between men of one
    lineage.

It is natural for an angry knight to be leader of a host,

And for ravens to stoop on carrion, and for flesh-hooks to be
    black.

It is unusual for the wicked to spare cheek or eye,

Or brain pan, though he be attacked...

– Thus Merlin sang.

Appendix 2

TWO MERLIN POEMS BY GIORDANO BRUNO

The following brief poems are taken from the text of *De Umbris Idearum*[1] by the Renaissance magician and philosopher Giordano Bruno, who in many ways resembles the character of Merlin. They are placed here as points of interest, showing how Merlin was perceived at the time. They are witty and a little mysterious, as one might expect. (Translations by the author.)

'Merlin the Temperate Judge'

In Phrygia lies a river named Gallus,
Whoever drinks from it,
Even just a little,
Cures the body of all ills.
According to the letters of the wise,
If you drink till you are full
Until you are utterly alive,
You need never drink again,
Be civil in your life,
Rejoice greatly –

For to drink too much brings trouble
Tosses you furiously about,
Flings you madly around.
Having made it thus far,
To avoid more pain
Choose mastery,
Seek to honour wisdom –
Touch with the lips,
Smell with the nose,
For it's not so good
When the judge is in a hurry
To pull the ears of Midas.

'Merlin the Knowing Judge'

There are those who would use a dog to pull a plough,
That would climb to the stars on a camel's back.
There's a frog who would cross the river on a shrew's back,
Those who would hunt from the backs of asses,
Those who use wolves to hunt cuckoos,
Those who would like pigs to fly,
Who always use the wrong tools.
This is like the organ maker's work,
From digging, or fishing,
Or learning to fly,
Or to hunt with the right steeds.
If you don't use the right kind of effort,
For flying, fishing, hunting,
It won't be me who weeps,
But you who navigates
The Labyrinth without a thread.

NOTES

Chapter 1

1. Matthews *The Shamanism Bible*, 2014
2. The Gododdin. Trans. Koch. 1997
3. Williams and Lewis, 2019
4. Bromwich, 2014
5. Ibid pp228-9
6. Matthews, Taliesin 2000 Chapters 2 and 5
7. Skene, 1995
8. Timothy Lewis, 2017
9. Anderson, 1991
10. Morris *British History and The Welsh Annals*, 1998
11. Bromwich, 2014
12. Bromwich, 1969 'Trioedd Ynys Prydein: the Myrvyrian Series' pp127-156
13. Parry 1925; Clarke, 1973
14. Ed. & Trans. Lewis Thorpe. Penguin Books, 1976
15. *British History & The Welsh Annals* Ed. & Trans. John Morris, 1988
16. Parry, 1925 Trans. Matthews

17. Ibid.
18. For a full exploration of Taliesin see Matthews, *Taliesin*, 2000
19. Matthews: *The Shamanism Bible*, 2014
20. *Historia* Ed. Reeve, Trans. Wright, 2007
21. Wace. Trans. J Weiss 2005
22. Trans. Winthrop Wetherbee, 2010
23. Barney, 2010. *The Etymologies of Isadore of Seville*
24. Parry, *Vita Merlini* 1925
25. See Forbes, A. P., 1894, for the Life of Kentigern by Joscelyn
26. McQueen (1989) *Vita Merlini Sylvestris*.
27. Ibid p83 trans. Matthews.
28. Scottichronicon, 1981-1983.

Chapter 2

1. Bromwich, 2014 pp14–16
2. Ed. Reeve; Trans. N. Wright, 2007
3. British History & The Welsh Annals Ed. & Trans. J. Morris, 1988
4. Vita Merlini Trans J. J. Parry, 1925
5. Kendrick, 1950 p7.
6. The original MSS of the *Prophecies* remains unedited in a modern edition. Most of the material is included in the *Historia* Book VII. For a commentary see Eckhardt, Caroline D. Ed. *The Prophetia Merlini of Geoffrey of Monmouth: A Fifteenth Century English Commentary*, 1982.
7. Lucan. *Pharsalia*. Trans R. Graves 1956
8. William of Newburgh, Trans. P.G. Walsh and M.J. Kennedy, 2007
9. Giraldus Cambrensis, *Expugnatio Hibernica* 2004
10. Michael Curley.1982 pp217–249
11. *Armes Prydain Fawr* Trans R. Bromwich 2014
12. Michael Feletra, 'Merlin in Cornwall' 2012, pp304–338

13. Matthews, 'Auguries, Dreams & Incubatory Sleep' in Stewart 1990; Ettlinger, E. 1948 pp97–111

14. Duggan, 2013

15. *Cormac's Glossary* Ed. Stokes; Trans. J. O'Donovan, 1868. Insertions in square brackets mine.

16. ibid

17. ibid

18. Chadwick 1934/5

19. ibid

20. *Cormac's Glossary*. Trans O'Donovan1868

21. *King Arthur's Raid*, Matthews & Matthews, 2003

22. 'The Three Cauldrons'. Trans. C. Matthews. *Encyclopaedia of Celtic Myth and Legend*, 2003.

23. Gerald of Wales Ed. Radice,1978

24. Ibid.

25. Meyer, K. *Eriu* 1, 1904.

26. Ibid.

27. Melia, 1983

28. *The Life of Merlin* by Thomas Heywood, Carmarthen,1985

29. Raphael Hollinshed, *Chronicles*, 2011

30. Heywood pp48–50

31. C. H. Herford, Percy Simpson, and Evelyn Simpson (eds), *Ben Jonson, Vol. 10:* 1950

32. Ibid

33. Lily, W. *England's Prophetical Merline*, Pareidge,1664

34. Swift, J. Ed. Williams, 1958

35. Ibid p244

36. Ibid p258

37. Historia pp124–125

38. Ibid.

39. R.J. Stewart, 1986 *The Prophetic Vision of Merlin*

40. Meixell, Amanda S. 2005[2006]. pp 59–82

41. Ibid.

42. Rowley and Shakespeare, Ed Stewart, 1998.

43. Dryden/Purcell *King Arthur, or Merlin, or the British Enchanter,* 2010

44. William Blake: From a Notebook of 1793, Open Book Publications,1977.

Chapter 3

1. Wace. *Arthurian Chronicles,* Trans. E. Mason, 1962

2. *Historia*: Trans. Sebastian Evens, 1963

3. Wace. *Arthurian Chronicles,* Trans. E. Mason, 1962

4. G. Ashe 'Merlin in the Earliest Records', 1987. P 37.

5. *Historia,* Trans. Sebastian Evens, 1963

6. Geoffrey of Monmouth, quoting *De Deo Socrate.* trans. G. Hudson Gurney, 1878

7. Quoted in Curley, 'Conjuring History' p232

8. 'De Deo Socrate,' 1878 p357

9. Curley, Michael J. 'Conjuring History' pp232

10. N Bryant, *Merlin and the Grail,* 2001 pp45–113

11. *Historia* trans L. Thorpe

12. Lacy et al. *Lancelot-Grail* Boydell, 2010 vol 1

13. Malcor and Littleton: *From Scythia to Camelot; The Roman King Arthur.* Malcor & Matthews (forthcoming)

14. *Le Morte D'Arthur,* Book 2, chapter xxv.

15. *Le Morte Darthur* Book I, Ch. xxv.

16. Wace. Trans. E. Mason 1962 p55

17. Lacey, L et al. *Lancelot-Grail.* Vol. 1

18. Tatlock, 1974. P201

19. Alexander Neckam, 1966

20. Trans J. Ford, 1977.

21. Virgil *Eclogue IV* Trans. Fairclough, 1916.

22. Malory Bk 2 ch. vi

Chapter 4

1. Jarman, 1969, p112
2. Paton, 1960.
3. Lacy, et al *Lancelot-Grail*. (Ystoria Merlin) 1980
4. Wheatley, Ed. *The English Prose Merlin*, vol 1. modernised by the author.
5. Ibid.
6. *Huth Merlin* included in Lacy, *Lancelot-Grail*, vol 2
7. Guest, *Mabinogion* pp62–65
8. *Le Morte D'Arthur* Ed. Matthews. Book III chs 1–2
9. Ibid. Book III chs 3–4
10. Ibid Bk IV ch.1.
11. Didot Perceval Trans D, Skeels, 1961 pp14–15
12. Ibid pp46–8
13. Adolf, 1946 pp173–193
14. Jarman, 1969 p73
15. Ibid. p74
16. *Vita Merlini*. Trans J.J. Parry, 1925
17. R Graves. *The White Goddess* pp213
18. *Historia*. Trans Lewis Thorpe, pp48–51
19. Ibid, pp 64–8
20. Varro. *Antiquitates rerum humanarum et divinarum*, 2019

Chapter 5

1. Bromwich, 1969 pp127–156.
2. *Faerie Queene*. Book 2.
3. *Historia* Trans. Thorpe, pp73–4
4. Mackley, J. S. 2014.
5. Matthews, J. & C., *Taliesin* pp73–4
6. Raoul de Houdenc, *Meraugis de la Portlesguez*, 2019.
7. Nennius. *Historia Britonum* p 27.
8. *Le Morte D'Arthur*. Bk. I. Ch xx.

9. Adolf, 1946. pp173–193.

10. *Legends of the Jews*. Vol 2 pp28–35.

11. Ibid pp41–42.

12. Ibid pp43–44.

13. Ibid pp 152–4.

14. *Voyage of Maelduin* Trans. Lady Gregory, Colin Smythe, 1973.

15. From Jes 3, a 16th century manuscript, it originally appeared in *Britannia After the Romans*, by Algernon Herbert. Henry Bohn Co., 1836. Trans by John Matthews.

16. Sperling and Simon, *Zohar* II.

17. ibid, III.

18. Matthews: *Taliesin*, 2000 p311.

19. Bromwich *Triodd Ynys Prydein* 2017, Appendix III.

20. Ibid.

21. Morris, 1878 pp30–35.

22. Verard, 2017.

23. Trans. Gareth Knight. Matthews, T*emples of the Grail*

24. *Vita Merlini* trans J.J. Parry.

25. *Chronicle of Ellis Gruffydd* trans. P.K. Ford, 1976.

26. Western Way vol 2 Chapters 1–4.

27. Ashmole, 2011.

28. Flamel, 2011.

29. Ford, 1976.

30. Wheatley, *The English Prose Merlin* vol 1.

Chapter 6

1. Fortune, *Glastonbury: Avalon of the Heart*. Red Wheel/Weiser, 2014

2. *Mists of Avalon*, p26.

3. Ibid pp150–152.

4. J.R.R. Tolkien: *Unfinished Tales*, pp27–8.

5. For full details of these and all books discussed here see: Further Reading.

6. *Porius*, p152.

7. *Lastborn of Elvinwood*, pp26–7.

8. Ibid. pp 24

9. Vansittart: *Lancelot*, pp00.

10. Tolstoy: *The Coming of the King*, pp88–89.

11. Lawhead: *Pendragon Cycle: Merlin, P135.*

12. Boulamie, 2004 pp181–193.

13. Bryant, p264 of the French edition.

14. Briant, Trans. Gareth Knight, P5.

15. Stuart: *The Last Enchantment, pp64–65.*

16. Cabell: *Something About Eve*, P49.

17. Attanasio: *The Dragon and the Unicorn*, pp97–8.

18. Godwin: *Firelord, p168.*

19. Ibid, p172.

20. White: *Sword in the Stone*, pp197–198.

21. Lerner: 'Merlyn's Magic ... And Ours,' p5.

22. Christian, *The Sword and the Flame*, p212.

23. Lewis, *That Hideous Strength*, p199.

24. Berger: *Arthur Rex*, p165.

25. Nye: *Merlin*, p12.

26. Yolen, *Merlin's Book*, pp60–61.

27. De Lint *Spiritwalk*, p80.

28. Godwin: *Firelord*, p66.

Chapter 7

1. Steven Morris 'Merlin Tale Fragments Discovered in Bristol Archives.' The Guardian, 30 January 2019

Appendix 2

1. Ed. and Trans. by Scott Gosnell. CreateSpace Independent Publishing Platform, 2013.

FURTHER READING

A Chronological List of the Most Important Works Relating to Merlin: AD 600–1862

Date	Title	Author (where known)
600 – 900	Poems	Attributed to Myrddin
1135	Prophecies of Merlin	Geoffrey of Monmouth
1136	*Historia Regum Brittania*	Geoffrey of Monmouth
1150	*Vita Merlini*	Geoffrey of Monmouth
1155	Prophecies of Merlin	John of Cornwall
1215	*L'Estoire de Merlin* (Vulgate Cycle)	Anon
1250	Merlinssupa	Gunnlag Liefson
1260	Merlin's Boek	Jacob van Maelent
1272	*Les Prophecies de Merlin*	Anon

1290	*Der Theure Morlin*	Alberecht von Scharfenburg
1300	Merlin	Robert de Boron
1310	The Prose Merlin	
1320	*La Storia di Merlin*	Paolino Peri
1350	Seven Sages of Rome	
1380	*La Estoria de Merlin*	
1390	*Roman de Silence*	Heldris de Cornualle
1395	Arthour and Merlin	
1410	Merlin	Henry Lonelich
1473	The English Merlin	
1480	*Le Morte D'Arthur*	Sir Thomas Malory
1588	The Birth of Merlin	William Rowley
1590	*Merlijn*	VoIsbroek
1590–1596	The Faerie Queene	Edmund Spenser
1610	Life & Prophecies of Merlin	Thomas Heywood
1615	*Don Quixote de la Mancha*	Miguel Cervantes
1644	England's Prophetical Merlin	William Lilly
1650	Merlin, or the British Enchanter	John Drayton
1683	The Mystery of Ambras Merlin	Anon
1734	Merlin or the Devil of Stonehenge	L. Theobald
1831	*Merlin der Wilde*	Ludwig Uhland
1857	Merlin and Vivien	Alfred Tennyson
1860	*Merlin l'Enchanteur*	Edgar Quinet
1862	*Myrdhinn ou 'l'enchanteur Merlin*	Hersant de la Villemarque

Texts and Critical Studies

Adolf, Helen, 'The Esplumoir Merlin: A Study of its Cabalistic Sources' *Speculum* 21 (1946) pp173–193.

Anales Cambriae in *British History and The Welsh Annals* ed. & trans. by John Morris (London & Chicester, Phillimore & Co, 1988).

Anderson, Alan Orr and Anderson, Marjorie Ogilvie, eds, *Adomnan's Life of Columba* (Clarendon Press, 1991).

Apuleius, *De Deo Socrate* (On the God of Socrates) in The Works of Apuleius trans. by G. Hudson Gurney (London, George Bell & Sons, 1878).

Ashe, Geoffrey, *Merlin in the Earliest Records*, The Book of Merlin ed. R.J. Stewart (Blandford Press, 1987) pp17–46.

Ashmole, Elias, *Theatrum Chemicum Britannicum* (Ouroboros Press, 2011).

Barney, Stephen A. ed., *The Etymologies of Isidore of Seville* (Cambridge University Press 2010.)

Bernardus Silvestris, *The Cosmographia* ed. and trans. Winthrop Wetherbee (Columbia University Press, 2010).

Blackburn, W., 'Spencer's Merlin' *Renaissance & Reformation* 4 (1980).

Blake, William, *Notebook of William Blake: A Photographic and Typographic Facsimile,* ed. David V. Erdman and Donald K. Moore (Open Book Publications, 1977).

Bouloumié, Arlette, The Myth of Merlin in 20th Century French *Literature Cahiers de recherches médiévales* 11 (2004) pp181–193.

Bromwich, Rachel ed. & trans., *Trioedd Ynys Prydein* (4th Edition) (Cardiff University of Wales Press, 2014).

Bromwich, Rachel, 'Trioedd Ynys Prydein: the Myrvyrian Series' *Transactions of the Honourable Society of Cymmrodorion* 1969 Pt. 1 pp299–301; Pt 2 pp127–156.

Bromwich, Rachel; A.O.H. Jarman; & B.F. Roberts, eds. *The Arthur of the Welsh* (Cardiff: University of Wales Press, 1993).

Brown, A. C. L 'The Esplumoire and Viviane' *Speculum* 20 (1945) pp426–432.

Butler, Alban. *Lives of the Saints*, Edited, revised, and supplemented by Herbert Thurston and Donald Attwater (Palm Publishers, 1956).

Chadwick. N.K., 'Dreams in Early European Literature' [in] *Celtic Studies,* ed. J. Carney & D. Greene (London: Routledge and Kegan Paul, 1968).

Chadwick, N.K., 'Imbas Forosnai,' *Scottish Gaelic Studies* 4 1934/5 pp97–135.

Chretien de Troyes, *Perceval, or the Story of the Grail,* trans. by Nigel Bryant. (Cambridge, D.S. Brewer, 1982).

Clarkson, Tim, 'Rhydderch Hael' *The Heroic Age* 2 Autumn/ Winter 1999.

Clarkson, Tim, *Scotland's Merlin* (John Donald, 2016).

Coe, John B. & Simon Young, *The Celtic Sources for the Arthurian Legend*. (Felinfach, Llanerch Publishers, 1995).

Colton, J. 'Merlin's Cave & Queen Caroline' *18th Century Studies* 10 (1976) pp1–20.

Conlee, John, *Prose Merlin* (Kalamazoo, Michigan Medieval Institute Publications, 1998).

Cormac's Glossary (Sanas Chormaic) Irish Archaeological and Celtic Society, ed. Whitley Stokes; trans. John O'Donovan. (Calcutta, O.T. Cutter, 1868).

Curley, Michael J., 'Animal Symbolism in the prophecies of Merlin' *Beasts and Birds of the Middle Ages,* ed. Willene B. Clark Meredith T. McMunn (University of Pennsylvania Press, 2017).

Curley, Michael J., 'A New Edition of John of Cornwall's Prophetia Merlini' *Speculum* 57 1982, pp217–249.

Curley, Michael J. 'Conjuring History: Mother, Nun and Incubus in Geoffrey of Monmouth's *Historia Regum Brittaniae*.' *JEGP*. 114, No.2, 2015, pp219–239.

Darrah, John, *Paganism in Arthurian Romance* (Boydell Press, Suffolk, 1994).

De Boron, Robert, trans. by Nigel Bryant, *Merlin & The Grail* (Cambridge, D.S. Brewer, 2001).

Doore, G., ed., *Shaman's Path* (Boston & London, Shambhala, 1988).

Dryden, John, *King Arthur; or, Merlin, the British enchanter. A dramatic opera, as it is performed at the Theatre in Goodman's Fields. The musick by Mr. Purcell* (Gale, ECCO, 2010).

Duggan, Catherine, *The Lost Laws of Ireland* (Glasnevin Publishing, 2013).

Eckhardt, Caroline D., 'The First English Translation of the Prophetia Merlini' *The Library* 6th Series 4 (1982) pp25–34.

Eckhardt, Caroline D. ed., *The Prophetia Merlini of Geoffrey of Monmouth: A Fifteenth Century English Commentary* (The Medieval Academy of America, 1982).

Escobar-Vargas, M. Carolina, 'Translating Merlin: Wace's Rendition of Merlin in his Translation of Geoffrey of Monmouth's *Historia Regum Britanniae*'. *Reading Medieval Studies* 44, 2018, pp 59–80.

Ettlinger, Ellen, 'Omens and Celtic Warfare' *Man* XLIII (1943) No 4, pp11–17.

Ettlinger, Ellen, 'Precognitive Dreams in Celtic Legend' *Folk-Lore* LIX (1948) pp97–111.

Evans, D. Sylvan, *Celtic Remains* (London, Alfred Nutt, 1878).

Feletra, Michael A., 'Merlin in Cornwall: The Source and Context of John of Cornwall's Prophetia Merlini' *JEGP* III, No. 3., 2012, pp304–338.

Flamel, Nicholas, *Testament of Flamel: and Other Works, Being a Collection on the Sacred Art and Science of Alchemy* (Theophania Publishing, 2011).

Forbes, Alexander P., *The Lives of S. Ninian and S. Kentigern, Compiled in the Twelfth Century.*(Edinburgh, Edmonton, 1894).

Ford, P. K., 'The Death of Merlin in the Chronicle of Elis Gruffydd', *Viator* no. 7, 1976, pp379–390.

Ford, Patrick K., *The Mabinogi and Other Medieval Welsh Tales* (Berkeley: University of California Press, 1977).

Fortune, Dione, *Glastonbury: Avalon of the Heart* (Red Wheel/ Weiser, 2014).

Gaster, M., 'The Legend of Merlin' *Folklore* 16, 1905, pp407–27.

Geoffrey of Monmouth, *Historia Regum Britanniae,* ed. & trans., Lewis Thorpe. (Penguin Books, 1976).

Geoffrey of Monmouth, *History of the Kings of Britain,* trans. Sebastian Evans, revised by C. W. Dunn. (Everyman's Library, 1963 [1912])

Geoffrey of Monmouth, *The History of the Kings of Britain: An Edition and Translation of the* De Gestis Britonum (Historia Regum Britanniae), ed. Michael D. Reeve, trans. N. Wright. (Boydell Press, 2007).

Geoffrey of Monmouth, *Life of Merlin,* ed. & trans. Basil Clarke. (Cardiff, University of Wales Press, 1973).

Ginsberg, Louis and Henrietta Szold, *Legends of the Jews* (4 Vols) Latest edition, Lulu 2018.

Giraldus Cambrensis, *Topographia Hibernica and Expugnatio Hibernica* (volume 5 of Complete Works) (Adamant Media Corporation, 24 Sept. 2004).

Giraldus Cambrensis, *The Journey Through Wales and the Description of Wales,* ed. and trans. Betty Radice. (Penguin Books, 1978).

Gollnick, James, ed. *Comparative Studies in Merlin from the Vedas to C.G. Jung* (Lewiston, New York, Edwin Mellen, 1990).

Goodrich, Peter, ed. *The Romance of Merlin* (New York and London, Garland Publishing, 1990).

Graves, Robert, *The White Goddess* (Faber, 1961).

Green, Miranda, *Symbol and Image in Celtic Religious Art* (London, Routledge, 1989).

Guest, Charlotte, *The Mabinogion* (London: Dent, Everyman's Library, 1906).

Gurney, Hudson, *Works of Apuleius* (London G. Bell, 1910).

Harding, Carol E., *Merlin & Legendary Romance* (New York: Garland, 1988).

Heywood, Thomas, *The Life of Merlin* (Carmarthen: J. Evans 1985).

Holinshed, Raphael, *The Historie of England, Books I-IV* (Benediction Classics, 2011).

Jarman, A.O.H., 'A Note on the Possible Derivation of Viviane' *Gallica*. (Cardiff, University of Wales Press, 1969), pp1–12.

Jarman, A.O.H., 'hwimleian, chwibleian'. *Bibliographic Bulletin of Celtic Studies* 16. 1954–6, pp71–6.

Jarman, A.O.H., *The Legend of Merlin* (Cardiff, University of Wales Press, 1976).

John of Cornwall, trans. by Julian Holmes, *The Prophecy of Merlin* (Cornish Language Board, 1988).

Johnson, Ben, 'The Speeches at Prince Henry's Barriers.' C. H. Herford, Percy Simpson, and Evelyn Simpson, eds, *Ben Jonson, Vol. 10: Play Commentary; Masque Commentary* (J.M. Dent, 1950).

Kendrick, T.D., *British Antiquity* (London, 1950).

Koch, J.T., *The Gododdin of Aneurin* (University of Wales Press, 1997).

Lacey, Norris J & Geoffrey Ashe, *The Arthurian Handbook* (New York, Garland Press, 1988).

Lacey, Norris J. *et al.*, ed. and trans., *The Lancelot-Grail: The Old French Arthurian Vulgate and Post-Vulgate in Translation.* (7 volumes), (Boydell Press, 2010).

Leclerc, Guillaume, *Fergus of Galloway: Knight of King Arthur,* trans. by D.D.R. Owen (London J.M Dent, 1991; Rutland, Vermont: Charles Tuttle, 1991).

Lerner, 'Merlyn's Magic ... And Ours'. *American Educator.* Summer 1996, pp pp3–8

Le Prophecies de Merlin, ed L. A. Paton (London: Oxford University Press, 1927.)

Lewis, Timothy, *A Glossary of Medieval Welsh Law.* (London, The Lawbook Exchange, 2017).

Lilly, John, *England's Prophetical Merline* (London: John Partridge, 1644).

Lilly, John, *Merlinus Anglicus Junior: The English Merlin Revised* (London, 1644).

Lloyd-Morgan, Ceridwen and Erich Poppe, eds, *Arthur in the Celtic Languages* (Cardiff, University of Wales Press, 2019).

Lovelich, Henry, *Merlin* (3 vols) (London: Oxford University Press, 1904–1932).

Lucan, *The Pharsalia: Dramatic Episodes of the Civil Wars,* trans. Robert Graves (Penguin Books, 1956).

MacDonald, Aileen *The Figure of Merlin in Thirteenth Century French Romance* (Lewiston, New York: Edwin Mellen, 1990).

Mackley, J.S. ed. & trans., *The Origin of the Giants: The First Settlers of Albion* (Dez Grantz Geanz) Isengrim Publishing, 2014.

Malcor, Linda A. and C. Scott-Littleton, *From Scythia to Camelot* (Garland, 2000).

Malcor, Linda A. and John Matthews. *The Roman King Arthur.* (Forthcoming, 2020).

Malory, Sir Thomas, ed. J. Matthews, *Le Morte D'Arthur* (London, Cassell, 2000. New annotated edition, Chaosium, 2020).

Markale, Jean, *King Arthur King of Kings* (Rochester, VT. Inner Traditions, 1999).

Merlin, Priest of Nature (Rochester, VT. Inner Traditions, 1995).

Matthews, Caitlín, *King Arthur & the Goddess of the Land* (Rochester, VT Inner Traditions, 2002).

Mabon & the Guardians of Celtic Britain (Rochester, VT. Inner Traditions, 2002).

The Celtic Book of the Dead (New York, St Martin's Press,1992).

Elements of the Celtic Tradition (Element Books,1990).

Matthews, C. & J., *The Complete King Arthur* (Rochester, VT. Inner Traditions, 2017).

King Arthur's Raid (Gothic Image Publishing, 2003).

Matthews, J., *An Arthurian Reader* (Aquarian Press, Wellingborough, 1988).

ed., *At the Table of the Grail* (London, Watkins Publishing, 2002).

'Auguries, Dreams & Incubatory Sleep', *Psychology & the Spiritual Traditions,* ed. R.J. Stewart (Element Books, 1990).

A Celtic Reader (Wellingborough, Aquarian Press, 1990).

Elements of the Arthurian Tradition (Shaftesbury, Element Books, 1989).

Gawain, Knight of the Goddess (Rochester VT. Inner Traditions, 2002).

Green Man, Spirit of Nature (Red Wheel/Weiser, 2002).

King Arthur: Dark Age Warrior and Mythic Hero (Carlton Books, 2004).

King Arthur and the Grail Quest (Poole, Blandford Press, 1994).

Legendary Britain: An Illustrated Journey (with R.J. Stewart) (Cassell, London, 1989).

Quest for the Green Man Wheaton, IL. (Quest Books).

Taliesin, the Last Celtic Shaman (Rochester, VT. Inner Traditions, 2002).

The Shamanism Bible (London, Hamlyn, 2014).

Matthews, J. & C., *The Encyclopaedia of Celtic Myth & Legend* (London, Rider, 2003).

The Encyclopedia of Celtic Wisdom (London, Rider, 2001).

Ladies of the Lake (Wellingborough, Aquarian Press, 1992).

MacQueen, Winifred and John, ed. and trans., *Vita Merlini Silvestris* (Scottish Studies 29, 1989) pp77–83.

Merlin, or The Early History of King Arthur (4 vols) ed. H.B. Wheatley (London: Kegan Paul, Trench, Trubner, 1865–1899).

Merlin: Roman en Prose du XIII Siecle (2 vols) ed. Gaston Paris & J. Ulrich (Paris: *Societe des Anciens Textes Francais*,1886).

Meixell, Amanda S., 'Queen Caroline's Merlin Grotto and the 1735 Lord Carteret Edition of Don Quijote: The Matter of Britain and Spain's Arthurian Tradition'. *Cervantes: Bulletin of the Cervantes Society of America* 25, 2. 2005[2006]. pp 59–82

Miexell, Amanda S., 'The *Espiritu de Merlin*, Renaissance magic, and the limitations of being human in *La casa de los celos*.' *Cervantes* 24 (2004) pp93–118.

Melia, D. F., 'The Irish Saint as Shaman,' *Pacific Coast Philology* 18 1983, pp37–42.

Meyer, K., 'The Boyish Exploits of Finn' *Eriu* 1, 1904. pp180–190

Morris, John, *The Age of Arthur* (London, Weidenfeld & Nicolson, 1973).

Morris, Lewis, *Celtic Remains* (Cambrian Archaeological Association, 1878).

Neckam, Alexander. *The Secret History of Virgil: From a Manuscript in Old Royal Library in the British Museum,* ed. and trans. Joannes Opsopoeus Brettanus (Nabu Press), 1996.

Nennius. *Historia Britonum* (in) *British History & The Welsh Annals,* ed. & trans. by John Morris (London & Chicester, Phillimore & Co.), 1988.

Nicholson, S. ed., *Shamanism* (Theosophical Publishing House),1987.

Neitz, W.A., 'The Esplumoir Merlin' *Speculum,* XVIII, 1943.

Noel, D.C., 'Archetypal Merlin & the New Shamanism' in *Psychology & the Spiritual Traditions,* ed. R.J. Stewart (Element Books,) 1990.

Of Arthour and Merlin (2 vols) ed. O.D. Macrae-Gibson. (London: Oxford University Press, 1973,1979).

O Hogain, D. *Myth, Legend, and Romance: An Encyclopaedia of the Irish Folk Traditions* Ryan Publishing, 1990.

Parry, J. J., *The Vita Merlini* (The Life of Merlin) (University of Illinois studies in language and Literature, Urbana, Illinois), 1925.

Paton, L.A., 'Merlin and Ganeida', *Publications of the Modern Language Association* 18 (1903).

Paton, L.A., *Studies in the Fairy Mythology of Arthurian Romance* (Burt Franklin), 1960.

Raoul de Houdenc. *Meraugis de Portlesguez: Roman de la Table Ronde* Forgotten Books, 2019.

Rhys, John, *Celtic Folklore, Welsh & Manx* (London: Wildwood House, 1980).

Rich, Deike & Ean Begg, *On the Trail of Merlin* (London, Aquarian Press), 1991.

Roman de Merlin, ed. H.O. Sommer (London: Ballantyne, Hanson), 1894.

Roman d'Ogier le Danois, a fourteenth-century prose romance (unpublished).

Rowley, William and William Shakespeare, *The Birth of Merlin* With additional chapters by R.J. Stewart, Denise Coffey and Roy Hudd (Shaftsbury, Element Books), 1998.

Russell, J. and R. Cohn, *The Boyhood Deeds of Fionn* (VSD), 2012.

Scottichronicon. John Fordun and Walter Bower (8 vols) (Mercat Press), 1981–1983.

Skeels, Dell. Trans. *The Romance of Perceval in Prose* [Didot Perceval] University of Washington 1961.

Skene, W.F., *The Four Ancient Books of Wales* (2 vols) (New York, AMS Press), 1995.

Spargo, John Webster, *Virgil the Necromancer: Studies in Virgilian Legends* (Kessinger), 2010.

Stephens, Meic, *The Oxford Companion to the Literature of Wales* (London & New York, Oxford University Press), 1986.

Stein, Walter Johannes, *The Death of Merlin* (Edinburgh, Floris Books), 1984.

Stewart, R.J. ed., *The Book of Merlin* (Poole, Dorset, Blandford Press), 1987.

Ed. *Merlin and Woman* (Poole Dorset, Blandford Press), 1988.

Stewart, R.J., *Celtic Gods, Celtic Goddesses* (Poole, Dorset Blandford Press), 1990.

The Merlin Tarot, illustrated by Miranda Gray (London: Aquarian Press), 1988.

Merlin Through the Ages, with J. Matthews (Poole, Blandford Press), 1995.

The Mystic Life of Merlin (London, Arkana), 1986.

The Prophetic Life of Merlin (London, Arkana), 1986.

The Way of Merlin (London, Aquarian Press), 1991.

Swift, Jonathan, *A Famous Prediction of Merlin, The British Wizard, written Above a Thousand Years Ago, and Relating to this year [1709]*, with Explanatory Notes by T.N. Philomath. *The Poems of Jonathan Swift* (Vol. 1: Occasional Poems 1698–1710). ed. Harold Williams (Oxford, Clarendon Press), 1958.

Tatlock, J.S.P., *The Legendary History of Britain* (New York, Gordian Press), 1974.

Toregrossa, Michael, 'Merlin Goes to the Movies: The Changing Role of Merlin in Cinema Arthuriana' *Film & History* vol 29 Numbers 3–4 1999, pp54–65.

Theobald, Lewis, *Merlin, or the Devil of Stonehenge* (London, John Watts), 1734.

Varro, *Antiquitates rerum humanarum et divinarum* (Antiquities of Human and Divine Things) OUP, 2019.

Verard, A., ed., *Le roman d'Ogier le Danois* (Hachette), 2017.

Virgil. *Eclogues, Georgics, Aeneid.* Translated by Fairclough, H R. Loeb Classical Library Volumes 63 & 64. (Cambridge, MA. Harvard University Press), 1916.

Voyage of Maelduin (in) *The Voyages of the St Brendan the Navigator and Tales of the Irish Saints,* trans. Lady Gregory (Colin Smythe), 1973.

Wace & Layamon, *Arthurian Chronicles,* trans E. Mason, Everyman's Library, 1962 (1912).

Wace, *Roman De Brut: A History of The British:* Text and translation Judith Weiss. (Exeter Medieval Texts and Studies) 2005

Ward, H L. D., 'Lailoken (or Merlin Silvester)', *Romania* 22 1893, pp504–526.

Wheatley, H. B., *Merlin: A Prose Romance* (3 volumes) (Greenwood Press), 1969–73.

William of Newburgh, *The History of English Affairs*, ed. and trans. William, P. G. Walsh and M. J. Kennedy, 1988 (Aris & Philips), 2007.

Williams, Robert, trans., *Y Seint Greal,* Jones (Wales) publishers, 1987.

Williams, Rowan and Gwyneth Lewis, *The Book of Taliesin* (Penguin Classics), 2019.

Zohar, trans. Harry Sperling and Maurice Simon (4 volumes) (Soncino Press), 1984.

Modern Retellings

Attanasio, A.A., *The Dragon & The Unicorn* (London, Hodder), 1994.
  Eagle and the Sword (New York, Harper Prism), 1997.
  Wolf and the Crown (New York, Harper Prism), 1998.
  Serpent and the Grail (New York, Harper Prism), 1999.

Barjavel, René, *The Enchanter* (Denoël), 1984.

Berger, Thomas, *Arthur Rex* (New York: Dell,) 1985.

Binyon, Lawrence, *The Madness of Merlin* (London, Macmillan), 1947.

Bradley, M.Z., *The Mists of Avalon* (N.Y., Knopf), 1982.

Briant, Théophile, *The Testament of Merlin,* trans. by Gareth Knight (Skylight Press), 2016.

Cabell, J. B., *Something About Eve* (N. Y., Ballantine), 1971.

Chopra, Deepak, *The Return of Merlin* (London, Century), 1995.

Christian, C., *The Sword and the Flame*, London, Macmillan, 1982.

Clare, H., *Merlin's Magic* (London, Bodley Head), 1953.

Cooper, S., *Over Sea, Under Stone* (Jonathan Cape), 1965.

Cunqueiro, Alvaro, *Merlin and Company* (London, Everyman), 1996.

De Angelo, M *Cyr Myrddin* (Seattle, Gododdin Press), 1979.

Drake, D, *The Dragon Lord* (Tom Doherty, N. Y.), 1982.

Durrell, L, *Revolt of Aphrodite* (Faber & Faber), 1974.

Erskine, J., 'The Tale of Merlin & one of the Ladies of the Lake' *American Weekly*, Feb. 4, 1940.

Fry, Christopher, *Thor, With Angels* (London: Oxford University Press), 1949.

Furst, Clyde B., *Merlin* (New York: Updike), 1930.

Godwin, P., *Firelord* (N. Y Doubleday), 1980.

Haldeman, L., *The Lastborn of Elvinwood* (London, Souvenir Press), 1980.

Hildebrandt, R. & T., *Merlin & the Dragons of Atlantis* (N. Y., Bobbs Merrill), 1983.

Hill, Geoffrey. 'Merlin' in *For the Unfallen* (London: Routledge), 1959.

Holdstock, Robert, *Celtika* (London, Gollancz), 2001.

Merlin's Wood (London, Collins), 1994.

The Iron Grail (London, Gollancz), 2002.

The Broken Kings (London, Gollancz) 2007.

Hume, M.K., *Clash of Kings* (London, Headline) 2011.

Death of an Empire (London, Headline), 2012.

Web of Deceit (London, Headline), 2013.

Kane, G., & J. Jakes, *Excalibur* (N. Y., Dell), 1983.

Lawhead, Stephen, *Taliesin* (Oxford: Lion Books),1988.
  Merlin (Oxford: Lion Books), 1988.
  Arthur (Oxford, Lion Books), 1989.
Lewis, C.S., *That Hideous Strength* (London: Bodley Head), 1945.

Mason, C. W., *Merlin: A Piratical Love Story* (London, Neville Beeman), 1986.
McIntosh, J. F., 'Merlin', *Fantastic* 9 no 3, Mar 1960.
Matthews, J. 'The Story of Grisandole' in *The Round Table* 4, 1 & 2 (1987).
Muir, Edwin. 'Merlin' in *Collected Poems* (London: Faber), 1952.

Munn, H. Warner. *Merlin's Godson* (New York, Ballantine), 1976.
  Merlin's Ring (N. Y., Ballantine), 1974.

Newman, Robert, *Merlin's Mistake* (London, Hutchinson), 1970.
  Testing of Tertius (N. Y., Atheneum), 1973.
Norton, Andre, *Merlin's Mirror* (New York: Daw), 1975.
Nye, Robert, *Merlin* (London, Hamish Hamilton), 1983.

Percy, W., *Lancelot* (London, Heinemann), 1979.
Powers, T., *The Drawing of the Dark* (N. Y., Ballantine), 1977.
Powys, John Cowper, *Porius* (London: Macdonald), 1951.

Quinet, Edgar, *The Enchanter Merlin*, translated and adapted by Brian Stableford (Black Coat Press), 2014

Roubaud, Jacques, *Grail fiction* (Gallimard), 1978.

Saberhagen, Fred, *Dominion* (New York, Tor), 1982.
Stewart, Mary, *The Crystal Cave* (London: Hodder), 1970.
  The Hollow Hills (London: Hodder), 1973.

The Last Enchantment (London: Hodder), 1979.

Tolkien, J.R.R., *Lord of the Rings* (London, Allen & Unwin), 1968.
  Unfinished Tales (London, Allen & Unwin), 1980.
Tolstoy, Nikolai, *The Coming of the King* (London: Bantam),
  1985.
Trevor, Meriol, *Merlin's Ring* (London, Collins), 1957.

Yolen, Jane, *Merlin's Booke* (New York, Ace), 1986.

White, Terence Hanbury, *The Once & Future King* (London:
  Collins), 1958.
  The Book of Merlin (London: Collins), 1978.
Whyte, Jack, *The Camulod Chronicles:*
  The Skystone (Tor), 2001.
  The Singing Sword (Tor) 2002.
  The Eagles Brood (Tor), 2002.
  The Saxon Shore (Tor), 2003.
  Fort at River's Bend (Tor), 2004.
  The Sorcerer: Metamorphosis (Tor), 2005.
  Uther (Tor), 2006.
  The Lance Thrower (Tor) 2007.
  The Eagle (Tor), 2008.
Williams, Charles, *The Arthurian Poems of Charles Williams*,
  ed. with Introduction by Grevel Lindop and John Matthews
  (Mythwood Books), 2017 (Kindle Edition).

Film and TV

A Connecticut Yankee in King Arthur's Court, directed by Tay Garnett, adapted by Edmund Beloin, 1949.

A Kid in King Arthur's Court, directed by Arthur Rankin Jr and Jules Bass, adapted by Romeo Muller, 1995.

Arthur the King, directed by Clive Donner, written by J. David Wyles, 1985.

Camelot (musical), directed by Joshua Logan, written by Alan J. Lerner and Frederic Lowe, 1967.

Camelot (TV series), directed by Mikael Salomon, Stefan Schwartz, Ciaran Donnelly, Jeremy Podeswa, Michelle MacLaren; written by Chris Chibnall, Michael Hirst, Louise Fox, Terry Cafolla, Steve Lightfoot, Sarah Phelps. 2011.

Excalibur, directed by John Boorman, written by Boorman and Rospo Pallenburg, 1981.

Guinevere directed by Jud Taylor, written by Ronni Kern, 1994.

Kids of the Round Table, directed by Robert Tinnell, screenplay by David Sherman, 1995.

King Arthur, directed by Antoine Fuqua, screenplay by David Franzoni, 2004.

King Arthur: Legend of the Sword, directed by Guy Ritchie, written by Joby Harold, Guy Ritchie, Lional Wigram, David Dobkin, 2017.

Merlin (TV series), directed by Jeremy Webb, Alice Troughton, David Moore, Justin Molotnikov, Ashley Way, Ed Fraiman, James Hawes, Metin Hüseyin, Alex Pillai, Stuert Orme, Declan

O'Dwer; written by Johnny Capps, Julien Jones, Jake Michie, Julian Murphy, Howard Overman, Ben Vanstone, Lucy Watkins, Richard McBrian, 2008–2012.

Merlin (miniseries), directed by Steve Barron, written by David Stephens and Ed Khmara, 1998.

Merlin: the Magic Begins (TV series), directed by David Winning, written by Tom Richards, 1998–1999.

Merlin, the Return, directed by Paul Matthews, written by Paul Matthews.

Mr Merlin (TV sitcom), various directors and writers; series ran from 1981 to 1982.

Sword in the Stone (animated), directed by Wolfgang Reitherman, story by Bill Peet based on the novel by T. H. White, 1963.

The Kid Who Would be King, directed by Joe Cornish, written by Joe Cornish, 2019.

INDEX

Firelord (Parke Godwin), 166,
185, 206
Flamel, Nicholas, 161
Flower Bride, 124-127
Fortune, Dion, 167-170
*Four Ancient Books of Wales,
The*, 15, 24, 37
Fourth Eclogue (Virgil), 258
Franzoni, David, 202
Fuqua, Antoine, 201

Galahad, Sir, 116
Gall, son of Dysgyfdawt, 102
Gandalf, 8, 171-2, 189, 195, 207
Gawain, Sir, 119, 125, 135
164ff, 198-9
Geoffrey of Monmouth, 29, 30,
41, 48, 59, 61, 184, 210-11
Gerald of Wales (Giraldus
Cambrensis), 70
Giant's Dance, 93, 149
Glastonbury Tor 192, 202
Godwin, Parke, 185, 206
Gorlois, Duke of Cornwall,
103-4
Graves, Robert, 134
Greetings (*Oianau*), 15, 33, 210
Gronw Pebyr, 124
Guinevere (film), 199
Gwasawg 45
Gwenddolau ap Ceidio, 16, 18ff,
153
Gwenddydd, 24, 25ff, 136-7
Gwion, 37-8
Gwyddno Garanhir, 38, 153

Haldeman, Linda 172-3
Halter of Clydno Eiddyn 153
Hamper of Gwyddno Garanhir
153
Hanes Taliesin, 17, 114

*Harry Potter and the
Philosopher's [Sorcerer's]
Stone* (J. K. Rowling), 187-8
Henry II, King, 59, 86
Henry IV, King, 77, 86
Herbertian Life, The, 46
Heywood, Thomas, 80
Historia Brittonum (*History of
the Britons*), 30, 37, 54
Historia Regum Brittanniae
(*History of the Kings of
Britain*), 55, 57ff, 143ff, 207,
210
History of Merlin, The, 25, 12,
209
Holdstock, Robert, 193-5
Hollow Hills, The (Mary
Stewart), 181
Holy Grail, 69
Horn of Bran the Niggard, 153
Hume, M. K., 179-181
Huth Merlin, The, 123-4
hwimleian, 133

Imbas Forosna, 64-68
Iona, 73
Iron Grail, The (Robert
Holdstock), 153ff
Istari, The, 172

James I, King, 82, 86
Janus, 135
John of Cornwall, 60-61, 86
Jonson, Ben, 81-2
Joseph of Arimathea, 110

Kid in King Arthur's Court, A,
196, 197-8
Kids of the Round Table, 196-7
King Arthur (2004), 202-3
*King Arthur, Legend of the
Sword* (2017), 203, 146, 163